REREADING TALMUD

Program in Judaic Studies
Brown University
BROWN JUDAIC STUDIES

Edited by
Shaye J. D. Cohen

Number 318

REREADING TALMUD
Gender, Law and the Poetics of *Sugyot*

by
Aryeh Cohen

REREADING TALMUD

Gender, Law and the Poetics of *Sugyot*

by
Aryeh Cohen

Scholars Press
Atlanta, Georgia

REREADING TALMUD
Gender, Law, and the Poetics of *Sugyot*

by
Aryeh Cohen

Copyright © 1998 by Brown University
Paperback edition published 2008

All rights reserved. No part of this work may be reproduced or transmitted in any form or by any means, electronic or mechanical, including photocopying and recording, or by means of any information storage or retrieval system, except as may be expressly permitted by the 1976 Copyright Act or in writing from Brown Judaic Studies, Brown University, Box 1826, Providence, RI 02912.

Library of Congress Cataloging-in-Publication Data
Cohen, Aryeh.
    Rereading Talmud : gender, law, and the poetics of sugyot / by Aryeh Cohen.
       p. cm. — (Brown Judaic studies ; no. 318)
       Includes bibliographical references and index.
       ISBN 0-7885-0499-1 (cloth : alk. paper)—ISBN 978-1-930675-53-7 (pbk. : alk. paper)
       1. Talmud—Criticism, interpretation, etc.—History—20th century.
    2. Women in rabbinical literature. I. Title. II. Series.
BM504.C65 1998
296.1'2506—dc21   98-41180
                      CIP

13 12 11 10 09 08   5 4 3 2

Printed in the United States of America
on acid-free paper

and then there's between

between cities
between times
between languages

living that instant when the sacred
meets the profane in a glory of chaos
gripped by the terror of not arriving

at times like these I seem drawn to the
courtyard of death where the dead can
teach the living, where the dead know.

once I sat all night and stared at my
grandfather's picture, his warm smile
his steely eyes, his handsome power.

when he lived I was too young to
learn from him, and now I am left
with all these questions; is this not exile?

he was a peddlar and I am of peddlar
stock. selling for street value at the
back door, for credit in the shop.

he was a scholar and I search for
his wisdom. often I have scanned
the pages of his worn copy of the Talmud

the leather bindings disintegrating as I
opened the volumes one after another,
the pages cracking under my touch – searching

for notes he might have left in the margins;
he hadn't, they were empty. his learning too
had been dispensed only in the market place

an Oral Law given over in weekly classes on
Saturday afternoons to others who also toiled
between a mythical Europe in flames and an

American dream just over the horizon. never
written down for there was never any purpose.
so i go to the courtyard to ask for the oral Torah

i do not go empty though. bringing my own pack
and setting it down on rough earth, i open it for
my grandfather's inspection. theories, understandings

choices, places, people. I wait for the moment
when the smile will light his face and we can sit
and talk and argue that I might learn at his feet.

yet the encounter always ends when he turns
with an enigmatic grin which seems to say: you
already know, why ask? and he heads for the academy

as i leave unsatisfied, not having gotten his
approval though never having asked for it, i
stand for another moment in the twilight

between night and day
between sacred and profane
between here and there.

CONTENTS

Chapter I: Introduction 1
    Chapters 5
Chapter II. Literary analysis for redaction history:
    source and form criticism 7
    Introduction 7
    Part 1. Avraham Weiss 8
    Part 2. David Halivni 25
        Appendix. b Gittin 36b 33
    Part 3. Shamma Friedman 34
    Conclusion 42
Chapter III. On Framing the Question: intertextuality,
    translation, literary analysis: Jacob Neusner 43
    Intertextuality 45
    Translation 49
    Literary analysis 57
Chapter IV. Talmud as Literature and Cultural Production 71
    Introduction 71
    I. Jonah Fraenkel 73
    II. Daniel Boyarin 89
    III. Boyarin, Fraenkel (and me) 97
    Conclusions 120
        Appendix: b Ketuboth 62b-63a 123
Chapter V. Towards a Poetics of *Sugyot* or Sugyaetics 131
    Introduction 131
    Reading and Context 132
    Reading Intertextually 135
    "Representation" and "Reality" 141
    Narrative 144
    Sugya 147
    Praxis 149

Chapter VI. Framing Women/Constructing Exile:
    b Gittin 34b-35b 153
    The *Sugya* 154
    Reading the *Sugya* 156
    Sugyaetics 158
    Framing Women/Constructing Exile 165
        Appendix I. David Weiss Halivni On b Gittin 35a 174
        Appendix II. Gendering (and) Halakhah 177
        Appendix III: סלקא דעתך אמינא... קמ"ל
        and Writing Under Erasure 188
        Appendix IV. The Text 190

Chapter VII: Women and Slaves: a Reading of Gittin 12a-13a 193
    Introduction 193
    The *Sugya* 194
    The *Sugya* At First Sight 198
    Reading 202
    Rereading 215
    Reaching Towards the End 217
    Appendix 220

Bibliography 225

Indexes 237

Preface

This book started its life as a doctoral dissertation at Brandeis University. During that time and since I have benefited from the generosity of spirit and intellectual rigor of Prof. Reuven Kimelman and Prof. Bernadette Brooten. This work is all the better for their comments and criticisms. Prof. Anthony Saldarini also read the dissertation and I benefited from his valuable comments.

I was fortunate to have been one of Prof. Marvin Fox's students in his last years at Brandeis and in his retirement. His death was a great loss to the world of Jewish scholarship, and the Jewish community in general. Prof. Fox was the model of a committed and caring educator and I hope that I can walk in his footsteps.

The revisions and rewriting were done in the wonderful atmosphere (and weather) at the University of Judaism. I am indebted to my colleagues here for the friendly and intellectually challenging environment at the UJ.

I would like to especially thank the following people who read and commented on the manuscript in part or in whole. Dr. Alan Brill, Dr. Denise Kimber Buell, Dr. Michael Carasik, Ruth Clements, Dr. John Lanci, Dr. Ruth Langer, Dr. Rebecca Lesses, Dr. Shaul Magid, Rachel Turkienicz, Dr. Julian Ungar, Dr. Maeera Schreiber, Prof. Eliezer Slomovic, Rabbi Ira F. Stone, Ari Elon, and Dr. Sarah Horowitz.

I am grateful to Prof. Shaye Cohen for his suggestions, and for accepting this volume into the Brown Judaic Studies series.

Andrea Hodos and Mark Borowitz did some much needed copy-editing, and I am grateful to them; and special thanks to Elon Sunshine for doing most of the work on the indexes.

This book is dedicated to Andrea Hodos, חברתי ואשת בריתי, in gratitude for her friendship, her love, her integrity.

"And one day I will sit at your feet
and you will tell me the secret of movement,
...
till then all I can give you
are flowers and words, till then..."

Abbreviations

M	Mishnah
T	Tosefta
b	Babylonian Talmud (Bavli)
p	Palestinian Talmud (Yerushalmi)
AZ	Abodah Zarah
Ar.	Arachin
BB	Baba Bathra
Ber.	Berachot
BK	Baba Kamma
BM	Baba Metzia
Erub.	Erubin
Git.	Gittin
Hag.	Ḥagigah
Ket.	Kethubot
Kid.	Kiddushin
Meg.	Megillah
Ned.	Nedarim
San.	Sanhedrin
Sot.	Sotah
Yeb.	Yebamot
Zeb.	Zebachim
Suc.	Succah
Rashi	R. Shlomo Yitzḥaki
RSB"A	R. Shlomo b. Avraham Adret
RTB"A	R. Yom Tov b. Avraham Alashvili

1

Introduction

אמר ריש לקיש מאי דכתיב זה ספר תולדות אדם וגו'
וכי ספר היה לו לאדם הראשון מלמד שהראה לו
הקדוש ברוך הוא לאדם הראשון דור דור ודורשיו...
(בבלי ע"ז ה ע"א)

In every generation, it seems, scholars are inexorably drawn to interpret anew those texts that are privileged as classics.[1] This is as true of the Bavli, whose history of interpretation begins at almost the same time as its final form took shape, as of other classics of Western and Eastern canons. The methods of interpretation of the Bavli and their theoretical presuppositions were always as varied as the schools of interpreters. While Alfasi attempted to read the Bavli for its halakhic decisions, the interpreters of the *'Iyyun* school of the generation after the Spanish expulsion practiced a form of proto-New Criticism in reading *sugyot*.[2] While Rashi was interested in understanding *sugyot* as units,[3] the Tosafists were more interested in reconciling Halakhic positions and interpretive inconsistencies across tractates.[4]

This revisiting of the Talmud by every generation of scholars continued into the modern and contemporary periods. While nineteenth and early twentieth century Talmud scholarship relied almost

---

[1] On the importance of institutional power in the history of interpretation, and in the definition of what are considered "legitimate and interesting" questions, see Frank Kermode, *Genesis of Secrecy: On the Interpretation of Narrative* (Cambridge, MA: Harvard University Press, 1979): 10-18.
[2] Daniel Boyarin, *Sephardi Speculation: A Study in Methods of Talmudic Interpretation* (Heb.) (Jerusalem: Ben Zvi Intstitute, 1989): 1-46.
[3] Though not exclusively so. Jonah Fraenkel, *Rashi's Methodology in His Exegesis of the Babylonian Talmud* (Heb) (The Magnes Press, Jerusalem, 1980).
[4] On the innovative understanding of the Tosafists, see Hyman Klein, "Gemara and Sebara," *Jewish Quarterly Review* vol. 38 (1947-48): 71.

exclusively on historical-philological methods, the "linguistic turn" in literary analysis brought in its wake source and form-critical analysis. I continue this process by critiquing the literary and historicist presuppositions of these analyses and developing a methodology for interpretation of the Bavli which accounts for contemporary theoretical understandings of text and textuality. This method opens the way for asking new questions of and about the *sugyot* in the Bavli.

One of the major focuses of the academic study of the Bavli, from the mid-nineteenth century and on, was the question of its redaction. When was the Bavli redacted? Who redacted it? What were the sources of the Bavli? The approaches to this question varied as did the subsequent theories.[5] Avraham Weiss entered this fray somewhat accidentally. A Jewish historian living and writing in Warsaw, he wanted to write an economic history of the Talmudic period.[6] When faced with the state of Talmudic research, he set out to first understand the development of the Bavli, in order to be able to say something about the development of economic terms as represented in the Bavli. While he never reached the second half of his intended project, he did manage to articulate a revolutionary theory of the redaction of the Bavli.

According to Weiss, one couldn't speak of a final redaction of the Bavli – that which is referred to as the closing of the Talmud (חתימת התלמוד). His understanding of the development of the Talmud was much more fluid. Every generation of sages studied the materials that they had received from their teachers. At a certain point, the comments that they made about these materials (Mishnah, Tosefta) started circulating with the received material. The new comments were "published" – that is they were given a fixed literary form – and studied alongside the earlier materials. This process would repeat itself in the next generation – with the Mishnah *and* the newer materials being studied together. One could, then, only talk of an ongoing process of compilation, study, and redaction.

This theory revolutionized thinking about the closing of the Talmud. Prior to Weiss, the redaction history question was stated in terms of the final editing. Out of this question grew other related concerns – were the editors using previously constructed (written or oral) materials? Did the editors *redact* or merely *collect*? Weiss' proposal reframed the whole

---

[5]For a summary of the state of the question at about the time that Avraham Weiss started to write about these issues, see Julius Kaplan, *The Redaction of the Babylonian Talmud* (New York: Bloch Publishing Company, 1933). Chapter one summarizes previous research. For a more recent survey see Richard Kalmin, *The Redaction of the Babylonian Talmud: Amoraic or Saboraic?* (Hebrew Union College Press, Cincinatti, 1989): 1-11.

[6]For Weiss' biography, see Chapter II, part 1.

Introduction

discussion by eliminating both the gap between production of the layers and redaction of the whole, and the orderly teleological conception of redaction.

Weiss' insight also opened the door for discussion of the Talmud as literature. The "literary character" of the Talmud had previously only meant the way in which the Talmud came to be. Weiss himself was also interested in this question. His answer was a developmental answer, yet his concerns were still within the parameters of the questions asked by previous scholars. However, implicit in Weiss' formulation of the idea that the קביעה ספרותית (the fixing of the literary form) of the statements of the sages was the basic building block of the *sugya* and the Talmud itself, was an even more radical notion. The fixing of the literary form of statements separated those statements from the sages who said them, and set them out as independent literary units. Their formulation wasn't a matter of whimsy, and therefore they needed to be attended to in the same manner as any other literary text. Weiss himself did not especially follow up this line of thinking.[7] Weiss devoted his efforts to constructing a theory of the development of the Talmud as a whole, and his students continued in his footsteps. I, in a sense, push Weiss' literary insight as far as it will go while at the same time moving away from his historical conclusions.

The organizing and limiting principle of the first half of this book is methodological. My interest in analyzing the scholarship that I review in Chapters II-IV is to understand the ways in which these scholars read and interpreted *sugyot*. Each scholar represents a different theoretical move. My interest in the work of these scholars is not their historical (or cultural) conclusions about the Bavli or *sugyot* in the Bavli. I am only interested in their interpretive method, and the theoretical presuppositions of that method.[8] Although there is some vague chronological order to these chapters, the real movement is the move away from historicism.

The methodological interest of the current work is a limiting principle in that I chose to regard the scholars whose work I reviewed as representative types, rather than do exhaustive analysis of all the works

---

[7]Although he continually brushed against it. His article, *The Literary Activities of the Saboraim* (Heb.) (Jerusalem: Magnes Press, 1953), discusses the possibility that the initial *sugyot* of many of the tractates (and even chapters) of the Bavli are actually Saboraic introductions to the tractates. This of course raises the literary question of how one is to read an introduction to a Tractate.

[8]This is also the reason that such a large part of this work is devoted to text studies.

that participate in some way in this discussion.⁹ The scholarship reviewed here represents the spectrum of theoretical stances of those who use "literature" as a category of analysis for Talmud.

My argument in this part of the work, in short, is that <u>literary analysis of sugyot</u> needs to take both subject and object equally seriously. Those who see literary analysis as a "mere tool" of historical inquiry, as, also, those who don't think about the issues of parameters and context of sugyot, fall short on both counts.

At the same time, this review is a gathering of insights which I incorporate into the method that I define and apply in the second half of the book. These include Weiss' basic insight about the literariness of sugyot; Halivni's understanding of the major transformative role of the *stam*; Friedman's insight into the literary structure of sugyot; and the ways of representing them; Neusner's argument for the importance of translation, and the unreliability of attributions; Fraenkel's stress on close reading; Boyarin's introduction of self-consciously theoretical, feminist analysis, and the challenge of cultural poetics. While in the end I present

---

⁹For this reason I didn't directly engage M. S. Feldblum's *Talmudic Law and Literature: Tractate Gittin* (New York: Yeshiva University Press, 1969), since the theoretical stance is a continuation of Feldblum's teacher Abraham Weiss.

A book that might have added to this study is Jack N. Lightstone, *The Rhetoric of the Babylonian Talmud, Its Social Meaning and Context* (Waterloo, Ontario: Wilfrid Laurier University Press, 1994). The stated purpose of Lightstone's study is close to some of the objectives of the present work. Lightstone is interested in the ways in which rhetoric helps to construct reality. His major theoretical claim is that: "Idiomatic modes of speech or the formal traits of particular groups of tradents have been assimilated to one of several variations of a limited number of rhetorical patterns. ...[T]hese pervasive rhetorical patterns convey meaning because of the lawlike, albeit implicit, rules governing (1) the elements of the structure (2) the relations among those elements and (3) the range of permissible content of any one element. ... One experiences these lawlike relations as the 'way things really are,' as part of one's knowledge of the world." (Ibid., 7) Unfortunately, Lightstone's text study of b AZ 14b-16a (one of his central text examples) is seriously flawed. By not using available manuscripts (especially the readily available Abramson facsimile edition of the JTS MS, which does not appear in Lightstone's list of editions, ibid. *xiii*.) Lightstone has not taken into account the possibility that some of the rhetorical phrases he numbers are not in the MSS or vice versa; e.g. Lightstone's line 10 on page 30 "וניחא" is not in the MSS, while the MSS have an ending שמע מינה at line 23 (bottom page 31). This latter missing phrase calls into question Lightstone's division of the unit at III (page 32, and the list on page 45) rather than after the closing phrase (acc. to the MS) שמע מינה...שמע מינה at 23. Additionally, there are some glaring errors of translation; e.g. דאמר רב תחליפא as "For Rav said the opposite [as well]" (29), thus adding a non-existent rhetorical term. (Cf. Chanoch Albeck, *Introduction to the Talmud, Babli and Yerushalmi* (Dvir, Tel Aviv, 1969): 382-3.)

Introduction

my own interpretive methodology as an alternative to these, scholarship is not a zero-sum game – we all stand on somebody's shoulders.

In the second half of this work I present my own interpretive method – a poetics of the *sugya* or "sugyaetics" – as a method which takes both literary analysis and *sugyot* seriously. The importance of any new method of analysis or interpretation is the extent to which it allows new insight into the texts which it is used to interpret. I conclude with two text studies which serve both as "proving grounds" for sugyaetic analysis, and, as a contribution towards the understanding of the relationship between law and narrative, and the construction of gender in Talmud.

Chapters

In Chapter II, I critique the work of Abraham Weiss, David Halivni, and Shamma Friedman. Both Halivni and Friedman acknowledge the influence of Hyman Klein's work,[10] and Friedman explicitly builds on it.[11] They have, however, developed Klein's work so significantly in different directions that Klein's theoretical insights would be subsumed under theirs – rather than *vice versa*.

In Chapter III, I engage some of Jacob Neusner's work. Neusner is a sharp critic of Halivni and Friedman, and is also a harsh critic of the direction taken by Boyarin and which I take up in the second half of the book. In this chapter I examine Neusner's alternative literary theory and argue that his project of interpretation and analysis of the Bavli (and his opposition to other approaches) flows from this understanding.

In Chapter IV, I analyze and critique the approaches of Jonah Fraenkel and Daniel Boyarin. While Fraenkel does not work with Halakhic *sugyot*, the engagement with his clearly articulated theoretical stance and serious study of Aggadot yields important insight into the significance of context.

The second half of the book is constructive. In Chapter V, I offer my own interpretive method – "sugyaetics" – and its theoretical grounding.

I conclude with two lengthy text studies (Chapters VI and VII) of Halakhic *sugyot* from b Gittin. Although I doubt that there is such a thing as a "random example" in a scholarly work, these two *sugyot* are representative to the extent that they are "about" different issues, and

---

[10] "Gemara and Sebara," *Jewish Quarterly Review* vol. 38 (1947-48): 67-91; "Gemara Quotations in Sebara," *Jewish Quarterly Review* vol. 43 (1952-3): 341-363; "Some Methods of Sebara," *Jewish Quarterly Review* vol. 50 (1959-60): 124-46.

[11] Shamma Friedman, "A Critical Study of Yevamot X with a Methodological Introduction," (Heb.) in H. Z. Dimitrovski ed. *Texts and Studies: Analecta Judaica*, vol. 1 (New York: Jewish Theological Seminary of America, 1978): 293-301.

differ in their structure. At the same time they intersect thematically. This, too, is not a matter of coincidence.

My intention is that these concluding studies actually begin a renewed discussion of the thematic issues they raise: the construction of gender in/by Talmudic law, and the impact of the midrashic discourse of divorce on the legal discourse.

2

Literary Analysis for Redaction History: Source and Form Criticism

Introduction

This chapter traces an arc which spans more than fifty years, three continents, and one basic theoretical program – the desire to write a history of the redaction of the Talmud. My purpose in engaging this scholarship, however, is to interrogate its interpretive methodologies, to explore what these scholars say about reading *sugyot*.

Starting in the nineteen thirties, Avraham Weiss set out to write about the development of economic theory in the Talmud. Finding contemporary paradigms for historical scholarship on the Talmud unsatisfactory, he developed a new paradigm for scholarship, and with it a new conception of Talmudic culture. While he never wrote his history of economic theory in the Talmud, he did initiate a new discussion about how to view the development of the Talmud. He questioned the then current notions of redaction and "sealing of the Talmud" (חתימת התלמוד) in favor of a more fluid conception which, he claimed, was of the essence of Talmudic culture itself.

My interest in the work of Avraham Weiss comes from the strong way in which he understood Talmud as a literary text. His novel understanding of the "literary formulation" (קביעה ספרותית) of attributed sayings in the Talmud and the ways he thought about the development of the *sugya*, opened the door for contemporary concerns about interpretation. Weiss' work, challenges the earlier binary opposition between viewing the Talmud as either book or chaotic anthology. He introduces a way of thinking about the textuality of Talmud by insisting that, in order to interpret *sugyot*, one needs to ask both rhetorical and cultural questions. While I differ from Weiss in his certainty that asking these questions can reveal the "archeology" or pre-history of the present *sugya*, I take from Weiss the insight that the very textured, layered feel of the *sugya* is part of its rhetoric.

David Halivni's source-critical work on Talmud stresses the transformative importance of the redactional layer (the *stam*) of *sugyot*. While ultimately differing with Halivni about the possibility of recovering earlier sources, I agree with him both that there were sources and a strong redactor. I learn from Halivni's understanding of the role of the redactor, the extent to which the stammaitic material is central to the rhetoric of the *sugya*.

Shamma Friedman's study of Yevamot Chapter Ten, brings the source-critical analysis of Talmud to a new level of formalization. He introduces a set of formal criteria to distinguish between layers. He also emphasizes the importance of understanding the literary structure of a *sugya* in order to interpret it. Indeed, half of his method consists of mapping the literary structure of each *sugya* he analyzes. While I differ with Friedman about the historical implications and assumptions of his method, I agree that interpretation of a *sugya* needs to include the mapping of its structure.

Part 1. Avraham Weiss

In this section I am going to analyze Avraham Weiss'[1] interpretive methodology as he applied it to the step by step reading of *sugyot*. I shall focus on three of Weiss' readings of *sugyot*.[2]

One of the problems in discussing Weiss' interpretive methodology is that it is never explicitly spelled out. Much of Weiss' work takes the

---

[1] Avraham Weiss was born in 1895 in Podhajce in Eastern Galicia. He was ordained in 1916 by Rabbi David Horowitz. From 1917 he studied History and Classical Philology at the University of Vienna, while simultaneously studying at the Rabbinical Seminary of Vienna. He received his Ph.D. in 1921 for his thesis "The Relationship of the Popes to the Jews during the Middle Ages."

From 1928 on he was docent for Talmud at the Institute for Jewish Science in Warsaw. He was involved in communal activities and religious Zionist affairs with the *Mizraḥi* movement. In 1939 he represented the Jews in futile negotiations with the Nazis over the Warsaw ghetto. In 1940 he was invited to Yeshiva University in New York, to be Professor of Talmud. He barely managed to escape the flames of the encroaching Holocaust with his wife and family. He taught at Yeshiva University until he moved to Israel, where he died in 1970. ("Biographical Note," in *The Abraham Weiss Jubilee Volume: Studies In His Honor Presented by His Colleagues and Disciples on the Occasion of His Completing Four Decades of Pioneering Scholarship* (New York: 1964): 7-9.)

[2] Two are from a late article, and one from his second book which is the starting point of his larger historical/interpretive project.

form of taxonomic discussion: at times he explains the uses of a certain phrase (e.g. איכא דאמרי[3] or אמר נמי[4]) through myriad examples; elsewhere he describes the various ways in which parallel *sugyot* relate to each other[5] (e.g. they originate in one place and are copied to the other; it is impossible to decide which was the original; it seems that both are original); or he presents the different types of *sugyot* (e.g. "simple" or "of normal historical development" etc.)[6]. In these situations, he refrains from explicit consideration of the issues which are most relevant to the present study, such as the assumptions one makes and the questions one asks when one is interpreting a *sugya*. In what follows I will attempt to make Weiss' assumptions explicit.

The bulk of Weiss' studies aim to understand the development of the Talmud. He develops, and then works within, a sophisticated historical understanding of the Talmud as an ongoing process of development. This conceptualization precludes the idea of a uniform "final redaction": "The entire essence of the Talmud which we have before us says 'becoming' and 'development', and not final redaction."[7]

In each generation, according to Weiss, the Sages made statements (מימרות)[8] which were at some point given a literary form (קביעה ספרותית) either by them or someone of their generation. The next generation subsequently studied these statements, together with the earlier material to which it referred – Mishnaic and other tannaitic statements. The

---

[3]*The Talmud in its Development*, Vol. One, (Heb.) (New York: Philipp Feldheim, 1954): 221-260. On Weiss' methods and results, see M. S. Feldblum, "Prof. Avraham Weiss – An Appreciation of His Method in Talmudic Research and A Summary of His Conclusions", (Heb.) in *The Abraham Weiss Jubilee Volume: Studies In His Honor Presented by His Colleagues and Disciples on the Occasion of His Completing Four Decades of Pioneering Scholarship* (New York: 1964): 27. This study by Feldblum is a very encompassing but rather uncritical review of Weiss' scholarship. Studies that are both narrower in focus and more critical are: Shammai Kanter, "Abraham Weiss: Source Criticism", in J. Neusner ed. *The Formation of the Babylonian Talmud*, (Leiden: E. J. Brill, 1970): 87-94; David Goodblatt, "Abraham Weiss: The Search For Literary Forms", in J. Neusner ed. *The Formation of the Babylonian Talmud*, (Leiden: E. J. Brill, 1970): 95-103; Roger Brooks and Joseph M. Davis, "Abraham Weiss as Exegete and Text-Critic: The Case of b Berakhot 35b," *Semeia* (27), (1983): 103-116.
[4]Ibid 70-80.
[5]Cf התהוות התלמוד בשלמותו, (New York: Alexander Kohut Memorial Foundation, 1943): 172-200.
[6]Cf. e.g. "On the Literary Development of the Amoraic Sugya in its Formative Period," (Heb.) in Avraham Weiss, *Studies in Talmud* (Jerusalem: Mossad Harav Kook, 1975) 124-159.
[7]Ibid 245. "כל מהותו של התלמוד המונח לפנינו אומרת התהוות והתפתחות ולא סדור אחרון".
[8]Weiss defines a מימרא as follows: "מאמר אמוראי קצר המכיל רעיון מסוים בלי כל שו"ט". "A short Amoraic saying which includes a specific idea, with no give and take." *Studies in the Literature of the Amoraim*, (New York: Horeb, 1962): 1.

comments of this next generation were then, at some point, given literary form. They were appended to and studied together with the earlier statements, and the Mishnaic and other tannaitic statements to which they all referred.

Starting with the third generation of Palestinian Amoraim (R. Yoḥanan and Resh Lakish in particular) statements of argumentation were given literary form and preserved along with the statements of direct commentary (מימרות). This last step – preserving argumentation along with other statements, constituted the crucial step toward the development of *sugyot*. *Sugyot*, therefore, Weiss claims, are the invention of third century Palestinian Amoraim,[9] though they were quickly exported to Babylonia.

Weiss defines *sugya* rather broadly:

> We give the name *sugya* to any Talmudic give and take, long or short, which is concerned with any subject, as long as it comprises a complete unit in itself.[10]

His definition includes two limiting principles: a unit of Talmud needs to have argumentation (or give and take [שו"ט or שקלא וטריא]) for it to be considered, and it must be "a complete unit in itself." While it may be relatively easy to establish whether or not a unit includes give and take, the latter criterion is rife with problems since the essence of the interpretive enterprise is to determine what exactly any specific *sugya* is about. We will however, forestall the theoretical discussion now for the practical.

This open-ended process: taught statement ⇒ literary formulation ⇒ study and comment ⇒ literary formulation and so on, continuing throughout the Amoraic and later periods, is the basic insight of Weiss' understanding of Talmud. In the words of Meir Simḥah Feldblum, a student of Weiss':

> ...the basis of his method is already inherent in his way of thinking about the literary formulation of the Talmudic material. According to this method, we see that the study created the material and its literary formulation made it into Talmudic material. By way of continued study and the ongoing establishment of literary form (קביעה ספרותית) the Talmudic material grew.[11]

---

[9] Ibid 14

[10] אנו מכנים בשם סוניא כל שקלא וטריא תלמודי, ארוך או קצר, העוסק באיזה ענין שהוא, ובלבד שהוא מהווה אחידה שלמה לעצמה. *The Talmud in its Development*, 3. Cf. *Studies in the Literature of the Amoraim* (Heb.): 1; Feldblum, 18.

[11] "...יסוד שיטתו כבר נעוץ בשיטתו על קביעותו הספרותית של החומר התלמודי. לפי שיטה זו, רואים אנו שהלימוד יצר את החומר וקביעתו הספרותית עשתה אותו לחומר תלמודי. על ידי לימוד ממושך וקביעה ספרותית בלתי פוסקת הלך וגדל החומר התלמודי." M. S. Feldblum, "Prof.

Literary Analysis for Redaction History

At a certain point, the changes that were made to a *sugya* became more stylistic than substantive (attempts to universalize technical terminology, etc. [שכלול]), and then the process of ordering the *sugyot* of a certain Mishnah began (סידור), but the sugyot were essentially in flux till very late.[12]

Weiss' Reading of b Gittin 32b-33a

In an article devoted to the literary development of the Amoraic *sugya*[13] Weiss gives a number of examples of what he calls the "simplest *sugya*," that is, the sugya out of which it is possible to detect the original parameters of the living debate.[14] This type of *sugya* contains only a single debate and no material from other sources. He offers a *sugya* from b Gittin 32b-33a as one of his examples.

This *sugya* is generated by a reading of the last part of M. Gittin 4:1:

> At first he would constitute a court in another place and nullify it. Rabban Gamaliel the Elder ordained that they should not do so for the good order of the world (*tikkun olam*).[15]

The discussion centers on the case which seemingly "no longer" happens. If a husband wished to nullify a divorce he had already sent his wife[16] by constituting a court in another place in order to go before that court to nullify the divorce – how many judges would need to sit on that court. R. Naḥman holds that a two judge panel is necessary, while R. Sheshet holds that three judges are needed:

> At first he would constitute [a court in another place...]:[17]

Avraham Weiss – An Appreciation of His Method in Talmudic Research and A Summary of His Conclusions," (Heb.): 27.

[12]Into the Gaonic period. For an overview of the different opinions about the date of the "final redaction" of the Talmud see Richard Kalmin, *The Redaction of the Babylonian Talmud: Amoraic or Saboraic?*, (Cincinnati: Hebrew Union College Press, 1989): 1-37.

[13]"On the Literary Development of the Amoraic Sugya in its Formative Period," (Heb.) in Avraham Weiss, *Studies in Talmud* (Jerusalem: Mossad Harav Kook, 1975): 124-159.

[14]Ibid 127. גם סיבו ונם היקפו היסדי של השו״ט והבירור הממשי

[15]Soncino translates מפני תיקון עולם as "to prevent abuses". This is a paraphrase which does, however, convey the local sense of the word.

[16]Presumably before the *get* reaches the wife. See the rest of Mishnah Gittin 4:1.

[17]
בראשונה היה עושה:
איתמר בפני כמה מבטלה?
רב נחמן אמר, בפני ב'.
רב ששת אמר, בפני ג'.
"רב ששת אמר בפני ג'," ב"ד קתני.
"ורב נחמן אמר בפני ב'," לבי תרי נמי ב"ד קרי להו.

It has been stated: In the presence of how many must he nullify it?
R. Naḥman said: In the presence of two.
R. Sheshet said: In the presence of three.
5   "R. Sheshet said: In the presence of three." – [the Mishnah] teaches *bet din*.
And "R. Naḥman said: In the presence of two." – before two is also called a *bet din*.
R. Naḥman said: From where do I say this?
For it is taught [in a Mishnah]: "I declare before you so-and-so and so-and-so (פלוני ופלוני) the judges in such-and-such place."
And R. Sheshet? Need the Tanna [of the Mishnah in Shebi'it] be like a peddler counting out his wares?[18]
10 R. Naḥman said: From where do I say this?
For it is taught [in that same Mishnah]: "The judges sign below or the witnesses."
Is it not that "judges" are like "witnesses" – just as witnesses [means] two, so judges [means] two.
And R. Sheshet? Is this an argument? This is as it is and this is as it is.
Why need I say judges, and why need I say witnesses?
15 This teaches us that it matters not if it is written in the language of judges and signed by witnesses,
or written in the language of witnesses and signed by judges.[19]

Weiss claims that the only parts of the *sugya* that can be attributed to the named sages (aside from the stated positions themselves) are R. Naḥman's explanations of his position in lines 7-8 and 10-12. The rest of the sugya is post-Amoraic and should be attributed to the anonymous redactional layer (*stam*).

Weiss' reasoning here is very illuminating. First he points out that R. Sheshet's refutations of R. Naḥman's explanations are at least as persuasive as R. Naḥman's explanations themselves. If the dispute was truly about whether or not a two person panel might be called a *bet din*

אמר רב נחמן, מנא אמינא לה? דתנן,
"מוסרני לפניכם | פלוני ופלוני הדיינין שבמקום פלוני." (שביעית י:ד)
ורב ששת, אטו תנא כי רוכלא, ליחשיב וליזיל?
10   אמר רב נחמן, מנא אמינא לה? דתנן,
"הדיינים חותמין למטה או העדים." (שם)
מאי לאו, דיינים דומיא דעדים. מה עדים בשנים אף דיינים נמי שנים.
ורב ששת מידי איריא, הא כדאיתא והא כדאיתא.
ל"ל למיתנא דיינים ל"ל למיתנא עדים?
15   הא קא משמע לן דלא שנא כתוב בלשון דיינים, וחתמי עדים.
ולא שנא כתוב בלשון עדים, וחתמי דיינים.

[18]That is, do we expect the author of the Mishnah to write that the person says "so-and-so and so-and-so and so-and-so," rather than "so-and-so and so-and-so," because there are actually three? Cf. Rashi b Gittin 33a.

[19]This last statement is somewhat puzzling, and the commentators also differ in its understanding. Rashi's explanation is that it makes no difference if the document of the *prozbul* is written from the point of view of the witnesses (i.e. "we witnessed that so-and-so said") or the judges (i.e. "on this day so-and-so came before us and said").

Literary Analysis for Redaction History

the result would be a draw, or R. Sheshet's position would be vindicated. Therefore, Weiss reasons, lines 5 and 6 must not reflect the original terms of the dispute, but rather lines 7-8 and 10-12. That is, R. Naḥman does not refer to the Mishnah in Shebi'it in order to back up his claim that a two person panel might sometimes be called a *bet din*. Rather, he refers to M Shebi'it in order to call attention to the similarity between the cases of *prozbul* and nullification of a divorce in the presence of a *bet din*. Both of these situations entail deposition or public announcement, which would not require a three person panel, as opposed to judgment, which might require a three person panel.

R. Naḥman's proof that the *prozbul* case is one of deposition is from the fact that at the end of the Mishnah in Shebi'it witnesses are introduced, whereas they are not mentioned before in that Mishnah – thus positing a relationship between the function of the witnesses and the judges. This would suggest a similarity between the *prozbul* proceedings and a testimony or deposition (הצהרה או מודעה). The proof therefore derives from the whole Mishnah, rather than any part thereof, as it would seem from the way in which the *sugya* appears before us. According to this line of thought, R. Sheshet's "refutations," are considered later than R. Naḥman's explanation(s).[20]

The reconstruction of the "original give and take" of this *sugya* would then be:

> At first he would constitute [a court in another place...]:
> R. Naḥman said: In the presence of two.
> R. Sheshet said: In the presence of three.
> R. Naḥman said: From where do I say this?
> For it is taught [in a Mishnah]: "I declare before you so-and-so and so-and-so (פלוני ופלוני) the judges in such-and-such place....The judges sign below or the witnesses." Is it not that "judges" are like "witnesses" – just as witnesses [means] two, so judges [means] two.

When this *sugya* was studied by the next generation, R. Naḥman's reasoning was misunderstood. These students assumed that his argument concerned whether or not one could understand the term *bet din* in Mishnah Gittin 4:1 as referring to a two person panel. This was given literary form in lines 5 and 6. The rest of the *sugya* proceeded from there – with R. Sheshet's "refutations" also on this basis – and ended in the final lines (14-15) which remain opaque.[21]

Weiss sees this as the normal development of a *sugya*. First there is a Mishnaic statement, then that statement is studied and commented

---

[20] "On the Literary Development of the Amoraic Sugya in its Formative Period," 125-127.
[21] Weiss (ibid 125 n. 6) suggests that these lines are later than the rest of the *sugya*.

upon. The comments are given a literary form, and then they too are studied and commented on or expanded, and so forth. Each stage of the process is preserved, and in order to get to an earlier stage we need only filter out the later accretions.

Reading Weiss I

When I analyze Weiss' analysis, I am struck by the major role that is played by reasoning or what we might refer to as סברא. At the same time a far less significant role is given to taxonomic criteria such as language (Aramaic or Hebrew) or form (e.g. explanatory or apodictic). When I attempt to reconstruct Weiss' interpretive process, and ask what questions he posed which brought him to this reconstruction or historical argument – they turn out to be similar to those asked by most medieval commentators on this *sugya*.

Many, if not most, of the medieval commentaries[22] on this *sugya* deal with two questions: 1) the question of this *sugya's*[23] placement, which does not concern us here; 2) the question of the derivation of the idea that "before two is also called a *bet din*." Most medieval commentators view the latter in light of the discussion (b Sanhedrin 3a) of whether the adjudication of two judges (instead of the requisite three) is valid.[24] Samuel rules for the validity of a two judge adjudication. The dominant interpretive tradition in the Talmud, however, within which the commentaries place R. Naḥman, rules that an adjudication by two judges is not valid.[25] Placing R. Naḥman in the camp that rules against the two

---

[22]Sheiltot #65 (ed. Mirsky 174), Alfasi, Rashi, Tosafot, RSB"A, RYTB"A, Meiri. The Sheiltot and Alfasi do not, of course, comment in a direct manner, however the Sheiltot juxtapose R. Naḥman's statement with the statement from b Sanhedrin 3a that is quoted by the rest of the commentaries, and Alfasi quotes the discussion in b Arachin 21b which attributes the statement to R. Sheshet which implies that nullifying a *get* is a מודעה (deposition or announcement).

[23]That is, why was this *sugya* placed here and not after the discussion following it (33a) of whether a husband can in fact nullify his wife's divorce without her knowledge. Since our *sugya* only has relevance to the side of that dispute (Rabbi) which says that a husband *can* nullify the divorce, why not place our *sugya* after that one. Weiss sees this as further proof of another principle of the ordering of *sugyot* which is articulated in *Studies in the Literature of the Amoraim* (Heb.), vis. on any specific Mishnah, the explanatory material (החומר הפרשני) is placed first, followed by the material which is only conceptually related. ("Literary Development..." 126 and n.7) It might also be pointed out that in the very next unit, the dispute between R. Naḥman and R. Sheshet is understood in terms of the resonance of a legal action קלא or קול. This seems to reinforce the reading of מודעה.

[24]שנים שדנו דיניהם דין אלא שנקראו בית דין חצוף. cf. b Sanhderin 30a and b Ketuboth 22a.

[25]The Tosafists, *ad locum*, argue that R. Naḥman could not have agreed with Samuel's statement, (even though he repeats the statement in the name of Samuel in b Sanhedrin 5b) since Rava doesn't accept Samuel's ruling and necessarily

Literary Analysis for Redaction History

judge adjudication is an important move. This forces all of the commentators to veer away from a simple reading of this line – since R. Naḥman cannot mean it literally, as that would contradict his general position on two judge adjudications. It is at this point, that is, in the understanding of lines 5 and 6 – but especially 6 – that Weiss parts company with the earlier commentaries.

The earlier commentaries reason that it is obvious that line 6 cannot mean that two is really a *bet din*.[26] Therefore, they claim, it must mean that a panel of two is an adequate *bet din* <u>for nullification of a *get*</u>, since this is just the giving of a deposition (מודעה). Lines 7-13 then follow as explication of these original positions. Weiss, on the other hand, takes lines 5 and 6 "literally," and then reads the *sugya* against its rhetoric. He claims that lines 5 and 6 are later (and mistaken) explanations of lines 7-8 and 10-12. Weiss' gain is in understanding this *sugya* without having to resort to the larger Talmudic matrix which the earlier commentators use. Nonetheless, his final understanding of the *sugya*'s meaning, as opposed to its development, remains very similar to the earlier commentators.

The difference, then, between Weiss and the medieval commentary tradition, lies in the interpretive framework. Weiss believes that textual difficulties[27] point to historical layers, or different sources. He offers his elegant solution to the anomalous lines of the *sugya*, based on his understanding of the historical development of *sugyot*. The medieval commentators, who do not employ this frame, interpret the textual problems within the matrix of the entire Talmud. Nevertheless, what prompted the questioning – for both Weiss and the medievals – was a *textual* problem.[28] Their respective answers depended in part upon their understandings of what a text is. Thus Weiss' answer, like those of the

---

agrees with R. Naḥman here. They derive this last from the fact that a) in the next unit (b Gittin 33a) R. Yoḥanan is said to agree with R. Naḥman; and b) in b Yebamoth 36a a statement is attributed to Rava in which he says that the Halakhah is according to Resh Lakish in (only) three places – implying that in the rest the Halakhah is according to R. Yoḥanan. ("הלכתא כוותיה דר״ל בתני חלת"). So, Rava holds according to R. Yoḥanan, R. Yoḥanan holds according to R. Naḥman, therefore Rava holds according to R. Naḥman.

Rashi *ad locum*, commenting on the phrase "in front of two" (בפני שנים) simply says: "...but here it is merely a deposition and it is enough with two." (אבל הכא אודועי בעלמא הוא ובתרי סני) In this way he differentiates between Samuel's ruling and ours by implication rather than explicitly (though the *sugya* b San. 3a is the obvious intertext of his comment).

RSB"A, *ad locum*, rehearses the general outline of the Tosafists argument without the explicit causuistry.

[26] See n. 25.
[27] That is, stylistic, syntactic or logical problems.
[28] Or ungrammaticality in contemporary literary terminology. See my discussion in Chapter 5.

medieval commentaries, is better viewed as a *product* rather than a *proof* of a particular historical/theoretical frame.

Weiss' Reading of b Gittin 15a-b

Further on in the same article, Weiss discusses a *sugya* (b Gittin 15a-b) which he sees as an example of a "*sugya* that has a normal layered development."[29] This discussion further illustrates Weiss' interpretive methodology.

The *sugya* is generated by the Mishnah's (Gittin 2:1) statement about a messenger who brings a *get* from far away – literally "from the countries of the sea." If that messenger then declares that the *get* was written in his presence, though not signed by both witnesses in his presence – the *get* is not valid.

> **The whole [document] was written in my presence, and half of it was signed in my presence it is not valid.**
> Said R. Ḥisda, and even if two testify to the signature of the second it is invalid.
> What is the reason?
> Either it is all [validated by the witnesses] for the validation of the *get*, or it is all [validated] through the sages' ordinance [that the messenger can validate instead of two witnesses].
> 5 Raba objected, Is there a situation [in which] if one had said [that it was valid, it would have been considered] valid, now that there are two [who say that it is valid] it is not valid?
> Rather, said Rava, Even if he and another testify to the signature of the second [witness] it is not valid.
> What is the reason?
> [Some] are liable to adopt this [manner of validation] with general contracts, and three quarters of the money would be removed [from one litigant] on the word of one witness.
> R. Ashi objected, Is there a situation [in which], if he had attested to the whole statement by himself, [it would have been considered] valid,
> 10 [but] now that there is another with him it is invalid?
> Rather, said R. Ashi, Even if he says 'I am the second witness.' It is not valid.
> What is the reason?
> Either it is all [validated by the witnesses] for the validation of the *get*, or it is all [validated] through the sages' ordinance [that the messenger can validate instead of two witnesses].
> We have learned in the Mishnah: The whole [document] was written in my presence, and half of it was signed in my presence.
> 15 What is the situation of the other half? If we say there was no one to testify to it all,

---

[29] סוניא בעלת התפתחות שכבתית נורמליח 128.

Literary Analysis for Redaction History

> Now [is this not the same as the Mishnah's case:] If one says it was written in my presence, and one says it was signed in my presence [it is invalid].
> For [in the case in which] this one testified to the complete writing [of the *get*], and this one testified to the complete signing it is not valid – need we ask of half?
> Rather, it is either according to Rava or according to R. Ashi and opposed to R. Ḥisda.
> R. Ḥisda would say to you, According to your reasoning, why do I need "It was written in my presence, but it was not signed in my presence"? Rather the Mishnah teaches 'not only this, but that too.'
> So, too, here, the Mishnah teaches 'not only this, but that, too.'[30]

A cursory glance at the *sugya* reveals that the three named Amoraim are from three generations, in chronological order. That is, R. Ḥisda is a third generation Babylonian Amora, Rava is fourth generation Amora, and R. Ashi is from the sixth generation. Weiss claims that that is exactly the way in which the *sugya* developed – first R. Ḥisda read the Mishnah and commented on it; then Rava studied the Mishnah with R. Hisda's comment and commented on that; finally R. Ashi studied the Mishnah and the other comments and commented on them. In his words:

30

בפני נכתב כולו ובפני נחתם חציו פסול.
אמר רב חסדא, ואפילו שנים מעידים על חתימת יד שני פסול.
מאי טעמא?
או כולו בקיום הגט או כולו בתקנת חכמים.
מתקיף לה רבא, מי איכא מידי דאילו אמר חד כשר, השתא דאיכא תרי פסול? 5
אלא אמר רבא, אפילו הוא ואחד מעידין על חתימת יד שני פסול.
מאי טעמא?
אתו לאיחלופי בקיום שטרות דעלמא, וקא נפיק נכי רובעא דממונא אפומא דחד סהדא.
מתקיף לה רב אשי, מי איכא מידי דאילו מסיק ליה אידו לכוליה דיבורא כשר,
השתא דאיכא חד בהדיה פסול!? 10
אלא אמר רב אשי, אפילו אומר אני הוא עד שני פסול.
מאי טעמא?
או כולו בקיום הגט או כולו בתקנת חכמים.
תנן בפני נכתב כולו ובפני נחתם חציו פסול.
אידך חציו היכי דמי? אילימא דליכא דקא מסהיד עליה כלל, 15
השתא אחד אומר בפני נכתב ואחד אומר בפני נחתם,
דהאי קמסהיד אכולה כתיבה והאי קמסהיד אכולה חתימה פסול,-חציו מיבעיא?
אלא או כדרבא או כדרב אשי, ולאפוקי מדרב חסדא.
אמר לך רב חסדא, ולטעמיך בפני נכתב אבל לא בפני נחתם ל"ל? אלא לא זו אף זו קתני.
הכא נמי לא זו אף זו קתני. 20

...here in the Bavli is a *sugya* with three layers. The first layer is R. Ḥisda's, the second is of Rava and the third is already from R. Ashi.[31]

From the discussion it emerges that, according to Weiss, only lines 15-20 are *stammaitic*,[32] that is, part of the later redactional layer.[33] The rest of the *sugya* reflects the actual continuing process of study, comment, literary formulation, repeated over generations.

Following Weiss' reasoning as he reads the *sugya* is, again, instructive. Weiss sees three major interpretive problems in this *sugya*. First, what is the relation between the statements attributed to the named sages (lines 2,6,11) and the Mishnah. Are they interpretations of the Mishnaic rule, expansions of that rule, or independent statements that are related by subject matter? The second problem concerns the statement given as both R. Ḥisda's and R. Ashi's "reason" (lines 4,13): או כולו בקיום הגט או כולו בתקנת חכמים.[34] What is the source of this statement? Is it an independent axiom that R. Ḥisda (and later R. Ashi) cites for support? Or is it a rule which R. Ḥisda derives from this Mishnah itself? Third, what is the relation between the three attributed statements themselves? Are they intrinsically contradictory, or is the contradiction a result of the way they are currently framed? To answer this last question we will have to take a closer look at the "attacks"[35] of Rava and R. Ashi.

As to the first problem, Rashi, in his commentary on this *sugya*, claims that R. Ḥisda's statement is an independent statement extrapolated from the Mishnah's ruling.[36] The stammaitic ending of the *sugya* (15-20) seems to support this interpretation by dismissing R. Ḥisda's ruling (18). Weiss rejects this interpretation, however, since it would require that we claim that the principle stated in line 4 was derived originally from this statement of R. Ḥisda's (2). This would be a problematic argument since Ḥisda's statement, according to Weiss, is "very strange" as an independent ruling, and especially since Rava's question (5) is "all too obvious."

---

[31] ...פה בבבלי סוגיא בת שלוש שכבות. השכבה הראשונה היא של רב חסדא והשניה מיסודו של רבא והשלישית היא כבר מרב אשי. "On the Literary Development of the Amoraic Sugya in its Formative Period," 132.
[32] 130.
[33] I suspect that Weiss would agree that the two מאי טעמא questions (ll. 3 and 12) are also later than the answers that they precede. He doesn't however say anything about this, nor is it clear how late he would date them. That is are they the result of the next generation's study of the former generation's remarks, or a *stammaitic* addition at the time of the final redaction or שכלול.
[34] I refrain from citing the translation here, since, as will be seen, the meaning of the statement itself is under contention.
[35] The literal meaning of the Aramaic מתקיף of lines 5 and 9.
[36] "סברא דידיה מוסיף ואמר רבותא..."

Weiss therefore contends that Ḥisda's statement (2) is a deduction from the principle of line 4, which he abstracted from the ruling of the Mishnah itself (1). That is, Ḥisda reads the Mishnah's statement "...and half of it was signed in my presence..." as saying that it does not matter whether or not there were witnesses to the other half. Since the Mishnah does not say that there were not, it means that even if there were – the *get* is still invalid. The only reason for this must be that the *get* must either be validated *in toto* (כולו) by the witnesses to the signing (הגם קיום), or by the messenger who is allowed by Rabbinic ordinance (תקנת חכמים) to testify to the validity of the *get* ("It was written and signed in my presence." M. Gittin 1:1) . The *method of validation* cannot be divided.

In contrast, Rava, according to Weiss, does not want to force the Mishnah, by dint of subordinating it to this principle (...או כולו), into supporting a conclusion as strange as Ḥisda's, especially because this principle is open to the objection of line 5. Rava therefore supports his own ruling by recourse to an argument from contracts in general (6-8).

R. Ashi objects to Rava's statement (9), and supports his own ruling (11) in the light of Ḥisda's original principle. However, Weiss argues that Ashi's understanding of the principle is different than Ḥisda's. For R. Ashi, the principle asserts that the messenger, as the validator of the *get*, must operate *in toto* (כולו) either as a witness to the *get* (הגם קיום) or as the messenger (תקנת חכמים). The *validator* cannot be divided into two functions.

Reading Weiss II

When we take a step back to analyze this reading of the *sugya* we are again struck by the paramount role of *sevara*, over and against linguistic or other formal criteria. In contrast to the *sugya* considered above, in Weiss' reading of this *sugya*, he resolves textual difficulties by accepting the attribution of statements to the three Sages as historically reliable. Weiss reads the fact of the three Sages being from somewhat consecutive generations back into his "master narrative." His only challenge is to smooth out the problems wrought by the movement from one moment of the *sugya* to the next. He sees no reason to rearrange the text as this is the "normal development" of the *sugya* according to the master narrative. Once again, though, the *sugya* has not supplied a proof of Weiss' theory of historical development. Once that theory was in place the *sevara* approach seemed the logical method. The generation to generation coherence that Weiss so elegantly showed, is not a function of "the *sugya* itself." It is, rather, one frame within which the *sugya* might be understood.

This last statement seems to call for a few comments on what might be the paths not taken by Weiss. First, if we compare the three attributed statements without the intervening questions and answers, they are not necessarily contradictory. They seem rather to build on each other, with R. Ashi supplying a crescendo: "Even if he himself was the second witness we do not believe him!"

They are, also, written in Hebrew while the surrounding objections are in Aramaic. This should pique the interest of source and form critics,[37] as should the observation that the commentaries hotly debate the meanings of both Rava's and R. Ashi's objections. Although the objections are far from clear, as Weiss himself mentions in the footnotes to his discussion, he dismisses this fact as unimportant.

Finally, the success of Weiss' reading depends upon the claim that the exact same statement can mean two very different things in the space of one *sugya*. It is nearly impossible to decide, however, whether this is the case. The statements occur only here; there is no parallel *sugya*.[38] Further, that which allows Weiss to read the statement in two different ways – the ambiguity of the referent of כולו – throws the meaning of the line into doubt at both occurrences. Weiss' confidence that his archaeology is correct emerges from his frame, and not the other way around.

To conclude this brief discussion I now look at the theoretical and textual point upon which Weiss constructs his understanding of Talmud.

קביעה ספרותית (Literary Formulation)

Weiss' major insight and contribution to the scholarly understanding of Talmud, is his idea of literary formulation or קביעה ספרותית. This insight is predicated on a theory of the culture of Rabbinic learning as consisting of an identifiable, and oftentimes traceable process of fluidity followed by definition, followed by fluidity and so on. A sage would teach

---

[37]E.g. the work of Hyman Klein. The distinction between Hebrew and Aramaic, both in the same statement and in different statements is essential to his method. Cf. "Gemara and Sebara", Jewish Quarterly Review, Vol 38 (1947-1948): 75ff. esp: "...a series of different Amoraic comments on a single text may as a result of interpretative discussion appear to have arisen because of successive objections. In all such cases it is necessary to distinguish carefully the additions of the Talmudic commentator from the original remarks....The Aramaic framework of question and discussion in which a series of Amoraic comments on a tannaitic text is embedded should be looked upon as a construction subsequent in date to that of the original statements." (79-80) See also my discussion of Shamma Friedman's form-critical criteria in section 3 of this chapter.

[38]Weiss claims that the corresponding *sugya* in the PT is a parallel *sugya*. His arguments though are not very convincing. He himself ends up making the argument in the Bavli without the aid of the other *sugya*. Second, there is no lexical parallel. None of the central phrases of our *sugya* are repeated in the PT. It is only through an ingenious interpretation – and a unique interpretation of one phrase used in PT – that the *sugyot* are shown to be even conceptually parallel.

something to a group of students or peers. The statement of this sage would then circulate orally for a period of time. At some point the statement would become so familiar or accepted that it would be given a definite literary form such as: "This law applies only Thursday nights in leap years." Often, the statement would be attributed to a specific sage ("Rabbi X says"). In the intervening time between the original teaching and its definitive literary formulation, however, the teaching was often dislodged from the association with the original speaker and popularly attributed to another.

Weiss posits a number of possibilities for why this happened. A certain student of the original sage, for example, would often repeat the teaching of his master – so much so that people would identify him with it. The specific reasons are not as important as the underlying theory of Rabbinic culture. Weiss theorizes that the Rabbis lived in a literary atmosphere (אוירה) which precluded "authorship" over specific sayings in the modern, legalistic understanding of the concept of authorship. Rather, the sayings belonged to the community, and therefore both literary formulation and attribution were not necessarily tied to the original "author." This could also account for statements which are attributed to more than one "author."[39]

Once a statement received its literary formulation, it then became a part of the common body of learned material, the Rabbinic curriculum – along with the Torah and the Mishnah. The "curriculum" constantly changed and grew as each generation added its layer of learning which eventually received literary formulation and passed over into the realm of that which is to be studied. This model views Talmud more as a process than as a fixed work, thus rendering meaningless the idea of a final redaction of the Talmud. (Or, in contemporary literary parlance, the Talmud is more text than book.)

Weiss attaches the process of a literary formulation (קביעה ספרותית) to the Talmudic phrase קבע, קבעיתו (69). The phrase אתמר נמי signals a statement in its final fixed literary form (73). Weiss sees this process explicitly at work in a *sugya* in b Erubin 32b. It should be noted that this *sugya* has occasioned much argumentation – both ancient[40] and modern[41] – about the redaction of the Babylonian Talmud.

---

[39]*The Talmud in its Development*, 62.
[40]The earliest post-Talmudic discussion is by Sherira Gaon. See *The Letter of R. Sherira Gaon* (ed. Levin): 63. Rashi in his commentary on this *sugya* also expands on the redaction history.
[41]Aside from Weiss, see *inter alia* Ḥanoch Albeck, *Introduction to the Talmud, Babli and Yerushalmi*, (Heb.) (Tel Aviv: Dvir, 1975): 576-578; David Halivni, *Sources and Traditions: Erubin and Pesaḥim*, (Jerusalem: Jewish Theological Seminary of America, 1982): 91-95. Cf. the translation of this *sugya* in the Soncino Talmud.

The sugya is generated by a Mishnah (Erubin 3:3) that discusses the place in which a person might place foodstuff before the Sabbath, so that that place would be considered his on the Sabbath. This has important ramifications for the radius of movement he might have on the Sabbath. The significance of the *sugya* for Weiss, is not, however, related to its substance, but the manner of its transmission.

Mishnah

1   If he deposited it[42] on a tree above ten handbreadths, his *erub* is ineffective;
Below ten handbreadths his *erub* is effective.
If he deposited it in a cistern, even if it is a hundred cubits deep, his *erub* is effective.

Gemara

R. Ḥiyya b. Abba and R. Assi and Raba b. Nathan were sitting[43] [and studying], and R. Naḥman was sitting beside them,
5   And [while they were] sitting they said: That tree [of the Mishnah] where was it standing?
If you would say that it stood in a private domain, what [difference is it] to me 'above' or 'below' – a private domain rises up to the sky!
Rather, it stood in the public domain.
The one who intended to abide [for the Sabbath], where [did he intend to make his abode]?
If you would say he intended to abide above [ten handbreadths] – he and his *erub* are in one place.
10   Rather, he intended to abide below – but is he not making use of the tree[44]?!
It may still maintained that [the tree] stood in the public domain, and he intended to abide below,
And this is [in accordance with] Rabbi who said: Any act forbidden by a rabbinical ordinance is not subject to that ordinance during twilight.
R. Naḥman said to them: Well spoken, and so also did Samuel say.
They said to him: Have you gone so far in your interpretation?
15   They too [however] have interpreted it in this way!
Rather, they said to him thus: did you set it in your teaching[45]?

---

[42]The foodstuff set aside as the *erub*, that is, as the symbolic joining of more than one domain.

[43]On the possible institutional implication of יתב see Isaiah M. Gafni, *The Jews of Babylonia in the Talmudic Era; A Social and Cultural History*, (Heb.) (Jerusalem: Zalman Shazar Center for Jewish History, 1990) Chapter 6 and appendix C.

[44]Such use being forbidden on the Sabbath.

[45]The Soncino interpretation "Did you embody it in the Gemara?" assumes a line of argumentation (only referred to in the footnoted reference to a Jewish Encyclopedia article) which is the opposite of the way Weiss, but also Albeck (*Introduction to the Talmud, Babli and Yerushalmi*, (Heb.)) and others understand the line. See n. 39 above.

Literary Analysis for Redaction History 23

He said to them: Yes.

It was also said (אתמר נמי): R Naḥman said Samuel said:
Here we are dealing with a tree that is standing in the public domain, ten [handbreadths] high and four wide, and he intended to abide [for the Sabbath] below.

20   And this is [in accordance with] Rabbi who said: Any act forbidden by a rabbinical ordinance is not subject to that ordinance during twilight.[46]

Weiss views lines 13-20 as the important section of the *sugya*, that is, R. Naḥman's approving response (l. 13) to the comments of those sitting with him, and especially their attribution of the resolution to the legal thinking of Rabbi: "יישר וכן אמר שמואל." R. Naḥman concurs with their opinion and claims that Samuel has said the same thing. They then seemingly challenge him, "Have you gone so far in your interpretation?" (l. 14).

At this point the editorial voice, or the *stam*, intervenes: "They too have interpreted it in this way." (l. 15) This exchange is then recapitulated (probably by the *stam*) as being a question about whether or not R. Naḥman had "set it" in his[47] tradition, or teaching.[48] The next

---

[46]

משנה
נתנו באילן למעלה מעשרה טפחים אין עירובו עירוב.   1
למטה מעשרה טפחים עירובו עירוב.
נתנו בבור אפילו עמוק מאה אמה עירובו עירוב:
גמרא
יתיב רבי חייא בר אבא, ורבי אסי, ורבא בר נתן, ויתיב רב נחמן גבייהו,
ויתבי וקאמרי: האי אילן דקאי היכא?   5
אילימא דקאי ברשות היחיד, מה לי למעלה מה לי למטה—רשות היחיד עולה עד לרקיע!
ואלא דקאי ברשות הרבים.
דמתכוין לשבות, היכא?
אילימא דנתכוון לשבות למעלה—הוא ועירובו במקום אחד הוא.
אלא ניכוון לשבות למטה—והא קא משתמש באילן!   10
לעולם דקאי ברשות הרבים, ונתכוון לשבות למטה.
ורבי היא דאמר: כל דבר שהוא משום שבות לא גזרו עליו בין השמשות.
אמר להו רב נחמן, 'יישר וכן אמר שמואל.
אמרו ליה, פתריתו בה כולי האי.
אינהו נמי הכי קא פתרי בה.   15
אלא הכי אמרו ליה, קבעיתו ליה בגמרא?
אמר להו, אין.

אתמר נמי אמר רב נחמן אמר שמואל,
הכא באילן העומד ברשות הרבים עסקינן, גבוה עשרה ורחב ארבעה, ונתכוון לשבות למטה.
ורבי היא דאמר כל דבר שהוא משום שבות לא גזרו עליו בין השמשות.   20

[47]Though Sherira (in the Spanish recension) has it as a question that R. Naḥman is asking them.

[48]See Weiss' discussion of גמרא, *The Talmud in its Development* 70-71, Albeck, *Introduction to the Talmud*, 599-601.

piece of the *sugya*, lines 18-20, clarifies what this phrase might mean. R. Naḥman answers "yes," that is, he has set it. Then, according to Weiss, his "setting" of the teaching is produced. This is what אמר נמי always means.⁴⁹

In lines 18-20, the "living exchange" between R. Naḥman and his friends is transformed into a statement in a set literary form, attributed to R. Naḥman in the name of Samuel. The phrase "קביעתו ליה בגמרא" sums up the move from lines 11-14 to lines 18-20.

Reading Weiss III

Two factors call into question whether the "history" that Weiss reconstructs results from the interpretation, as opposed to his interpretive framework. First, he precedes the discussion of this *sugya* with five pages of theoretical discussion of התהוות ספרותית and קביעה ספרותית.⁵⁰ Second, after presenting various texts in which the term קבע appears, Weiss makes the following statement:

> In every one of these places, the term קבע does have a shade of meaning of its own, but when we try to define the action to which they are referring to with this expression, using a definition which will encompass all the places together, we come to the definition of the action which we have named קביעה ספרותית.⁵¹

That is, no single occurrence of the phrase has, as its simple meaning, that action that he calls קביעה ספרותית. In fact, on the basis of the same evidence, Weiss and Albeck come to opposing readings of the phrase in certain *sugyot*.⁵² Only in the light of the theory does this meaning present itself. The compelling part of this understanding for Weiss seems to be that it solves the major problem of the *sugya*, namely, interpreting the purpose of lines 18-20. Since they seem to reiterate the earlier statement, they cannot be a proof for it. According to Weiss' understanding, they are not meant as a proof at all. Rather, these lines constitute R. Naḥman's answer to the question posed in line 16: "Yes there is a set literary form to Shmuel's statement, and here it is."⁵³

This is the crux of Weiss' interpretive methodology. His interpretation starts at the point of syntactical, grammatical, lexical or logical problem in a *sugya*. He subordinates these questions about the

---

⁴⁹Ibid 78
⁵⁰*The Talmud in its Development* 61-66.
⁵¹69. בכל מקום ממקומות אלה אמנם לביטוי קבע איזה גוון משלו, אבל כשנכנסה להגדיר את הפעולה שאליה מתכוונים בביטוי זה בהגדרה שתכלול את כל המקומות גם יחד, נבוא לידי הגדרת פעולה שקראנו אותה בשם קביעה ספרותית.
⁵²E.g. b Rosh Hashana 31b (Weiss 68, and Albeck 577).
⁵³Halivni and Albeck each offer their interpretation of these lines – in line with their understanding of the redaction history of the Bavli.

sugya as a literary text,⁵⁴ to an overarching historical frame which he employs to ascertain the meaning of the specific *sugya*. While the frame might be correct, its inadequacy lies in its privileged position as presupposed rather than proven. This privileging masks its relativity, as only one possible frame.

In the three *sugyot* that I read closely, I pointed out a disjunction between interpretive method and historical framework. That is, the problems, which Weiss dealt with, arose from tensions, roughness, or the inability to read the text as is. The readings that were offered, were inspired by a historical setting which preexisted the reading of the specific *sugya*. While Weiss' ability to read closely, and interpret brilliantly is never called into question, we have seen that the historical conclusions that Weiss draws are not based on his reading. They are, rather, presupposed and then applied as an interpretive framework.

Part 2. David Halivni

David Halivni has maintained a consistent methodological approach to Talmud from his first volume of *Sources and Traditions*. This approach might be categorized as a strict source-critical approach. Halivni defines source criticism as a method

> ...that seeks to differentiate between the original statements as they were enunciated by their authors and the forms they took as a consequence of being orally transmitted: that is, between the sources and their later traditions.⁵⁵

In its specific application to Talmud, a source-critical method strives to identify and isolate the "sources," that is, "the statements that reached us in their original form, as they were enunciated by their authors,"⁵⁶ from the "traditions," additions or distortions which resulted from the process of transmission.⁵⁷

---

⁵⁴The phrases which usually signal the literary discussions of specific texts are words such as: תמוה, מחו ("On the Literary Development of the Amoraic Sugya in its Formative Period," 130, 140), the often recurring yet undefined "טיב מהותה של הסוגיא" (e.g. *Studies in the Literature of the Amoraim*, 32), "עושה רושם" (*Studies...*, 87), "קרוב הדבר" (*Studies...* 129). These phrases give way to a more precise "scientific" vocabulary for the statement of the theoretical premises/conclusions.

⁵⁵"Talmud: Source Criticism," in *Encyclopedia Britannica*, vol. XXI (1963): 645. Quoted in *Sources and Traditions: A Source Critical Commentary on Seder Nashim* (Tel Aviv: Dvir Publishing House, 1968) on back of English title page. Cf. *Sources and Traditions: A Source Critical Commentary on Seder Moed: Tractate Shabbath* 14 n. 25*.

⁵⁶למימרות שהגיעו אלינו בצורתן המקורית, כפי שיצאו מפי המחבר (*ipsissima verba*)

⁵⁷*Sources and Traditions: A Source Critical Commentary on Seder Nashim* 7 n.1.

The historical picture that Halivni sketches with this method changes from the first *Sources and Traditions* to the third[58] although the method remains the same. In the first volume, Halivni attributes a narrow role to the *stammaim*. He is also less clear about the dating of the *stammaim*.[59] In the third volume he concludes that the Talmud as we know it – that is, the argumentation and the give and take, and even large parts of many statements attributed to earlier sages – is all the product of the anonymous layer, the layer of the *stammaim*. These anonymous redactors lived in the period after R. Ashi's death. Prior to the *stammaim*, apodictic statements were recorded, but the reasoning or argumentation either wasn't recorded or was recorded in a fragmented way.

> The *stammaim* received from the previous generations dialogues, cryptic explanations and fragmentary give and take, which were appended to the Mishnah and the beraitta. They filled out and widened that which they received, they added rhetorical questions and answers, close or distant associations, and attended to it minutely.[60]

The *stammaim* are redactors, that is they are

> partners to the creation (if of a lesser rank). They complete, broaden, and add to the text whenever it is necessary to bring it to completion.[61]

The typical Talmudic *sugya* then, is the creation of the *stammaim*. According to Halivni, even some apparently Amoraic statements, or parts of statements, are in reality *stammaitic*.

Halivni's major interpretive procedure is identifying what he calls דחוקים or deviations from the "simple interpretation" (פירוש הפשוט).

> Deviations from the simple interpretation – that is the interpretation which comes out of the text without taking from it or adding on to it,... – prove that those who deviated did not have in front of them

---

[58]*Sources and Traditions: A Source Critical Commentary on Seder Moed: Tractate Shabbath* (Jerusalem: JTSA, 1982).

[59]Even in the second volume he is hesitant about stating that all the *stammaitic* additions are late. *Sources and Traditions: A Source Critical Commentary on Seder Moed: Yoma-Hagiga*, 9.

[60]הסתמאים קיבלו מהדורות הקודמים דיאלונים, פירושים מצומצמים ושקלא וטריא מקוטעת, שהיו טפלים למשנה ולברייתא. הם השלימו והרחיבו את קבלתם, הוסיפו לה שאלות ותשובות ריטוריות, אסוציאציות קרובות ורחוקות ודייקו בה דיוק מרובה Ibid. 6-7.

[61]רידקטור (המתקין את הטקסט, מכין ומכשיר אותו...) הוא שותף ליצירה (אם כי נחות דרגה). הלה משלים מרחיב ומוסיף לטקסט כל אימת שיש צורך להביאו לידי גמר. *Sources and Traditions: A Source Critical Commentary on Seder Moed: Tractate Shabbath*, (16 n. 37*). Halivni never clearly defines what it would mean to bring a text "to completion." The only implied meaning is that the text as we have it has usually been brought "to completion."

Literary Analysis for Redaction History

the sources in their totality and their original form, and [that their sources] were deficient.⁶²

The *deḥukim* point to the places at which the "source" has been corrupted. At these spots, the critical scholar can intervene to recover the original text.

This method presupposes a certain textual ideology – that is, there was an original pristine text which its transmitters corrupted, wittingly or unwittingly, and must be recovered by the scholars/protectors of the text.⁶³ Although, Halivni affirms the notion that meaning is a function of context,⁶⁴ he seems to ignore the implications of that notion. If, indeed, meaning is a function of context, then recovering a supposedly original statement without recovering its context cannot help us recover an original meaning.⁶⁵

---

⁶² סטיות מן הפירוש הפשוט – דהיינו הפירוש העולה מתוך הטכסט מבלי לגרוע או להוסיף עליו, והן רבות בתלמוד – מוכיחות שלו היו לפני בעלי הסטייה, המקורות בשלימותם כהוויתם ושלקו חסר ויתר. *Sources and Traditions: A Source Critical Commentary on Seder Nashim*, 8.

⁶³There is a hint of the theological implications of this ideology in the following note: ...שכיחותם של דחוקים בתלמוד מעוררת גם בעיה כללית היסטורית, והיא: חנן שכולו אומר הכנעה לטכסט, איך הוליד פירושים המעבירים את האדם מן הטכסט? אלה שמושבעים ועומדים להיות נאמנים לטכסט, איך נשאו בחיקם פירושים הפוגעים בתמימותם של הטכסט? Ibid. 13 n.16. It seems to me that it is this very problem of textual corruption, or seemingly faulty textual transmission, that is at the core of Halivni's later theological writings. Halivni's theology sets out to explain how this text based culture lost track of the text so that midrashic means were necessary to retrieve the original meaning (the *peshat*). See *Peshat and Derash: Plain and Applied Meaning in Biblical Exegesis*, (Oxford: Oxford University Press, 1991) especially chapter 5, e.g. "The implied lack of such public instruction in the centuries preceding Ezra suggests a general inattention to the sacred writ that could very well have directly resulted in the neglect and abuse of its text. The absence of public, communal reading of the Torah meant that it was in the possession and guardianship of various 'private' parties, a situation which may have fostered textual multiplicity and adulteration." (135)

⁶⁴ משמעות כידוע נקבעת במידה לא קטנה על ידי המסגרת. ויש שעל ידי הצירוף של הלכות שונות ממקורות שונים בלי ההתאמה הראויה נוצרה מסגרת חדשה במשנה שהשפיעה גם על המשמעות. *Sources and Traditions: A Source Critical Commentary on Seder Nashim*, (11 n.11).

⁶⁵"A sentence is never not in a context. We are never not in a situation.... Consider, as an example, the sentence 'I will go.' Depending on the context in which it is uttered, 'I will go' can be understood as a promise, a threat, a warning, a report, a prediction, or whatever, but it will always be understood as one of these, and it will never be an unsituated kernel of pure semantic value. In other words, 'I will go' does not have a basic or primary meaning which is then put to various illocutionary uses [Illocutionary refers to the way an utterance is taken – as an order, a warning, and so on. AC] ; rather, 'I will go' is known only in its illocutionary lives, and in each of them its meaning will be different. Moreover, if the meaning of a sentence is a function of its illocutionary force (the way it is taken), and if illocutionary force varies with circumstances, then illocutionary force is not a property of sentences but of situations." Stanley Fish, *Is There a Text*

There is a problem raised by the source critical approach beyond differentiating the words of the *stammaim* from the words of their sources. Even if I grant that this may be possible through an intelligent use of linguistic criteria and parallel sources (in those cases where they exist), the more fundamental question is: how does one establish the original context of the Amoraic statement(s)?[66] Without the original context, how can one know what the statement might have meant?[67] If there is no *original* context, as opposed to merely *another* context in which the statement appears, why is a reconstructed (speculative) context more compelling than the present context? Finally, what is missed in the current context by trying to get to an original context? To pursue these questions further, I will analyze Halivni's interpretation of b Gittin 36b.

The *sugya*, b Gittin 36b,[68] actually forms part of a larger unit which is generated by the last line in M Gittin 4:3. The line is not obviously connected to the rest of the Mishnah:

Hillel ordained the *prozbul* for the good order of the world.

The *prozbul*, as explained in M Shebi'ith 10:3-4, is a way of collecting debts even though they should have been forgiven as a result of the seventh year *shmitah* release of debts.[69] The mechanism, attributed to Hillel, is justified there as social reform. If the debts couldn't be collected, people wouldn't lend money to the poor. The other source for both the Hillel attribution and the explanation – with slight differences – is Sifri Deut. 112.

The first *sugya* generated by this line from the Mishnah uses these sources – naming the Mishnah, and referring to Sifri as a *beraitta*. The general subject concerns the power of the court to override a law of the Torah. Our *sugya*, which follows this one, takes up the question of the intended length of time of the *prozbul* ordinance. Was it intended as a short term stop-gap measure, or a long term piece of legislation?

---

in This Class?: The Authority of Interpretive Communities, (Cambridge, MA: Harvard University Press, 1980): 284.
[66]In addition to the following discussion, see my discussion of Halivni's interpretation of b Gittin 35a in the appendix to Chapter VI.
[67]On these issues generally, see Stanley Fish, *Is There a Text in This Class?* 268-292. Cf. n. 11 above.
[68]In a note to his article "David Weiss Halivni, *Meqorot Umesorot 1. Ketuvot*," in J. Neusner, ed., *The Formation of the Babylonian Talmud*, Robert Goldenberg writes: "In a letter to Professor Jacob Neusner, dated May 7, 1969, Professor Weiss recommended a number of *sugyot* as particularly useful to the student trying to study his method. ... Those numbers in *italics* are highly recommended;..." (135 n.2) b Gittin 36b is one of the highly recommended *sugyot*.
[69]Deut. 15.

Literary Analysis for Redaction History 29

It was asked by them: When Hillel ordained the *prozbul* – [did] he ordain it for his generation or, perhaps, [did] he ordain it for all time, too.
In what [case] might it make [a difference]? [In regards to] abolishing it. If you would say that he ordained it for his generation, we [might] abolish it,
but if you say [that] he ordained it for all time, too,
is it not [the rule] that "a court cannot abolish the decisions of a fellow court,

5   unless it is greater than the other in wisdom and number"?
What [is the answer]?

Come and hear that Shmuel said, We do not write a *prozbul*, except in the court of Sura or in the court of Nehardea.
If you conclude [that] he ordained [it] for all time, [let it be] written in all other courts also.
Perhaps when Hillel ordained for all time, [he intended] a court like his own,

10   and like R. Ami and R. Asi which have the power to wrest money[70] [from a litigant], but not all other[71] courts.
Come and hear that Shmuel said, This *prozbul* is the arrogance (*'ulb'na*) of judges, if I garner enough strength I will abolish it.
"I will abolish it"? Is it not [the rule] that "a court cannot abolish the decisions of a fellow court, unless it is greater than the other in wisdom and number"?
This is what he said, if I garner more strength than Hillel, I would abolish it.
And R. Naḥman said, I would confirm it.

15   "I would confirm it"? It is already confirmed. Rather, I would make a declaration such that even though [a *prozbul*] were not written it would be as if it were written.

It was asked by them: This *'ulb'na* [from line 11], [does it] mean arrogance or [does it] mean convenience?
Come and hear that 'Ulla said, Arrogant [*'alubah*] is the bride who prostituted herself [while still] within her bridal canopy.
Said R. Mari the son of the daughter of Shmuel, What is [the meaning of] the verse, "While the king was on his couch, my nard gave forth its fragrance?" (Song of Songs 1:12)

20   Said Raba, And yet the love is still with us, for it is written "gave forth" and not "stank."
Our Rabbis have taught: Those who are insulted [*ne'elabin*] and do not insult [*'olbin*], hear themselves reviled and do not answer, do [religious duties] out of love and rejoice in suffering,

---

[70]Neusner translates לאפקועי ממונא as "to enforce payment". While the end result might be the same, a) that is not what the words mean (cf. b BB 171a), and b) the mechanism of *prozbul* works by the power of the court to take over the collection of the loan. Additionally, Translating "enforce payment" also loses the resonance of another action of the court in this chapter "wresting away betrothal" אפקעה קידושין (b Gittin 33a).
[71]MS. See the Hebrew text.

of these Scripture says: "But may His friends be as the sun rising in might!" (Judges 5:31).⁷²

Halivni takes two *dehukim* as his starting point. First, why is the opening question understood in terms of invalidating the *prozbul*, as opposed to establishing it? That is, the simple sense of the first line seems to be questioning the very notion of the *prozbul's* legislation for every generation. The explanatory or "rhetorical" question of line 2, however, posits the opposite – the *prozbul* obviously exists, the question is whether or not it can be abolished. Rashi, reading line 1 in light of line 2, comments on the phrase "to abolish it":

> To impanel a court [so that] if the generation is worthy, that is, they won't refuse to lend, [the court] would abolish the ordinance of Hillel, so that even if one wrote a *prozbul*, [the debt] would still be forgiven.⁷³

Second, it is not clear that the general rule, that a court can only overturn or abolish a ruling of an earlier court if it is greater in number and wisdom than that earlier court, should apply to this situation – i.e. *prozbul*. The rule itself is found in M Eduyoth 1:5. According to a tradition cited in b Abodah Zarah 36a, this ban extends only to those ordinances which the students of Shammai managed to pass over the objections of the students of Hillel in the loft of the house of Natsha (M Shabbat 1:4).⁷⁴ *Prozbul* is not explicitly mentioned as one of those ordinances.⁷⁵ The introduction of this rule into the *sugya* also complicates the gemara's explication in line 12 (a line that is missing in the Munich MS) of Shmuel's statement in line 11 – forcing the restatement in line 13.

R. Nahman's statement (line 14) also doesn't make sense within the context of a discussion that assumes the unproblematic contemporary institutionalization of *prozbul*. If it was already the accepted law to use the *prozbul*, what is the purpose of his declaration. This elicits the *stammaitic* question of line 15.

Halivni claims that, in its original setting, the question of line 1 concerned whether or not a *prozbul* could be enacted in a generation subsequent to Hillel's. He thus construes R. Shmuel's and R. Nahman's statements as originally about whether or not the *prozbul* itself was a good idea. Shmuel opposed *prozbul* and would have preferred to abolish

---

⁷²The Hebrew/Aramaic text and apparatus is in the appendix to this section, page 33.
⁷³לבטולי' – להושיב ב"ד אי אכשור דרי שלא יהו מונעין מלהלוות לבטל את תקנת הלל שאפילו כתב פרוזבול ישמט:
⁷⁴see Tosafot here *s.v. elah im ken*.
⁷⁵Tosafot has a long and detailed discussion as to why *prozbul* might or might not be included in the ban.

it all together (13). On the other hand, R. Naḥman would have enacted it. He locates the composition of the question of line 2 at a time when the enactment of the *prozbul* was no longer an issue; therefore it was understood that the question concerned the *cancelling* of the *prozbul*.

Despite the intuitive sense of Halivni's interpretation, as well as its ability to account for the problems he identified, it raises its own set of concerns. First, the statements attributed to R. Naḥman and R. Shmuel are not attested elsewhere in the Talmud, Bavli or Yerushalmi. This leaves us without "outside" criteria by which to judge what the original statements might have been. Even if we follow Halivni and excise their immediate statements from the *sugya*, it is obvious that without a frame we have no way of interpreting them. From Shmuel's statement in line 7 we could conclude that he is either 1) narrowing an existing law (it can *only* be written), 2) enacting a law where there was none before (it *can* only be *written...in*), 3) claiming that the practice of *prozbul* is either so important, so involved, so weighty, so [fill in the blank] that it can only be done in the court of the Academy – regardless of the prevalence or absence of the practice in his day. Actually, these are only a few of the possible contexts of Shmuel's statement. A comparable number of settings might be imagined for the other statements (11 and 14). Moreover, even if there were some outside, parallel, source it would still be difficult to determine which, if either, was "original."

The identification of *deḥukim* in a text doesn't provide the key to a historical solution. Moreover, as I have implied here, there is no clear direction in which one must go to interpret the pre-edited text. I will argue later that *deḥukim* or ungrammaticalities are indeed hermeneutic indices, but they need not be interpreted as merely indices of a layered text; rather, they point towards literary or intertextual solutions.

I will conclude this section by indicating the road which Halivni did not travel. The above *sugya* (or part of a *sugya*) is sandwiched between lines 16-21 and the previous piece. The previous piece discusses the power of *bet din* in the context of the confiscation of property[76] citing a prooftext from Ezra; while the next piece discusses the weakness of *bet din*, or its humility/lack of power. In the context of the previous *sugyot* in

---

[76] הפקר בית דין הפקר.

this chapter,[77] this is a very suggestive setting.[78] The *deḥukim* all seem to point at the *bet din* as a problematic or conflicted institution, something which is a recurring theme of the previous and the following *sugyot*.

---

[77]See my discussion in chapter six.

[78]Some comment must be made about Jacob Neusner's outrageous critique of Halivni. "Did the Talmud's Authorship Utilize Prior 'Sources'? A Response to Halivni's *Sources and Traditions*," in *Ancient Judaism: Debates and Disputes (Second Series)*, ed. Jacob Neusner (Atlanta, Georgia: Scholars Press,). First, Neusner only quotes Halivni from the articles about Halivni that his student Robert Goldenberg wrote (David Halivni Weiss, *Meqorot Umesorot: 1. Ketuvot*), and that he published in a volume in 1973. There is not a single direct quote from Halivni's work. Second the *ad hominem* attack on Halivni and the charge of "[Halivni's] unwillingness to read other scholars' treatment of the same literature and problems..." is obviously false. That Neusner quotes it in the name of "book reviewers" (137) doesn't lend it any more credibility. In the first volume of *Sources and Traditions* Halivni refers to, in either the text or the footnotes, Albeck, Lieberman, I. Heinemann and others. In the subsequent volumes he refers to *inter alia* Abraham Weiss, Shamma Friedman, Hyman Klein. It seems that the only scholar that he didn't refer to is Jacob Neusner. Third, Neusner's premise that a null hypothesis for the Bavli should be constructed by analyzing the Yerushalmi ("Did..." 136) is startling. If we are to say, with Neusner, that the Bavli and the Yerushalmi have two completely separate authorships, and are a product of two different Judaisms, how can one prove anything about the Bavli merely by proving something about the Yerushalmi? Further, Halivni himself is inconclusive about the role of the *stammaim* in the Yerushalmi, and he doesn't extend his argument to that document (*Sources and Traditions: A Source Critical Commentary on Seder Moed: Tractate Shabbath* 16 n.37**) Fourth, ignoring the recklessness of his critique, it seems that Neusner has not read Halivni very closely (despite his students' articles in note 7.). Neusner characterizes the conclusion of his experiment with a null hypothesis as follows:

"When I claim that the Talmud's focus of interest is in the logical exposition of the law, here is a good instance of what I mean. The materials are organized so as to facilitate explanations of the law's inner structure and potentiality, not to present a mere repertoire of ideas and opinions of interest for their own sake. **The upshot is a sustained argument, not an anthology of relevant sayings. But Halivni's theory requires the opposite, that is, an anthology of diverse materials, some changed some not changed, from their 'original' formulation.** A null hypothesis offered by Halivni should turn up precisely the document as we now have it. A null hypothesis offered by me should turn up the opposite of what the Yerushalmi gives us.

Such a cogent and ongoing argument as we find characteristic of both Talmuds is more likely the work of a single mind than of a committee, let alone of writers who lived over a period of ten or fifteen decades." (emphasis added) (152)

Compare this with Halivni: הפרשנות הכריעה איפוא שהגמרא כפי שהיא לפנינו ברחבותה הגדולה, היא של הסתמאים, של העורכים המאוחרים (בתוכנה ובסגנונה, ואילו סידורה והטרמינולוגיה שבה הם כנראה מרבנן סבוראי). קודם לסתמאים לא היתה הגמרא כה רחבה, אלא ספלה למשנה (p.16) ולבריתא, קטנה ומצומצמת ובלא עצמאות ובלא רצף. סגולות אלה באו לה מן הסתמאים. לא כן הסתמאים, ידם היתה בתלמוד כולו ומהם יצא הכל. (emphasis added) Or the following: ההשלמה, ההרחבה וההוספה של הסתמאים נעשו מדעת. הללו הם חלק מן העריכה והחלטתם ליצור...

Appendix: b Gittin 36b

איבעיא להו: כי התקין הלל פרוסבול לדרה הוא דתקין או דלמא לדרי עלמא נמי[79] תקין?
למאי נפקא מינה? לבטולה. אי אמרת לדריה הוא דתקין מבטלינן לה,
אלא אי אמרי לדרי עלמא נמי[80] תקין,
הא אין בית דין יכול לבטל דברי בית דין חברו,
5   אלא אם כן גדול הימנו בחכמה ובמנין.
מאי?

תא שמע דאמר שמואל לא כתבינן פרוסבול אלא אי בבי דינא דסורא אי בבי דינא דנהרדעא.
ואי סלקא דעתך לדרי עלמא נמי[81] תקין בשאר בי דינא נמי לכתבו.
דלמא כי תקין הלל לדרי עלמא כגון בי דינא דידיה
10 וכרבי אמי ורבי אסי דאלימי לאפקועי ממונא, אבל לכולי עלמא לא[82].

תא שמע דאמר שמואל הא פרוסבלא עולבנא דדייני הוא אי איישר חיל אבטליני'.
אבטליני'[83] הא אין ב"ד יכול לבטל דברי ב"ד חברו אלא אם כן גדול הימנו בחכמה ובמנין
הכי קאמר, איל[84] איישר חיל יותר מהלל אבטלינה.
ורב נחמן אמר אקיימנה.

15 אקיימנה, הא מיקיים וקאי? אלא[85] אימא ביה מילתא דאף על גב דלא כתוב ככתוב דמי.
איבעיא להו האי עולבנא דחוצפא הוא או לישנא דניחותא הוא?

תא שמע: דאמר עולא, עלובה כלה שזינתה בקרב חופתה.
אמר רב מרי ברה דבת שמואל, מאי קרא עד שהמלך במסבו נרדי נתן ריחו (ש"ש א:י"ב).
אמר רבא עדיין[86] חביבותא הוא גבן דכתיב נתן ולא כתיב הסריח.
20 תנו רבנן הנעלבין ואינן עולבים שומעין חרפתן ואין משיבין עושין מאהבה ושמחין ביסורין,
עליהן הכתוב אומר ואוהביו כצאת השמש בגבורתו (שופטים ה:ל"א).

ספר שונה מן המשנה (והברייתא) בתוכן (שקלא וטריא ונוקדני) ובסגנון (דיאלקטי, ריטורי וארכני).
and n. 11) השינויים שחלו בעקבות התוספות היו שינויים מודעים לא כן השינויים שחלו בעקבות המסירה.
21*)

Neusner has a valid point in claiming that Halivni seems to assume that attributions are reliable. This point, however, loses its force since Neusner, for some reason, assumes it to mean that, for Halivni, chronology is the single most determinative characteristic of a *sugya*. (E.g. Neusner ibid. 157) This is blatantly false as can be seen from the paragraphs quoted above, and from most of Halivni's introduction to *Sources and Traditions: A Source Critical Commentary on Seder Moed: Tractate Shabbath*.

79 נמי] ליתא ו ו ן
80 נמי] ליתא ו ו
81 נמי] ליתא ו ו ן א
82 שאר דייני לא]ון ;שאר בידיני' לא] ם
83 אבטליני'... ובמנין] ליתא ם
84 אם דפוס ו אי] ם
85 דפוס אלא] ם ו ו ן הכי קאמר
86 עדיין]אכתי ם

Part 3. Shamma Friedman

I turn now to the work of Shamma Friedman. Though very sensitive to the literary character of *sugyot* in his approach, Shamma Friedman's methodology is still firmly ensconced in the source critical school. He sets as the goal of his analysis of *sugyot*:

> 1.To completely separate the words of the Amoraim from the words of the anonymous Talmud (סתם התלמוד), in order to be able to discuss the words of the Amoraim by themselves, **and as they were originally presented.** 2. to discern the literary structure of each and every *sugya*. (emphasis added)[87]

It is important to clarify Friedman's claims. With most source critics, Friedman needs to claim, that one can, by "objective means,"[88] separate strata of material and assign them to different historical layers. Second, he holds that by this means one can recover or reconstruct a statement "as originally presented," and then sketch the construction of the *sugya* in front of us. There is no need for Friedman to claim that the statement "as originally presented," is the statement as originally spoken by the named Amora, only that it is a statement which was spoken or presented by *an* Amora. It remains unclear whether or not Friedman is making the stronger claim.[89]

---

[87]1. – להפריד הפרדה שלמה בין דברי האמוראים לבין דברי סתם התלמוד, וזו כדי לדון בדברי האמוראים בפני עצמם,. – וכפי שניתנו מחוילתם; 2.– לעמוד על המבנה הספרותי של כל סוגיא וסוגיא. Shamma Friedman, "A Critical Study of *Yevamot* X with a Methodological Introduction," (Heb.) in H. Z. Dimitrovski ed. *Texts and Studies: Analecta Judaica*, vol. 1 (New York: Jewish Theological Seminary of America, 1978): 283.

[88]Friedman uses the phrase to describe Klein's work. (294)

[89]See, e.g., Friedman's remark about the "sixth *sugya*": רב "בפי" ש הדומים והסגנון הניסוח הונא ור' יוחנן מעוררים את השאלה אם לא הותאמו דברי האחד בכדי להקבילם לדברי חברו. (Scare quotes in the original.), or his remark about the statement attributed to רב הונא בריה דרב יהושע in the seventh *sugya* (367), or the following, also on the seventh *sugya* הנמנע מן כמעט דבר של לאחתו להניע על סמך החומר שבידינו ללשון המקורית שאמר רב ששת עצמו. ... וספק אם אמרו הם עצמם ניסוח זה, או שניסחו כן נסחים מיוחדים ... כיום אין לך "דברי רב ששת" עצמו, זולת ניסוח זה,. (Scare quotes in the original.)

I stress this in opposition to one line of criticism originating in what might be called the Neusnerian school. *Semeia*'s issue devoted to "Law as Literature" had a section devoted to Shamma Friedman's monograph on *Yevamot* X. In the article on Friedman's methodology David Weiner ("Shamma Friedman's Methodological Principles," *Semeia* 27 (1983): 47-51.) makes two problematic assertions. I single them out since I think that they are symptomatic of the Neusnerian school as a whole. First, he claims that "Friedman takes for granted that the person who formulated the Amoraic sayings in the Talmud recorded the actual views of the Amoraim themselves. ...Even if Friedman could somehow succeed in recovering the 'original version' of a saying attributed to Rabbi x, he still has no way of knowing that the saying represents the actual views of Rabbi

Literary Analysis for Redaction History

Friedman's second objective – discerning the literary structure of *sugyot* – is not totally dependent on the first objective. It is possible to map the literary structure without making any historical claims about its development. Thus it follows that one may accept the mapping of the literary structure of a *sugya*, and agree that the mapping points out the textured or layered form of the *sugya*, without having to agree that the results are a developmental map.

His unique contribution is an elaborate set of formal criteria by which to differentiate sources. Friedman enumerates twelve different criteria which can be roughly divided into three categories:

1. Evolutionary markings; that is, the more concise, and brief is earlier. The longer, clumsier, and explanatory is later.
2. Linguistic criteria. Much of this, as Friedman notes, derives from the work of Hyman Klein.[90] Klein was a form critic who developed rules

---

x." (51) As we just showed it is nowhere clear that Friedman makes this latter claim, and further there is no reason for him to make it, that is, his methodology could work easily well if the Amoraic statements originally came from the named Amoraim, or others in the Amoraic period. Second, Weiner states that "Friedman's method of substantive and literary analysis presupposes *a priori* that the Amoraic sayings antedate the anonymous materials of the Talmud." (Ibid.) Whether or not one agrees with Friedman's conclusions or even his mode of argumentation, one cannot say that he "presupposed" the dating of the *stam*. He argues the position at length in his introduction (283-299, and n. 42). It seems that the Neusnerians are blinded by the glare of the attribution question. (Cf. in this regard Jack Lightstone's criticism of Kraemer and Halivni: "Both Kraemer and Halivni maintain that attributions in the text to rabbinic tradents are in some significant sense a reliable means of pulling apart the Talmud in order to identify and isolate its historical layers." *The Rhetoric of the Babylonian Talmud, Its Social Meaning and Context* (Waterloo, Ontario: Wilfrid Laurier University Press, 1994):15) While this question has interesting and important historical implications – it should not end the discussion. First, there is the possibility that while attributions to specific persons are unreliable, attributions to a period are more reliable. For exegetical and even many historical purposes, dating a statement to the Amoraic period, whether Rab or R. Sheshet "really" said it, is significant. As I will argue further in the next chapter, reviewing Neusner's work, there is a binary fallacy at work here. One need not claim that either attributed statements are the *ipssisima verba* of the named tradents, or they were created out of whole cloth in sixth or seventh century. Linguistic criteria (Hebrew or Aramaic), attributions (to people *and* to otherwise unattested *beraittot*), and chronology ("real" or "fictional") are, at the least, important hermeneutic indices. This is not to discount some of the important points made by some of the Neusnerian critique of Friedman, e.g. Judith Romney Wegner's critique of Friedman's use of parallels from Yerushalmi in the fourth *sugya* ("Shamma Friedman on b. Yebamot 88b-89a," *Semeia*, 27, 1983: 86-89).

[90]See the references in "A Critical Study of *Yevamot X* with a Methodological Introduction," p. 293 n. 40, and add to them Hyman Klein, *"Gemara" and "Sebara"* in *Baba Metziah 60b - 64a* (Jerusalem: Akademon, 1978).

of language (Hebrew vs. Aramaic) and logic to distinguish layers of *sugyot*. He claimed that the Talmud was divided into *gemara* and *sebara*, the former being the "original" statements, and the latter being the subsequent commentary.[91] He considered Hebrew to be earlier, and Aramaic later. In the case of a sentence or phrase from which the Aramaic could be removed and still leave an intelligible Hebrew sentence he held the remaining Hebrew sentence as original. Friedman adopts Klein's rules and related general criteria about the editing: phrases that refer ahead in the *sugya* are editorial, as are words or phrases mainly found in later Amoraic and stammaitic material.

3. Textual variants. The abundance of variant readings in the manuscripts, the clustering of variants, the absence of phrases in manuscripts or in Rishonim, etc. In this category, Friedman breaks new ground for the source critics that we have examined.[92] While Weiss and Halivni often refer to variant readings in the course of their analyses neither of them presents a methodological justification and rationale for the way in which the manuscripts are to be weighed. Friedman adopts as a rule that an abundance of variants of a specific phrase in a *sugya* suggests a later dating for that phrase. Likewise if a certain phrase is missing when the *sugya* is quoted in most of the early commentaries it is probably a later addition.

Friedman's basic goal is to separate the named Amoraic statements from the later editorial, anonymous material in service of his long term goal of writing the history of Talmudic law.[93] In Friedman's words:

> Only in this way is it possible to investigate the history of Talmudic law, that is, the positions of the Amoraim by themselves, separate from the understandings (שיטות) of the *stam* which were added by them, and which are sometimes different than the understanding of the Amoraim.[94]

It is this evolution of the law that interests Friedman. To understand how he goes about his work, we turn now to his analysis.

---

[91]This is, of course, not unlike Halivni's "Sources" and "Traditions." See my discussion of Halivni in section 2 above.
[92]See, e.g., Friedman's article, "להתהוות שינויי הגירסאות בתלמוד הבבלי", *Sidra* vol. 7 (1991): 67-102.
[93]For an attempt to do this very kind of history, based on the source-critical method see Michael Satlow, "'Wasted Seed': The History of a Rabbinic Idea," in HUCA, forthcoming.
[94]רק בדרך זו ניתן לחקור את תולדות המשפט התלמדי, דהיינו עמדות האמוראים בפני עצמן, בנפרד משיטות הסתמא שנוספו על ידן, שהן שונות לפעמים משיטות האמוראים. "A Critical Study of *Yevamot X* with a Methodological Introduction," 293.

Friedman divides Chapter Ten of b Yebamoth into sixteen sugyot plus a number of collections of statements that did not adhere as sugyot. We will take a look at what he labels the sixth sugya[95] (b Yebamoth 91a).

The sixth sugya is generated by the last lines of M Yebamoth 10:1. This Mishnah, in general, deals with the situation of a woman whose husband has gone overseas. Witness(es) then come and report that her husband has died. She subsequently marries another man. The situation turns tragic when the first husband shows up – for she is now, apparently, married to two men. The Mishnah forces her to leave both husbands, and not to derive benefit from connection with either. After the anonymous Mishnaic voice spells out a long list of items which she suffers, three named Tannaim offer differing opinions of some of the issues.

M Yebamoth 10:1

R. Yosi says, her dowry[96] [is a lien] upon the estate of the first husband.
R. Elazar says, the first [husband] has rights to her findings and the products of her labor, and the abrogation of her vows.
R. Shimon says, the coition or *ḥaliẓah* of the brother of the first [husband], excuses her co-wife [from levirate marriage/*ḥaliẓah* obligations], and the offspring from him is not a *mamzer*.[97]

This *sugya* is an attempt to determine what the organizing principle of these three opinions is. That is, why are they written in this order? The *sugya* includes two named Amoraic statements, offering opposite views of the issue. The graphic arrangement of the *sugya* is Friedman's:

b. Yebamoth 91a

R. Yosi says, her dowry [is a lien] upon the estate of the first husband, etc.

Said R. Huna, the [Sages listed] later [in the Mishnah] consent to the [rulings of the Sages listed] earlier.

---

[95]The analyses of the first, second, and fourth *sugyot* were critiqued in *Semeia* 27. See Louis Newman, "Shamma Friedman on b. Yebamot 87b-88a," *Semeia* 27 (1983): 53-61; Roger Brooks, "Shamma Friedman on b. Yebamot 88a-b," *Semeia* 27 (1983): 63-75; Judith Romney Wegner, "Shamma Friedman on b. Yebamot 88b-89a," *Semeia*, 27, 1983: 77-91. See above note 89 for analysis of their approach.
[96]For the interpretation of כתובה as "dowry" here, and elsewhere in Mishnaic literature, see "A Critical Study of *Yevamot X* with a Methodological Introduction," 361 and Mordechai Akiva Friedman, *Jewish Marriage in Palestine: A Cairo Geniza Study, vol. 1: The Ketubba Traditions of Eretz Israel* (New York: Tel Aviv University and The Jewish Theological Seminary of America, 1980): 310-311.
[97]

משנה יבמות י:א
רבי יוסי אומר כתובתה על נכסי בעלה הראשון.
רבי אלעזר, אומר הראשון זכאי במציאתה ובמעשה ידיה, ובהפרת נדריה.
ורבי שמעון אומר, ביאתה או חליצתה מאחיו של ראשון פוטרת צרתה, ואין הולד ממנו ממזר.

R. Shimon consents to [the ruling of] R. Elazar,
[arguing that] since coition which is primarily [in the realm of] forbidden [acts] is not penalized, all the more so her findings and the products of her labor which are monetary [would not be penalized].
And R. Elazar does not consent to [the ruling] of R. Shimon,
[arguing that] her findings and the product of her labor are not penalized since they are monetary [matters], but coition which is [in the realm of] forbidden [acts] is penalized.
And both of them consent to [the ruling] of R. Yosi,
[arguing that] these [i.e. coition, her findings and the products of her labor], [which are in effect] when she lives under him are penalized, all the more so the dowry which is there so as to be taken and [thereby] to leave [i.e. be divorced].
And R. Yosi does not consent to them,
[arguing that] the dowry which is there to be taken and [thereby] to leave [i.e. be divorced] is that which is not penalized, but these [which are in effect] when she lives under him are penalized.

And R. Yoḥanan said, the [Sages listed] earlier [in the Mishnah] consent to the [rulings of the Sages listed] later.
R. Yosi consents to [the ruling] of R. Elazar,
[arguing that the] dowry which [is transferred] from him to her is not penalized, all the more so her findings and the products of her labor which [are transferred] from her to him.
And R. Elazar does not consent to him,
[arguing that] her findings and the products of her labor which [are transferred] from her to him are [those which are] not penalized, but [the] dowry which [is transferred] from him to her [is] penalized.
And both consent to [the ruling] of R. Shimon,
[arguing that] since these [i.e. her findings and the products of her labor] which are [in effect during the] life [of the husband], are not penalized, coition [to excuse the co-wife from levirate marriage/ḥaliẓah obligations] all the more so.
And R. Shimon does not consent to them,
It is coition, which [is only in effect] after the death [of the husband], [which is] not penalized, but these [i.e. her findings and the products of her labor] which are [in effect during the] life [of the husband], are penalized.[98]

98

בבלי יבמות צא ע״א
רבי יוסי אומר כתובתה על נכסי בעלה וכו׳:
אמר רב הונא בתראי מודו לקמאי קמאי לא מודו לבתראי.
ר׳ שמעון מודי ליה לר׳ אלעזר,
דמה ביאה דעיקר איסורא לא קניס, וכ״ש מציאתה ומעשה ידיה דממונא הוא.
ור׳ אלעזר לא מודי ליה לר׳ שמעון,
מציאתה ומעשה ידיה דממונא הוא לא קניס, אבל ביאה דאיסורא הוא קניס.
ותרוייהו מודו ליה לר׳ יוסי,
הני דיתבא תותיה לא קניס וכל שכן כתובה דלמשקל ומיפק קאי.
ורבי יוסי לא מודי להו,

Literary Analysis for Redaction History

This presentation affords a concise illustration of a number of the central devices of Friedman's method. First, the graphic layout, highlighting the two named Amoraic statements, makes it an easy matter to read the two in relation to each other. Moreover, it compels one to read the statements in relation to each other, rather than in relation to the flow of the *sugya* (lines 3-10 & 12-19). Read in relation to each other, the "dispute form" (צורת המחלוקת) becomes apparent. This form, noted already in the Gaonic literature, is "Said R. X... **And** R. Y said...."[99] Although the connective *vav*, which is emblematic of this form, is missing in the printed editions of the Talmud, it appears in two important manuscripts.[100]

Setting off the named statements in this way, also makes the identification of, and the differentiation from the *stammaitic* material, clearer. In this *sugya* there is no clear linguistic criteria, with which to differentiate Amoraic from *stammaitic* material. The entire *sugya* is written in Aramaic. The criteria that comes into play is Friedman's rule that explanatory material often postdates the statements that it explains. Supporting this contention are the facts that 1) the explanations that are given are artificial, and 2) they don't cover all the laws mentioned by the three named sages of the Mishnah.

The Rishonim already noticed that the explanations are a stretch, at best. For example, how would the wife have been penalized by the fact that her first husband would no longer own her finds and her labor, as line 3 implies she would be. The Tosafists[101] need to claim that this would cause the husband to hate her, or alternately, it would ultimately deprive her of her support. On the other hand, there is no explanation given which accounts for abrogation of vows. We should note, however,

---

10 כתובה דלמשקל ומיפק הוא דלא קניס אבל הני דיתבא תותיה קניס.
ורבי יוחנן אמר קמאי מודו לבתראי בתראי לא מודו לקמאי.
ר' יוסי מודי ליה לר' אלעזר,
כתובה דמדידה לדידיה לא קניס וכ"ש מציאתה ומעשה ידיה דמדידה לדידיה.
ור' אעזר לא מודי ליה,
15 מציאתה ומעשה ידיה הוא דמדידה לדידיה לא קניס אבל כתובה דמדידה לדידיה קניס.
ותרוייהו מודו ליה לר' שמעון,
ומה הני דמחיים קנסי ביאה דלאחר מיתה לא כ"ש.
ור' שמעון לא מודי להו,
ביאה הוא דלאחר מיתה לא קניס אבל הני דמחיים קניס:

[99] see Friedman's discussion "A Critical Study of *Yevamot* X with a Methodological Introduction," 349 and n. 30.
[100] Vatican 111 (1381) and Oxford 367/Oppenheimer 248 (1691).
[101] *s.v.* כל שכן מציאתה ומעשה ידיה.

that the literary style is symmetrical in a manner that seems to suggest completion.[102]

A comparison with the Yerushalmi is revealing:

> What does R. Lazar say with regard to the dowry? [i.e. R. Yosi's statement] If things [her labor, finds] which fell [to the first husband] in a forbidden way [i.e. now that she is forbidden to him] you hold [that they] belong to him; the dowry which fell to him in a permissible way, all the more so [it should belong to him].

Here, the anonymous voice of the Yerushalmi claims that there is no agreement at all between R. Lazar and R. Yosi. R. Lazar holds that just as the first husband has a claim to her labor and finds so, all the more so, he should have a claim to her dowry. R. Yosi, on the other hand, holds that the first husband doesn't even have a claim to the dowry (כתובה), and, all the more so, not to her labor and finds.

The continuation of the Yerushalmi offers a different opinion, one that is similar in part to R. Huna's statement and in part similar to R. Yohanan's:

> It seems that R. Lazar consents to R. Yosi,
> [though] R. Yosi does not consent to R. Lazar.
> R. Yosi and R. Lazar consent to R. Shimon,
> [though] R. Shimon does not consent to R. Yosi or R. Lazar.

The first two lines are like R. Huna (as spelled out in lines 7 and 9), and the last two lines are similar to R. Yohanan (as spelled out in lines 16 and 18). The major difference, of course, is that there is no attempt to arrive at an organizing principle as in the Bavli.

There are then three different understandings of the attributed statements in the Mishnah: R. Huna, R. Yohanan, and the anonymous voice of the Yerushalmi. Friedman wants to chart the development of the *sugya* from the Mishnah to the Bavli as follows:

1. The Mishnah ordered the statements of Elazar, Yosi, and Shimon according to the topics that were discussed in the beginning of the Mishnah i.e. *ketubah*, her finds, labor, abrogation of vows and *halitzah*.

2. The Yerushalmi's first statement interprets with this understanding, that is, the order in the Mishnah is only the order of topics, and doesn't correspond to the consenting – *since there is none* – of the tradents.

---

[102] A similar point about the artificiality of an argumentative style which seems to denote completeness is made by the Tosafists about M Baba Kama 1:1 הדתנא האריך לצריך תורה ולהאריכה (ולא כל שכן) (s.v.).

Literary Analysis for Redaction History

3. The Yerushalmi's second statement holds that there is some consent but it has nothing to do with the order of the Mishnah.
4. The Bavli claims that the order, is the order in which the tradents consent to each other. R. Yoḥanan's statement probably originated in a Palestinian tradition, which was essentially like the second statement of the Yerushalmi.
5. The statements were fleshed out, and stylized, in order to make them systematic and oppositional. The *stammaim* added the explanations which seemed to logically flow from the order of consenting.

Reading Friedman's reading, we can see his mapping the *sugya* encourages a reading of the *sugya* against its rhetoric. That is, instead of following the linear pull of the *sugya*'s narrative and reading line 3 as a direct continuation of R. Huna's comments, the mapping suggests a structural connection between R. Huna and R. Yoḥanan. This allows Friedman to see the anonymous explanations as artificial and stylistic, essentially comprising another narrative line.

If we read Friedman from another angle, we can see his reading as precipitated by the *deḥukim* of the anonymous explanation. These *deḥukim* or ungrammaticalities point towards other texts, namely the Yerushalmi and the language that it shares with the anonymous explanation. This intertextual relation reinforces the existence of alternative, non-linear ways of reading the *sugya*.

The reading moves to shakier ground when Friedman introduces the historical development as an explanatory frame. To convince, Friedman needs to posit a Palestinian tradition analogous to the Yerushalmi, but of which no record exists. It is unnecessary to posit a historical, rather than a literary connection between the two *sugyot*, especially since the lexical links are suggestive but tenuous.[103] Further, if we stop at the point of identifying the two narratives that Friedman has mapped – without attempting to harmonize them within the historical construct – we are able to ask questions that otherwise disappear. For example, what is the significance of the *stammaitic* framing of this *sugya* in terms of קנס (penalty)? The word קנס – in its various verb permutations – occurs in this *sugya* more than any place else in Yebamot – by two or three times.[104] קנס figures prominently in the comments earlier on 91a, as

---

[103] And cf. Judith Romney Wegner's remark on the fourth *sugya*, note 3 above.
[104] קניס or קנסי occurs 12 times in this *sugya*. It occurs 3 times earlier on 91a. The largest occurrence in any other *sugya* in Yebamoth is 86b, where it occurs 5 times, in a *sugya* which is dealing with the issue of the relative rights of collection of *kohanim* and *leviim*, of priestly dues.

Friedman points out.[105] The power of *bet din*, which is, by definition, what a קנס is, figures prominently in the very next Mishnah (10:2). This is all the more interesting in that קנס itself is a site of conflicted interpretations,[106] something that points to an unstable frame. These questions can't be asked if the historical frame serves to create a single harmonized meaning, which covers the roughness of the text.

Conclusion

The scholarly arc that I traced in this chapter constitutes an important move in the concept of literary analysis as it refers to understanding Talmud. For Weiss, literary analysis describes a method by which a literary text developed. For Friedman, literary analysis also includes understanding the constituent units (i.e. *sugyot*) as literature. At the end of this chapter then, we are poised to press the understanding of Talmud as literature, or literary text, beyond the historical-redactional realm. This we will accomplish through a discussion of Jacob Neusner's work, followed by a discussion of the work of Jonah Fraenkel and Daniel Boyarin.

---

[105]. "A Critical Study of *Yevamot* X with a Methodological Introduction,": 358-359.
[106]. See in addition to the Tosafot mentioned above, the references cited in ibid 360 n. 4.

3

On Framing the Question: Intertextuality, Translation, Literary Analysis: Jacob Neusner

Easily the most prolific writer on Rabbinic literature,[1] Jacob Neusner is also one of the most influential voices in the discussion of that literature in the American academy. He and his circle have translated most of the works that are included in the corpus of Rabbinic texts. His

---

[1] Neusner's writings, of course, cover all of Rabbinic literature. For the purposes of this chapter I am interested in his works that deal with the literary interpretation of the Bavli, and the translation of the Bavli. The works pertinent to this chapter are: Jacob Neusner, *Judaism, The Classical Statement: The Evidence of the Bavli* (Chicago: University of Chicago Press, 1986); *Midrash as Literature: The Primacy of Documentary Discourse* (Lanham, New York, London: University Press of America, 1987); *Canon and Connection: Intertextuality in Judaism* (New York: University Press of America, 1987); *Translating the Classics of Judaism: In Theory and In Practice* (Atlanta, Georgia: Scholars Press, 1989); *The Talmud of Babylonia: An American Translation: XVIII.A:Gittin Chapters 1-3* (Atlanta, Georgia: Scholars Press, 1992); *The Talmud of Babylonia: An American Translation: XVIII.B:Gittin Chapters 4-5* (Atlanta, Georgia: Scholars Press, 1992). *Sources and Traditions: Types of Compositions in the Talmud of Babylonia* (Atlanta, Georgia: Scholars Press, 1992); *The Bavli's One Voice: Types and Forms of Analytical Discourse and their Fixed Order of Appearance* (Atlanta, Georgia: Scholars Press,, 1991); *The Rules of Composition of the Talmud of Babylonia: The Cogency of the Bavli's Composite* (Atlanta, Georgia: Scholars Press, 1991) *How to Study the Bavli: The Languages, Literatures, and Lessons of the Talmud of Babylonia* (Atlanta, Georgia: Scholars Press, 1992) *The Principal Parts of the Bavli's Discourse: A Preliminary Taxonomy* (Atlanta, Georgia: Scholars Press, 1992). *How to Study...* is "in a single statement the results of several monographs, all of which are aimed at investigating problems concerning the literary character of the document." The previous two works are among those monographs.

research has brought about a rethinking of some of the issues central to the history of the Talmudic period.[2]

One of Neusner's most influential contributions to the contemporary study of Talmud has been his thorough skepticism about attributed statements. He has developed this position beyond a skeptical agnosticism towards redaction history, to the point where he attributes the Bavli as a whole to one "authorship" that lived around the seventh century.[3] On this basis he is violently[4] opposed to the approaches of Halivni and Friedman.

Neusner is also a literary formalist. The only salient features of any work, for him, are its "rhetoric, topic and program." As a result of this theoretical stance, Neusner doesn't have a method of reading *sugyot*. In fact he denies the use of doing this.[5] Neusner only reads "books," as a whole, to identify their rhetoric topic and program, and to differentiate them from other books. Each book, per definition, is seen as autonomous, a creation of its authorship and unrelated in any important literary way with any other book.[6] The relations between books are of a secondary order, a sociological construct.[7] For this reason Neusner violently rejects

---

[2] Cf e.g. "Judaic Uses of History in Talmudic Times," in Ada Rapaport-Albert, ed., *Essays in Jewish Historiography*, History and Theory: Studies in the Philosophy of History, Beiheft 27, 17ff.

[3] *Rules of Composition*, 191-192, "Did the Talmud's Authorship Utilize Prior 'Sources'? A Response to Halivni's *Sources and Traditions*", in *Ancient Judaism, Debates and Disputes* (Scholars Press, Atlanta, Georgia, 1984): 159-160.

[4] I use the word "violently" advisedly, as in addition to the "free and encompassing debate, reasoned discourse, [and] honorable contention," there are also pages of *ad hominem* attacks. See, e.g., *Sources and Traditions: Types of Compositions in the Talmud of Babylonia* (Atlanta, Georgia: Scholars Press, 1992): x-xii. This is in addition to the *ad hominem* attacks in Neusner's critique of Halivni: "Did the Talmud's Authorship Utilize Prior 'Sources'? A Response to Halivni's *Sources and Traditions*," in *Ancient Judaism, Debates and Disputes* (Scholars Press, Atlanta, Georgia, 1984): 136.

[5] "I reject the assumption that the building block of documents is the smallest whole unit, the lemma, nor can we proceed in the premise that a lemma traverses the boundaries of various documents and is unaffected by the journey. The opposite premise is that we start our work with the traits of documents as a whole, rather than with the traits of the lemmas of which documents are (supposedly) composed." *The Talmud of Babylonia: An American Translation: XVIII.A:Gittin Chapters 1-3* (Atlanta, Georgia: Scholars Press, 1992): 133.

[6] "When I say that the Talmud speaks in a single voice, I mean to say it everywhere speaks uniformly, consistently, and predictably. The voice is the voice of a book." *The Rules of Composition of the Talmud of Babylonia: The Cogency of the Bavli's Composite* (Atlanta: Scholars Press, 1991): 189.

[7] "Let me spell out what I find puzzling. It is, specifically, why in the world we should ever have wondered how – on the basis of *intrinsic* and not imputed traits – one document connects to others. Seeing each document on its own or viewing

any notion of intertextuality. Since intertextuality is central to the rest of this work, and to my understanding of Talmud, it is necessary to address Neusner's objections to it before going any further.

In this chapter, then, I review Neusner's brand of "formalism" and claim that the rest of his project flows from it – his objections to intertextuality, his theory and practice of translation, and ultimately, his way of reading individual units of the Bavli.

Intertextuality

> "Someone writes a document, someone buys it, an entire society sustains the labor of literature."
> (3)

> "A book exists in three dimensions: on its own, within its cover, thus *autonomously*; then on the shelf of books, along with others of its classification, thus, *connected* to other books of the same type; and finally, within the larger collection, the library as a whole. The staff of a library – to continue the metaphor – forms the textual community, for it has chosen these books in particular – and no others – for its community of users. By decision of the library staff the book is *continuous* not only with other books on its shelf but with all the books in the same building." (15)

> "Intertextuality takes place when two or more documents go over the same materials, and the connection at hand derives from that intersection." (31)

> "...anyone can replicate my experiments and test my results." (97)
> Jacob Neusner[8]

One of the most striking facets of Neusner's work, is its grounding in a discourse of scientific empiricism.[9] That is, there are certain "literary

---

all documents together by reason of a social consensus pose no special problems of logic or interpretation. The one perspective derives from the very definitive trait of a book or a document: its uniqueness. The other constitutes a social, not a textual issue: why do people see as one what in fact are several?" *Canon and Connection* 12. Cf *inter alia. How to Study the Bavli*, p.15.

[8]*Canon and Connection: Intertextuality in Judaism* (New York: University Press of America, 1987).

[9]The word "discourse" is used by theorists to indicate a language that, by way of a specific lexicon, contains certain logical, cultural or political assumptions. So, for example, scientific discourse – indicated by the use of a lexicon which

facts" that can be established by "experiments" which are "reproducible." The first step in this process, for Neusner, is the preparation of the material by way of translation. The process of translation is like that of preparing slides for the researcher.[10] It demands a certain skill, thoroughness and meticulousness – but is essentially a preparatory job, which does not take a "position" on the question of what is being examined.

Interestingly enough, this is not the case in biology. Biologists refer to "artifacts" to signify unwanted results (data or images) which are the result of the technique and do not reflect the biological reality and to distinguish them from those same objects as they are "in nature." This is to explicitly acknowledge the contribution that the slide preparation makes to the "argument."[11]

Be the reality of scientific practice as it may, the ultimate source of Neusner's empiricist discourse is a conception of literature that can be called formalism, or genre criticism. The proper way to begin the study of any book, for Neusner, is to identify its type. Is it a novel or a law code, for example? This is established by looking at the book as a whole and characterizing its rhetoric, topic and program. The types of literature within which one might characterize Talmud are, for Neusner, either traditional or systemic. "Traditional literature" is literature which does not have an independent program, but is dependent for its program and

---

includes terms such as experiment, fact, empirically verifiable matters – also has the cultural assumption of authority, truth, and objectivity. On discourse see, e.g. Terry Eagleton, *Literary Theory: An Introduction* (Minneapolis: University of Minnesota Press, 1983): 115-117; idem, *Ideology: An Introduction* (London:Verso, 1991): 193ff.

[10]In addition to the phrase quoted above, Neusner repeat this description of the work of translation in the preface to the Gittin translations, and adds to it: "For me, translation is the same type of work as is, for the biologist and pathologist, the preparation of slides, and for the demographer, the opinion survey." *Gittin Chapters 1-3*, x.

[11]"Thoughtful pathologists know that everything we look at is some sort of artifact, the tissue is not really the vibrant shades of blue and pink that we stain it, and of course when it is alive it has a different appearance, etc. and slides stained by different labs, even with the same chemicals, will look different. The point is, artifacts that we are used to and know how to interpret are useful, and the others we ignore.

"The image on a slide can be varied tremendously, depending on how it is prepared. In fact, certain criteria we use for diagnosis are only seen with certain fixatives i.e. when you use them you get a useful, reproducible artifact. You can take the same slide, stain it one way and demonstrate a structure or cell, and stain it another way and that structure/cell will not be visible i.e. different stains stain different structures within the same cell, that are otherwise invisible." Personal communication from Dr. Isaac Ely Stillman, Dept. of Pathology Beth Israel Hospital and Harvard Medical School Boston, MA.

topics on another body of literature. Traditional literature "merely collect[s] and arrange[s] what it has received, that is, [it is] merely a medium of tradition." The rhetoric of traditional literature is merely explanatory and does not foster its own agenda.[12]

Systemic literature is not dependent on its sources for its program and topics. Its rhetoric is the rhetoric of independent logical inquiry and not mere commentary. Systemic literature leaves its own imprint on its sources, and uses them for its own program.[13]

The method of establishing whether a book is traditional or systemic, according to Neusner, is by way of statistical taxonomic inquiries. One asks, for example, what percentage of the literature quotes outside sources; what percentage of the literature is scriptural commentary; what percentage of the literature is inquiry that is independent of the agenda of its sources.

There is a paradox at the heart of this project, though. In order for one to talk about the rhetoric of a book, and in order to get a statistical pool that is significant, one has to first assume that the reading process itself is transparent. That is, one must assume that understanding the words, lines, units, "composites," etc., is a simple and straightforward task. If it were not a simple and straightforward task, there would be no way to gather the initial *data* in order to scientifically classify the whole as a "type." In fact, Neusner does seem to assume that understanding the words, lines, etc. of the Bavli is an uncomplicated task.[14]

A second paradox is that one needs to have a clear idea of what the boundaries of a book are before one can proceed to define what type of book it is. Here Neusner seems to have a naive belief in book covers. He seems to ground his understanding of what a book is in the notion of the identifiable artifact which in commerce is referred to as a "book."[15]

Both of these assumptions – that reading is a transparent and straightforward activity, and the naive acceptance of book covers to identify a book – are highly contested by contemporary theorists. These assumptions also lie at the heart of the polemic Neusner has had with

---

[12]*Sources and Traditions: Types of Compositions in the Talmud of Babylonia*, 1-3.
[13]Ibid.
[14]A typical comment is the following one after printing two Mishnah units (Zebahim 5:1-2) and a page and a half of Talmud (Bavli Zebahim 47a- 48a).:
> We open with two entirely conventional questions, namely, analysis of the formulation of the Mishnah's rule, within the premise that the wording in all of its patterns yields meaning. The solution of the initial problem, in appeal to a verse of Scripture, provides only a routine demonstration of the metaproposition that Scripture forms the court of final appeal. The second entry follows suit. (*How to Study the Bavli*, 153.)

[15]See the first two epigraphs above.

those whom he calls the "proponents of the intertextualist approach to the canon of Judaism."[16]

Neusner comes to the field, to battle the "intertextualists," armed with ignorance. By his own admission, when he wrote *Canon and Connection* he had read only one article on intertextuality, and had only understood one of the theories in that article.[17] For this reason Neusner sets up the debate on the basis of his own definition of intertextuality, and a caricature of his "opponents'" definition.

The position that Neusner critiques is as follows:

> [The intertextualists] maintain that these writings form a primary arena for intertextual reading of texts, which, they clearly propose, means that we always are to understand everything in light of everything else.[18]

Neusner's own definition of intertextuality is as follows:

> Intertextuality takes place when two or more documents go over the same materials, and the connection at hand derives from that intersection.[19]

It is obvious that, for Neusner, by the terms of his own theoretical stance, the "intertextualist" position is wrong. If every text is hermetically sealed, and is to be read by itself[20] then clearly it cannot be read in light

---

[16]*Canon and Connection*, xii.
[17]"Among the diverse theories at hand, the one of greatest relevance [or, at any rate the only one I could understand] is that of Genette... *Canon and Connection* 151 and n. 4. From his discussion of Genette, it is not clear that he has understood this theory either. Daniel Boyarin has also pointed out Neusner's lack of understanding of intertextuality:

> "I think it would not be too speculative to suggest in the context of Neusner's recent writing that he has a kind of obsession with arguing against his misconceived notion of 'intertextuality' as a characteristic of midrash (or rabbinic literature in general). He believes that the use of this term implies that all rabbinic literature is a "seamless whole" without history or contestation. Since this straw man has become his nemesis, he sees him hiding under every bed.... That this is indeed Neusner's animating obsession here is eminently clear from his having devoted an entire monograph solely to his subject.... Neusner's entire discussion both in the monograph on the subject and here [Neusner's critique of James Kugel's essay "Two Introductions to Midrash"] is founded on an entirely mistaken conception of the notion of intertextuality as it appears in myriad discussions in literary theory." *Intertextuality and the Reading of Midrash* (Bloomington: Indiana University Press, 1990): 13, 14. The monograph referred to is *Canon and Connection*.

[18]*Canon and Connection*, xii.
[19]Ibid., 31.
[20]"Each document, *as a matter of theory*, is to be seen all by itself." (Emphasis added.) *Judaism, The Classical Statement*, 2.

of everything else. On the other hand, what Neusner defines as intertextuality, is actually a discussion of sources.

I have no intention, nor is it my place here, to defend the scholars that Neusner attacks in *Canon and Connection* as intertextualists.[21] I will, however, attempt to explain why Neusner persists in an obdurate tone-deafness towards the idea of intertextuality.

The theory on which intertextuality is based questioned the naive belief in the stability of meaning.[22] That is, the idea that there is an essential or objective connection between a word and its meaning was challenged. The reading process was revisioned as the activity of bringing words (signs) into line with meanings (signifieds). This process posits that words, sentences, lines and on have more than one possible meaning. Further, language is not merely an intermediary between an author and a reader, a speaker and a listener, or a "reality" and an audience. Language exists in a world of texts, and negotiating the polysemy of language – that is, the essential plurality of meaning of the units of language – is the process of reading or interpretation, According to this understanding of language, intertextuality is a characteristic of all texts. Language doesn't mean anything in a vacuum, language relates first to other language. Interpretation is the process of mediating or negotiating that relationship. One author's use of language, by definition of this semiotic understanding, intersects with and is informed by other uses of language in other texts. The theory that informs intertextuality challenges the notion of hermetic or monadic texts which is at the heart of Neusner's whole project. There is no useful dialogue between Neusner and the "intertextualists" since the terms of the debate, as Neusner sets them up, precludes any common language. I will argue in Chapter V that there is a useful and significant way of incorporating intertextuality into a poetics of the *sugya* – a sugyaetics – which is not "reading everything in the light of everything else everywhere."

Translation

A significant part of Neusner's scholarly work has been devoted to the project of translating or retranslating most of Rabbinic literature. Since the Bavli was already translated, Neusner felt the need to justify his retranslation. In doing so, he does not lay claim to any philological innovation. The Soncino translations, according to Neusner, are accurate

---

[21]The grouping together of Schiffman, Cohen and Handelman in one theoretical space in *Canon and Connection*, seems to me additional proof of Neusner's essential tone-deafness towards intertextuality.
[22]On intertextuality, see my discussion in Chapter V, and the literature cited there.

on philological grounds. Neusner is not attempting to render the language more precisely or to correct errors of translation. Neusner's sole explanation for retranslating the Bavli is that the current translation is unusable for scholarly analysis. By this Neusner means that there is no adequate system of reference for the Soncino translations.

> Our principal contribution lies in the more analytical character of our translation than that which came before. We do not present long columns of undifferentiated type, broken up merely by paragraphs. We distinguish from one another the large-scale discussions and complete discussions of problems or topics....[23]

A usable translation, for Neusner, is one in which the discussions are laid out in such a way as to enable analysis. This entails a reliable system by which all scholars can refer to the text at hand. The only "reference system" of the traditional Vilna edition of the Bavli is page and side, which is far from helpful in being able to perform the types of analyses that Neusner is interested in. The Soncino translations break up the pages of the Vilna edition into paragraphs, but these are still unable to be referenced in any manner other than page and side.

A second innovation of Neusner's translation is the stated attempt to render the text in an American idiom.[24] In this attempt Neusner follows the Soncino translators in not pursuing a literal translation.

> I, therefore, depart from a literal translation, which for the Bavli would produce gibberish, and offer a clear sense of the passage. That is, I set forth what I think our authors would say, if they were speaking in American rather than in Eastern Aramaic and Mishnaic Hebrew, and if their intent were to set forth not notes from which a discussion can be reconstructed, but the fully articulated discussion

---

[23]*Translating the Classics* 39. And cf. "I do not claim to have improved in any important way on the exegetical and philological work of most of my predecessors..." *Translating the Classics*, 4. "The foundation of my analytical translation is the reference system..." *Translating the Classics* 1. "Throughout I have followed Mishcon's and Cohen's translation [the Soncino translation] for every line an generally reproduce their sense, though not their language." *The Talmud of Babylonia: An American Translation: XXV.A: Tractate Abodah Zarah Chapters 1-2* (Atlanta, Georgia: Scholar's Press, 1991): *xi*. " Throughout I have followed Simon's translation [the Soncino translation] for every line and generally reproduce his sense, though not his exact language except where indicated." *The Talmud of Babylonia: An American Translation: XVIII.A: Gittin Chapters 1-3* (Atlanta, Georgia: Scholar's Press, 1991): *xii*.

[24]It is unclear to me that the translation accomplishes the goal of being rendered in idiomatic American, aside from the occasional "Yup" which introduces a colloquialism not obviously justified by the original. Cf. *Gittin Chapters 1-3*, 38, I.1 C.

itself. ...my translation does not signal the character of the rhetoric of the original. [25]

This quote also hints at Neusner's hypothesis that the Bavli is only notes for an actual discourse which needs to be reconstructed " by those essentially familiar with the (original) discourse."[26]

Neusner's translations do accomplish one goal that is important to his analytic project. They allow immediate access to various formal features of the text. Since Mishnaic material and Toseftan material is set off by typeface, as is Aramaic material and Hebrew material, it is easy to explore the formal relations between them. Further, the reference system allows the reader to immediately apprehend the beginning and end of units of discourse. All these are important in ascertaining the rhetoric topic and program of the Bavli. I will claim that there is a flip side to this coin. First, there is the near impossibility of grasping from the translation what is involved in the reading of the *sugya* in the original.[27] Second, the *unexplained* division into lines, units, etc. naturalizes that division, and precludes, from the reader, the possibility of challenging that division – especially the reader without recourse to the original.

I proceed now to an example of the translation, and analyze the theory in practice. The translation is Arachin 2a, chosen since it is the translation which Neusner presents as a model of his method.[28]

The background to M Arachin 1:1, are the laws of Valuation in Lev. 27:2-8. "Valuation" is a specific method of pledge to the Temple. One pledges his or her worth, and is then required to pay it. The verses in Leviticus sketch out the various payments. The Mishnah extends, explicates, expounds or expands these laws.

Mishnah

A. *All pledge the valuation [of others] and are subject to the pledge of Valuation [by others].*

B. *Vow [the worth of another] and are subject to the vow [of payment of their worth by another]:*

C. *Priests and Levites and Israelites, women and slaves.*

D. *A person of doubtful sexual traits and a person who exhibits traits of both sexes vow [the worth of another] and are subject to the vow [of payment of their worth by another], pledge the valuation [of others], but are not subject to the pledge of Valuation by others,*

E. *for evaluated is only one who is certainly a male or certainly a female.*

---

[25] *The Talmud of Babylonia: An American Translation: XVIII.A:Gittin Chapters 1-3* (Atlanta, Georgia: Scholars Press, 1992): x.
[26] *Translating the Classics* 22.
[27] Neusner grants this, and doesn't consider it a major problem since the important features of a text are its formal features.
[28] *Translating the Classics* Chapter 2.

This Mishnah then generates the first *sugya*.

Gemara

I.   A.   [When the framer explicitly refers to] *all*, [in framing the Mishnah-paragraph at hand, saying *All pledge...*,] what [classification of persons does he intend] to encompass, [seeing that in what follows C, he lists the available classifications of persons in any event, and, further at D-G specifies categories of persons that are excluded. Accordingly, to what purpose does he add the encompassing language, *all*, at the outset?]

    B.   It serves to encompass a male nearing puberty [who has not yet passed puberty. Such a one is subject to examination to determine whether he grasps the meaning of a vow, such as is under discussion. A child younger than the specified age, twelve years to thirteen, is assumed not to have such understanding, and one older is taken for granted to have it.]

    C.   [When the framer explicitly frames matters as *all*] *are subject to the pledge of Valuation*, what [classification of persons does he intend] to encompass?

    D.   It is to encompass a person who is disfigured or afflicted with a skin ailment.

    E.   [Why in any event should one imagine that persons of that classification would be omitted?] I might have supposed that, since it is written, "A vow... according to your Valuation" (Lev. 27:2), [with Scripture using as equivalent terms "vow" and Valuation,"] the rule is that whoever is possessed of worth [e.g., whoever would be purchased for a sum of money in the marketplace, hence excluding the disfigured persons under discussion, who are worthless] also would be subject to a vow of Valuation [at fixed price, such as Scripture specified].

    F.   Accordingly, [the formulation of the Mishnah-passage at hand] tells us, [to the contrary, that a pledge of Valuation represents an absolute charge and is not relative to the subject's market-value.]

    G.   [How does Scripture so signify? When the framer of scripture refers at Lev. 287:2 to] "persons," [the meaning is that a pledge of Valuation applies] to anyone at all.

    H.   [When the framer of the Mishnah, further, states that *all*] *vow* [the worth of another], what [classification of persons does he thereby intend] to encompass [seeing that at C we go over the same matter, specifying those who may make such a vow]?

    I.   It is necessary for him [to specify that all take such a vow] on account of those concerning whom such a vow is taken.

    J.   [And along these same lines, when the framer specifies that *all*] are subject to a vow, what [classification or persons does he thereby intend] to encompass?

    K.   [Here matters are not so self-evident, for] if the intention is to encompass a person of doubtful sexual traits and a person who exhibits the traits of both sexes, both of those classifications are explicitly stated [in the formulation of the Mishnah-passage itself].

    L.   And if the intention is to encompass a deaf-mute, an imbecile, and a minor, these classifications also are explicitly stated. [So what can have been omitted in the explicit specification of the pertinent classifications, that the framer of the Mishnah-passage found it necessary to make use of such amplificatory language as *all*?]

M. If, furthermore, the intent was to encompass an infant less than a month old, that classification also is explicitly included [below].

N. If, furthermore, the intent was to encompass an idolator, that classification furthermore is explicitly included as well. [Accordingly, what classification of persons can possibly have been omitted in the framing of the Mishnah-passage at hand, that the author found it necessary to add the emphatic inclusionary language?]

O. In point of fact, [the purpose of adding the emphatic language of inclusion] was to encompass an infant less than a month in age.

P. [The framer of the passage] taught [that such a category is included] and then he went and restated the matter once again, so as to make explicit the inclusion of that category.

The most obvious thing about the translation, is that it is indeed written as if reconstructing a conversation from cue cards. There is far more bracketed text than not. In analyzing the translation, I ask what options were cut out by this way of framing the *sugya*. I then need to determine if the fact that certain options were denied, affects the characterization of the document as a whole.

The *sugya* in the original follows.

משנה

הכל מעריכין ונערכין, נודרין ונידרין, כהנים לוים וישראלים, נשים ועבדים. ונקבה ודאית.

טומטום ואנדרוגינוס נודרין ונידרין ומעריכין, אבל לא נערכין, שאינו נערך אלא הזכר ודאי חרש שוטה וקטן נידרין ונערכין, אבל לא נודרין ולא מעריכין, מפני שאין בהם דעת:

גמרא

A 'הכל מעריכין' לאתויי מאי?

B לאתויי מופלא סמוך לאיש.

C 'נערכין' לאתויי מאי?

D לאתויי מנוול ומוכה שחין.

E סלקא דעתך אמינא, נדר בערכך כתיב כל שישנו בדמים ישנו בערכין, וכל שאינו בדמים אינו בערכין,

F קא משמע לן.

G 'נפשות' כל דהו.

H 'נודרין' לאתויי מאי?

I נידרין איצטריך ליה.

J 'נידרין' לאתויי מאי?

K אי לאתויי טומטום ואנדרוגינוס בהדיא קתני להו.

L ואי לאתויי חרש שוטה וקטן בהדיא קתני להו.

M אי לאתויי פחות מבן חודש בהדיא קתני להו.

N ואי לאתויי עובד כוכבים בהדיא קתני להו.

O   לעולם לאתויי פחות מבן חודש.
P   ותני והדר מפרש.

Already at A., Neusner engages and answers one of the central questions of the translation of Talmud, without letting the reader know that there was a question. There is an important ambiguity in the question: "לאתויי מאי?." Literally, it means "to bring in what?" Leo Jung in the Soncino translation renders the phrase: "What does [ALL PERSONS] ARE FIT TO EVALUATE mean to include?" This translation retains the ambiguity of the object of the question. Is the anonymous questioner asking a question of original intent? That is, should the question be understood as Neusner has formulated it:

> [When the framer explicitly refers to] *all*, [in framing the Mishnah-paragraph at hand, saying *All pledge*...,] what [classification of persons does he intend] to encompass...

Or is it a question of reading: what do I understand when I read the word *All*? This latter question is like the midrashic formulation of *ribbui* – the word *All* implies that there are more cases here than just the ones listed, for if the ones listed were all the cases there would have been no need for the word *All*.

The evidence in favor of reading A. as a "midrashic" question rather than a question of original intent is twofold. First, lines E. and G. are midrashic. E. states that it is "doing midrash," by explicit citation: "it is written" (כתיב), while G. is more subtly midrashic. Second, line A. appears in b Nazir 62a, as a midrash:

איש כי יפליא בערכין למה לי?
אלא האי איש מיבעי ליה לאיתויי מופלא סמוך לאיש.

> What is the necessity of the phrase "When a man explicitly" (Lev. 27:2) in [the context of] Valuation?
> Rather this "man" is needed to include one who is "discerning"[29] and close to manhood.

Whether line A. is actually midrashic, or not, Neusner's translation closes off the possibility that it is, without acknowledging that he is doing that.

In a similar manner, the translation at P.,

> [The framer of the passage] taught [that such a category is included] and then he went and restated the matter [once again, so as] to make explicit the inclusion of that category.

---

[29]Cf. Rashi and Tosafot b. Arachin 2a *s.v. Mufla.*: ומופלא קרי ליה על שם שבודקין אותו אם יודע להפלות It seems that Jung has mistranslated Rashi's comment in his note. Neusner translated Rashi's comment, correctly, into the bracketed remarks, but then mistranslated מופלא as "a male nearing puberty."

belies the midrashic implication of this term. As a technical term, ותני והדר מפרש is employed[30] as a result of an encompassing reading (*ribbui*), or a narrowing reading (*mi`ut*) of a Mishnaic phrase. At some point in the ensuing discussion, the encompassing phrase becomes redundant[31] since "everything" that can be encompassed has been so encompassed explicitly – as is the case here. At this point in the *sugya* the stam introduces the ותני והדר מפרש, to reread the original *ribbui* or *mi`ut* as a general principle which is later clarified or expanded upon. Neusner's translation gives the reader no idea that this statement is a known rhetorical device.

It is clear from this sample that Neusner's understanding of *sugyot* in the Bavli as "cue cards," or "sherds and remnants of coherent speech" has led him to "reconstruct" the *sugya*. The other option, of course is to treat the *sugya* as closer to poetry, or prose-poetry, and trying in a translation to retain the rhythm and, at times, the ambiguity of the original.

An even cursory review of some of Neusner's translation of Gittin, reveals that the sample we have just looked at is not unique. In one *sugya*[32] the same phrase: אם כן מה כח בית דין יפה is translated first as "for otherwise what power does the court have," and subsequently, "what value is the ruling of the court." Without some sort of apparatus, or access to the original, the reader has no way of knowing that these two are the same exact phrase.

This is also the case with the *sugya* b Gittin 12a-13a. The phrase מהו דתימא...קא משמע לן is translated three different ways in this one *sugya*.

> What might you otherwise have imagined? ... So we are informed that this is not the case. (II.1 M p.39)
> What might you otherwise have supposed? ... so we are informed that that is not the principal consideration. [33] (II.1 U p.40)

---

[30]Cf. Baba Kama 13b, 50b; Horayot 2b; Zebahim 20b, 68b.
[31]On the talmudic "fear" of redundancy as a midrashic "move" see e.g. Hyman Kaplan, "Some Methods of Sebara", *Jewish Quarterly Review* vol. 50 (1959-60) 126ff.
[32]Gittin 33a-33b, Neusner 12-14.
[33]For a full discussion of this *sugya* see chapter seven. Neusner completely mistranslates this whole second unit. He translates Psalms 45:14: כל כבודה בת מלך פנימה as "The honor of the king's daughter lies in her enjoying rights to privacy." [All glorious is the princess within,... (KJV); ...with all kinds of wealth. The princess is decked... (RSV); ...goods of all sorts. The royal princess,... (NJPS)] While Neusner is trying to translate the verse as it is read *midrashically*, a) he makes no mention of this in the translation, thereby leaving the reader either ignorant, or, if the reader looks up the verse in another translation, confused. b) the midrashic translation is wrong. The point of the midrash is that a woman is *confined* – and therefore not *allowed* to work, rather

You might suppose that, ... but we are informed that that is not the fact. (II.3 E p.41)

In fact, all ten occurrences of this formulation in the first chapter are translated differently. Additionally, while throughout Gittin it is recorded as one "thought" in other tractates (e.g. Arachin) it is two "thoughts." While these differences might seem merely nuanced when we have access to the original, Neusner's claim is that his is an analytical translation. That is, it was written for the express purpose of researching, and analyzing the Talmud, without recourse to the original.[34]

I would further argue, that the present system of reference (page and side for the Bavli) has distinct advantages. As Neusner points out, the sole purpose behind the present division is an attempt to get as many words of Talmud on a page along with the relevant comments of Rashi and Tosafot.[35] The fact then that a comment is on 23a rather than 22b, is purely coincidental, and therefore neutral. If a scholar wishes to argue or interpret on the basis of the division of a *sugya* into units, lines, etc. – the

---

than *enjoying rights to privacy*. The former point is important if one is to attempt any sort of understanding of how a *sugya* "works" at odds with Neusner's own. The latter is important for the understanding of the *sugya* itself.

[34] Neusner doesn't explain his division of specific texts into units, lines, etc. This division is far from self-explanatory. A brief review of his reference apparatus to b AZ 2a-3b bears this out. (This is the text that Neusner uses as the example in *The Rules of Composition of the Talmud of Babylonia*, Chapter 2; also in *How To Study the Bavli*, Chapter 3; the major portion of the analysis is originally in the translation *Tractate Abodah Zarah Chapters 1-2*, 32-34.) The organizing principle of this unit is the verse from Isaiah 43:9: כל הגוים נקבצו יחדו ויאספו לאמים מי בהם יגיד זאת וראשנות ישמיענו, יתנו עדיהם ויצדקו וישמעו ויאמרו אמת. (NJPS: All the nations assemble as one, the peoples gather. Who among them declared this, foretold to us the things that have happened? Let them produce their witnesses and be vindicated, the men, hearing them may say, "It is true!") Neusner missteps when, at the beginning of his second sub-unit (I.2 A) he misidentifies the verse that R. Simlai is exegeting. It is obvious that the verse is Isaiah 43:9. (It is quoted in the comment, and the images are all from the verse.) Neusner's A-G are all based on the first phrase כל הגוים נקבצו יחדו ויאספו לאמים. Neusner's H, however, should be another unit (I.3 ?) since it is based on the next phrase in the verse: מי בהם יגיד זאת. (MS JTS, ed. Abramson, has an indented division here. Neusner obviously didn't consult MSS.) The next division, I would argue, should be at Neusner's CC, since this is based on the next phrase וראשנות ישמיענו. This division is more obvious in the MS JTS since the Vilna has an added ומי, which ties it to the previous line. From Neusner's translation here one also misses the play off the word וישמע which was midrashically explained earlier (I.1 L).

On the other hand, Neusner's division at I.4 is unclear. This is a continuation of I.3. The MSS have both questions at I.3 B, in which case I.4 is merely a continuation of I.3.

[35] The other commentaries on the Vilna page do not affect the graphic layout in the same way.

division will immediately be recognized as part of the argument or interpretation.[36] A translation which includes the elaborate referencing that Neusner has included, "naturalizes" that referencing. It skips the step of noting that the division into units and lines is not of a piece with the translating of the material. It is an interpretive move of a different order.[37]

Its important to notice that Neusner's translation follows from his understanding of text. The reading process, the move from line to line, is not an important focus for understanding texts, according to Neusner. The reading process is straightforward, and the important questions, as I pointed out above, are about the work as a whole.

Literary analysis

One of Neusner's major contributions to the study of the Bavli is his questioning of the authority of attributions. While several scholars before him raised the question, no one has pursued the skeptical line of thought as consistently as has Neusner. The end of this line of thought is that the Bavli is a composition of its authorship, that is the last group of like minded scholars who put it together. At different times Neusner has been more or less certain about how long the time period of this authorship was. The certainty is that the student of the Bavli cannot get beyond the text to an original statement of a named author. This leaves open some questions about the style of a text which seems to claim for itself that it is passing down a tradition in the names and languages of its tradents. What this style or character of the Bavli is, and what it signifies, is the subject of the monographs that led up to the book *How to Study the Bavli*.[38]

In *The Bavli's One Voice*, Neusner comes to the following conclusion:

> The Bavli throughout speaks in a single and singular voice. It is single because it is a voice that expresses the same limited set of notes everywhere. It is singular because these notes are arranged in

---

[36]As is the case with Shamma Friedman's work. See Chapter Two. (See also Michael Satlow, "'Wasted Seed': The History of a Rabbinic Idea," in *HUCA*, forthcoming.) This is also the case with Jonah Frankel's work. See Chapter Four.
[37]The same comment can be made about Steinsaltz's edition of the Talmud. His division into units is also an interpretive move which is not unproblematic. A cursory glance at the Manuscript evidence reveals that this is not a new "problem." There have been many divisions of the text along the lines of the colons that are found in the Vilna edition. Some are the same as our texts, others are very different. This is an interesting avenue of exploration for the understanding and definition of "*sugya.*"
[38]*How to Study the Bavli: The Languages, Literatures, and Lessons of the Talmud of Babylonia* (Atlanta, Georgia: Scholars Press, 1992).

> one and the same way throughout. The Bavli's one voice, sounding through all tractates, is the voice of exegetes of the Mishnah. The document is organized around the Mishnah, and that is not a merely formal, but a substantive order. At every point, if the framers have chosen a passage of Mishnah exegesis, that passage will stand at the head of all further discussion. Every turning point brings the editors back to the Mishnah, always read in its own order and sequence.[39]

This conclusion was reached by first classifying all the "composites" in Bavli Temurah in one of three categories: 1. Exegesis and amplification of the law of the Mishnah; 2. exegesis and exposition of verses of, or topics in, Scripture; 3. Freestanding composites devoted to topics other than those defined by the Mishnah or Scripture.[40] Then, the averages of proportions of the various types of composites are calculated. The result is that most of the composites of the Bavli (by percentage) are devoted to Mishnah exegesis.[41]

This then leads to the claim that since the rhetoric of the Bavli is uniform everywhere, it is the work of the final authors who framed the document. One can then speak of "The Bavli" as one uniform book. Further, the fact that such an overwhelmingly large percentage of the Bavli is concerned with Mishnah exegesis points to the further conclusion "that the purpose of the Talmud is to clarify and amplify selected passages of the Mishnah."[42] For the framers of the Talmud, the Mishnah had a "near monopoly over serious discourse" and was the "text of ultimate concern." For Neusner, then, the concerns of the Bavli are those of the Mishnah. The Bavli merely works on the details.

This multifaceted conclusion is, of course, dependent on the accuracy of the taxonomic system. If the categorization is faulty, the conclusions are unproven. In order to examine this taxonomy at close quarters, we now examine b Temurah 2a-3a. In this examination I again use Neusner's translation. My comments on the translation itself will be relegated to the notes.

Mishnah

A. [2A] All effect a valid substitution [substitute a beast for one they have first designated as a sacrifice for that the second beast enters the status of the originally consecrated one] –
B. all the same are men and women.
C. Not that a man is permitted to effect a substitution.

---

[39]453.
[40]454. These results were then compared with the results of ten other tractates.
[41]455.
[42]464.

On Framing the Question: Intertextuality, Translation, Literary Analysis   59

       D.   But if one has effected a substitution, it [that which is designated instead of the beast already consecrated] is deemed a substitute [and also consecrated].
       E.   And the man [who does so] incurs the penalty of forty stripes.

I.1   A.   *The very statement of the Mishnah's rule contains an internal contradiction. You first say,* **All effect a valid substitution,** *which means, to begin with. But then you go on,* **But if one has effected a substitution, it [that which is designated instead of the beast already consecrated] is deemed a substitute [and also consecrated],** *and that means, only after the fact!*
       B.   *But do you think that* **All effect a valid substitution,** *means, to begin with? [If that is your reading, then] instead of raising your problem to the formulation of our Mishnah passage, address it to the formulation of Scripture, for it is written, "[If it is an animal such men offer as an offering to the Lord, all of such that any man gives to the Lord is holy.] He shall not substitute anything for it or exchange it, a good for a bad or a bad for a good; and if he makes any exchange of beast for beast, then both it and that for which it is exchanged shall be holy" (Lev. 27:9-10).*
       C.   *Rather, said R. Judah, "This is the sense of the Mishnah passage:* **All** *can be involved so as to* **effect a valid substitution** *[substitute a beast for one they have first designated as a sacrifice for that the second beast enters the status of the originally consecrated one] – all the same are men and women. Not that a man is permitted to effect a substitution.* **But if one has effected a substitution, it [that which is designated instead of the beast already consecrated] is deemed a substitute [and also consecrated]. And the man [who does so] incurs the penalty of forty stripes.**

Neusner classifies this unit as "Mishnah exegesis," that is, the "passage takes shape around the requirement of explaining the language or meaning of a statement of the Mishnah. ...A composition that is classified as Mishnah exegesis is one that makes sense only within the framework of a Mishnah paragraph, one that cannot have been composed without the immediate presence of a sentence of the Mishnah."[43]

This classification is dependent on an understanding of reading and interpretation as a simple and transparent process. That is, any reader can "obviously" see that the Mishnah's language is "unclear" and therefore is in need of clarification. The comment (of the Bavli) is therefore true to its rhetoric – its purpose is to untangle a seeming contradiction. This understanding of the function of commentary is clear from Neusner's remarks about this unit. "Composite" I.1, for Neusner,

---

[43]*Bavli's One Voice*, 155-156.

"simply clarifies the sense of the Mishnah passage so as to eliminate an unwanted implication of a contradiction."[44]

The question that Neusner doesn't ask is: Does the contradiction exist prior to the Bavli's intervention? I would argue that if one reads M Temurah I:1 not within the context of the Bavli, one would not necessarily raise the question that the Bavli raises. There is no necessary "contradiction." The Mishnah standing alone seems to be a simple reiteration of the verses from Lev. 27.

> 9. If it is an animal such as men offer as an offering to the Lord, all of such that any man gives to the Lord is holy. 10. He shall not substitute any thing for it or exchange it, a good for a bad, or a bad for a good; and if he makes any exchange of beast for beast, then both it and that for which it is exchanged shall be holy.

Therefore, the sugya first needs to argue for **ambiguity** (I.1A and B). It needs to be established that A and C of the Mishnah are contradictory, rather than merely related as a priori and a posteriori events. Once this has been established the Bavli can proceed to clarify (C). The gain of this rhetorical move is the innovation of a Halakhic category not found in the Mishnah – the category of effecting a substitution (מחפיסין בתמורה), different from the Mishnah's substituting (ממירים), which is how A in the Mishnah should be translated.[45] This is far from "transparent," as Neusner claims.[46]

Similarly strong objections might be raised about the classification of the next "composite."

I.2 A. **All effect:**
B. *What does the language, "all" serve to encompass?*
C. *It serves to encompass the heir* [who effects a substitution while father is still alive. He does not yet own the beast, and only the owner of a beast can designate it as holy. But he is presumed to be heir and therefore future owner of the beast. The legal effect of his presumptive ownership then is at issue.]
D. *That is not in accord with the position of R. Judah. For it has been taught on Tannaite authority:*
E. "The heir of the owner of a beast may lay on hands, and the heir of the owner of a beast may effect a valid substitution," the words of R. Meir.

---

[44]Ibid. 43.
[45]The Soncino translation of Rabbi L. Miller, does make the distinction. *Temurah: Translated into English with Notes, Glossary and Indices* (London: The Soncino Press, 1948):1.
[46]"The purpose of the discussion [I.1] is transparent: the clarification of the meaning of the passage before us." ibid 156.

F. And R. Judah says, "The heir of the owner of a beast may not lay on hands, and the heir of the owner of a beast may not effect a valid substitution."

G. What is the reasoning behind the position of R. Judah?

H. It is that R. Judah draws an analogy from the end of the act of consecration for the beginning of the act of consecration. Just as, in the final act, the presumptive heir of a beast cannot lay on hands [but only the actual owner of the beast does so], so at the beginning of the act of consecration, the presumptive heir cannot effect a valid substitution.

I. Then how do we know the rule governing the laying on of hands anyhow?

J. We find a reference to "his offering" three times [Lev. 3:1, "and if his offering is a sacrifice of a peace offering"; Lev. 3:6, "and if his offering for a sacrifice to the Lord be of the flock"; Lev. 3:7 "and if he offer a lamb for his offering"]. One bears the sense, "his offering," and not the offering of a gentile; one bears the sense of, "his offering", and not the offering of somebody else; and the third bears the sense of, "his offering," and not the offering of his father.

K. And so far as R. Meir is concerned, who has said, "A presumptive heir lays on hands," do we not have written, "his offering"?

L. He requires that to make the point that all members of a partnership that owns a beast must lay hands on the beast.

M. And does R. Judah not concur that all members of a partnership that owns a beast must lay hands the beast?[47] How come?

N. It is because their offering is not designated [to belong specifically to any one of the several partners, so the language "his offering" does not pertain].

O. If you prefer, I shall say, in point of fact he does concur [that all members of a partnership that owns a beast must lay hands on the beast], but he derives the rule governing both the offering of a gentile and the offering of one's fellow from the same verse, leaving over a reference that serves to make the point that all partners in the ownership of a beast that is to be sacrificed lay hands on the beast.

P. And R. Meir, who maintains that a presumptive heir does not lay on hands[48] – what is the scriptural basis for his position?

Q. He will say to you, "'If he makes any exchange of beast for beast, then both it and that for which it is exchanged shall be holy' serves to encompass the presumptive heir of the beast.' One then infers from the initial act of dedication the rule governing the final act of consecration [done just before the animal is killed]. Just as, at the initiation of the process of consecration, the presumptive heir may effect a valid act of substitution, so at the end of the process of consecration, the presumptive heir may lay on hands."

---

[47]A more accurate translation would be:
And R. Judah? He does not hold that all the members of a partnership must lay hands on the beast.
What is the reason?
[48]The translation should be:
And R. Meir, who maintains that a presumptive heir effects a substitution.

R. *And as for R. Judah, how does he deal with the verse, "if he makes any exchange of beast for beast, then both it and that for which it is exchanged shall be holy"?*

S. *It serves to encompass within the law the power of a woman, and that is in accord with that which has been taught on Tannaite authority:*

T. Since the entire passage [governing the act substitution] speaks only of men, as it is said, "[If it is an animal such as men offer as an offering to the Lord, all of such that any man gives to the Lord is holy.] He shall not substitute anything for it or exchange it," how do we know that a woman is subject to the same law? Scripture says, "If he makes any exchange of beast for beast," which serves to encompass a woman.

U. *And as for R. Meir, how does he know that a woman is subject to the law?*

V. *He derives that fact from the language, "and if...."*[49]

W. *And how does R. Judah deal with that possible proof?*

X. *He derives no lesson from the language, "and if...."*

Y. *Now so far as both R. Meir and R. Judah are concerned, the operative consideration is that Scripture has served expressly to include the case of a woman, but if the woman had not been encompassed by Scripture, then I might have reached the conclusion that, if she made a statement of substitution of a secular beast for an already consecrated one, [while the former may be deemed consecrated] she does not incur the penalty of a flogging.*[50]

Z. But has not R. Judah said Rab said, and so, too, has a Tannaite authority of the household of R. Ishmael stated, "'When a man or a woman commits any sin that men commit' (Num. 5:6). In this language, Scripture has treated the woman as comparable to the man for the purpose of all the penalties that are imposed by the Torah."

AA. [The explicit proof in the present] is required. For what might you have thought? These words pertain to a sanction that is equivalent for either an individual or the community, but here, since we deal with a penalty that is not equivalent for every body, as we have learned, **A congregation and partners do not produce a substitute,**[51] **since it is said, "He shall not change it" (Lev. 27:10). The individual produces a substitute, and neither a congregation nor partners produce a substitute,**

BB. *in consequence of which, a woman also, if she should do such a deed, would not be flogged. So we are informed that she would be flogged.*[52]

Neusner characterizes this unit as Mishnah exegesis, too. According to Neusner, "I.2 proceeds to the more interesting problem of language

---

[49]Here and in X the MSS and Rashi have "waw" (ואו). The parallel in B Nidah 83a has "and if..." (ואם).

[50]MS Vat. 119 has: "then I might have reached the conclusion that she had not effected a substitution." ה"א לא עבדא תמורה.

[51]From here till the end of AA is a continuation of the quote from M Temurah 1:6, but is not found in the Vilna Talmud nor in the MSS. It is also not clear why Neusner thinks it is important to add it.

[52]MS Vat. 119 has: "a woman does not effect [a substitution]." אשה לא עבדה.

analysis. It is not particular to our passage but must be investigated in connection with all parallel usages of the encompassing language, 'all.' This rapidly moves into an analysis of the position of Judah on several parallel matters, with the effect of showing us how these parallel matters interrelate. The issues are several: the facts of our case, rules for deriving proof from Scripture, the general principles governing the status of women in context, and the like."[53]

A number of points must be raised here. First, if at all, this is "language analysis" of a very specific type. This is a midrashic reading of the Mishnah. Moreover, this technique of exploiting the Mishnah's use of "All" (הכל) is a frequent part of the Bavli's rhetoric.[54] The purpose of the Bavli is not "language analysis" but, it would seem, the deconstruction of the category of "all."[55] Whereas the Mishnah proposes a seamless category, the Bavli's rhetoric generates multiple differences – gentiles, women and, in the next unit, children. Further, the discussion of women introduces a comment on the equity between men and women in regard to responsibility and punishment. This is far from a simple analysis of the language of the Mishnah. The *sugya* in the Bavli moves the discussion to uncharted territory.

Further, returning to Neusner's original definition of "Mishnah exegesis," this unit could just as easily have been found without the Mishnah – and in fact much of it is found in Sifra,[56] the Tannaitic midrash to Leviticus. Again, there is nothing simple or transparent about what the Bavli is doing here.

The same manner of objection might be raised to most of Neusner's classifications.[57] The problem is not that there are better categories that

---

[53] *Voice of the Bavli*, 44.
[54] See *inter alia* b Hag. 2a, b Suc. 56a, b Ket. 110b, b Kid. 76b, b San. 36b, b Ar. 2a.
[55] I use this somewhat loose sense of the word deconstruction, to contrast this interpretation to Neusner's statement in *Voice of the Bavli*: "Dismantling ('deconstructing') [the Bavli's] components and identifying them, perhaps even describing the kinds of compilation that the authors of those components can have had in mind in writing their compositions – these activities of literary criticism yield no insight into the religious system that guided the document's framers." (465)
[56] *Behukotai* 9:6.
[57] E.g., while Neusner classifies I.3 as "Speculation and Abstract Thought on Law," it is actually a continuation of I.2, inserting children into the discussion. Further, it can easily be classified as a Midrashic reading of Lev. 17:8, which has no need of our Mishnah. At the same time I.4-9, which Neusner also classifies as "Speculation and Abstract Thought on Law," is based on the interpretation of a *beraitta*, which is not very theoretical though it is midrashic. The fact that Neusner doesn't recognize the significance of midrashic reading practice as part of the Bavli's legal poetics seems to stem from his general inattention to the importance of reading line to line as opposed to reading books.

Neusner hasn't identified as of yet. The problem is methodological. Neusner's method is based on the scientific accuracy of taxonomic categorization. For this to be correct, the categories themselves need to be neutral, and the categorization a simple manner of fitting square pegs into square holes. However, the categorization itself is an argument, an interpretation rather than a neutral classification. When, as in this case, the interpretation is faulty, the classification is then unhelpful if not unintelligible and the percentages are meaningless.[58]

A second result of the premise that the Bavli is a composition of its final authorship is that the choice of language of a statement, either Hebrew or Aramaic, is not a result of the "historical sequence ('biography') let alone authentic reproduction of things actually said ('ipsissima verba')"[59] by named authorities. What then does it signify? Neusner claims that "the choice of language serves a taxonomic purpose."[60] That is:

> In the Talmud of Babylonia what is said in Hebrew is represented as authoritative and formulates a normative thought or rule. What is said in Aramaic is analytical and commonly signals an argument and formulates a process of inquiry and criticism.[61]

This abstract definition is concretized in the following way:

> Where we find Hebrew, the language of quotation, it will commonly signal one of three facts, which, through the very choice of language, our author wishes to tell us:
>
> 1. A passage is from the Hebrew Scriptures. 2. A passage is from the Mishnah or the Tosefta (or from a corpus of sayings out of which the Tosefta as we have it was selected; for our purposes that is a distinction that makes no difference). 3. A statement is authoritative and forms a normative formulation, a rule to be generalized and obeyed even where not from the Mishnah or Scripture, but from a named or anonymous authority of the time of the document itself.[62]

The first two of the objectives of the taxonomic use of Hebrew are pretty obvious. The third is less than obvious. In the example that Neusner cites, from Bavli Bekhorot 28a,[63] this third type of statement is found:

> *It further supports the position of R. Eleazar, for R. Eleazar has said,* "They assign to the animal thirty days from the moment at which the blemish appeared on the beast."

---

[58] These same observations are also applicable to Neusner's discussion of b Moed Katan in *The Principal Parts of the Bavli's Discourse*, 1-70.
[59] *How to Study the Bavli* 17.
[60] *How to Study the Bavli* 18.
[61] *How to Study the Bavli* 19.
[62] *How to Study the Bavli* 20.
[63] *How to Study the Bavli* 22.

On Framing the Question: Intertextuality, Translation, Literary Analysis

The italics represent Aramaic, and the plain type letters are Hebrew. The Aramaic phrase in the thought-unit is making an argument, while the Hebrew "is authoritative and forms a normative formulation" which is being pointed to for support. Neusner stresses this point saying:

> The use of Hebrew therefore forms part of the conventional substrate of the document, conveying a claim and a meaning, and what it signals is not 'quoting from the original source,' though that is, as a matter of fact, part of the message of facticity, the classification of a statement as a datum, that the use of Hebrew is meant to convey.

Hebrew, then, carries no chronological or historical significance in the Bavli. It is merely a taxonomic device, a means to classify statements. Or in the words of literary theory, a hermeneutic index – a signpost that points to the way a statement is supposed to be interpreted.

Aramaic is also then a hermeneutic index with a different significance. Aramaic signifies that:

> 1. A passage formulates an analytical or critical problem and is engaged in solving it.

> 2. A passage is particular and episodic, for example, commonly case reports about things decided in courts of the time of the document set forth in Aramaic, or stories about things authorities have done, told in Aramaic; these invariably are asked to exemplify a point beyond themselves.[64]

Both of these taxonomic categories are problematic. The first category is open to several interpretations. Is midrashic exegesis, for example, an analytical or critical problem? In a review of all the statements attributed to Rava, with the attribution "Said Rava,"[65] in Bavli Megillah, it was often hard to decide whether a statement was analytical or authoritative. Further, some of the statements obviously did not comply with the taxonomic categories above. For example on 7b we find the following:

> Said Rava,[66] *a person is obligated to become intoxicated on Purim to the point that he can no longer distinguish between "cursed is Haman" and "blessed is Mordechai."*[67]

---

[64]*How to Study the Bavli* 24.
[65]This methodology for choosing statements to survey attempted to fulfill two criteria: 1. That there be enough of a sample – and Rava is well represented, 2. That the sample be in some way randomized. Choosing Rava statements as opposed to statements based on a rhetorical or linguistic signifier, fulfilled this criteria.
[66]One can only tell contextually whether "Said" is Aramaic or Hebrew, since the difference is only in the pointing: אֲמַר (Aramaic) vs. אָמַר (Hebrew).
[67]אמר רבא, מחייב איניש לבסומי בפוריא עד דלא ידע בין ארור המן לברוך מרדכי

This is an obviously Aramaic, authoritative sentence.[68] It is neither analyzing nor solving – it is a rule to be obeyed. This sort of evidence, though plentiful, will not settle the question of whether Neusner's categories hold water. It seems to me, however, that two other statements found later in Bavli Megillah, might.

There are a number of comments, large and small, generated by the Mishnah (2:3) at 19a. The Mishnah deals with concerns that arise from the fact that regular cities and walled cities have different appointed times to read the Esther scroll for Purim.

Mishnah

A resident of an [unwalled] city who travelled to a walled city,
and a resident of a walled city who travelled to an [unwalled] city.
If he intends to return to his place [of origin], he reads as
    [they do in] his place,
if not, he reads with them.

Gemara

Said Rava, this [rule is stated] only when he intends to return on the
    night of the fourteenth,
but if he does not intend to return on the night of the fourteenth he
    reads with them.
Said Rava, *From where do I know this? For it is written* "That is why
    village Jews who live in unwalled towns" (Esther 9:19).
Since it says "village (*prazim*) Jews," *why need it say* "who live in
    unwalled towns (*prazot*)?"
It comes to teach us that a villager (*paroz*) for a day is considered a
    villager.

This extended comment, follows the Neusnerian categories perfectly. The first Rava statement is in Hebrew, it is authoritative and a normative formulation. The second Rava statement is Aramaic. It is also analytic (and exegetical).

A doubt forms when we look again at the first Rava statement. We see that it is also analytic and engaged in solving a problem. The problem, of course, is what does the Mishnah mean by "If he intends to return to his place [of origin]"? Rava answers that it means "intends to return on the night of the fourteenth." This doubt about the categories

---

[68] Among others see also the following from Bavli Succah (38b and 39a):

אמר רבא לא לימא איניש ברוך הבא והדר בשם ה' אלא ברוך הבא בשם ה' בהדדי.
אמר רבא, לא לימא איניש יהא שמיה רבא והדר מברך אלא יהא שמיה רבא מברך בהדדי.

Said Rava, a person should not say: "blessed is the one who comes," and then "in the name of God" but rather "blessed is the one who comes in the name of God" together.
Said Rava, a person should not say: "May his great name" and then "be blessed," but rather "May his great name be blessed" together.
These too, are Aramaic, authoritative sentences.

grows as we look to the bottom of the same page. The discussion has come round to the physical scroll of Esther, and what it must be like (physically) in order that one who reads from it fulfills their obligation.

> R. Yehudah said in the name of Shmuel, one who reads from an [Esther] scroll, which is written in a scroll with other Writings, did not fulfill [his obligation].
> Said Rava, this [rule is stated] only when it is neither slightly shorter nor longer, if however, it is slightly shorter or longer there is no problem.

Shmuel's statement legislates that the Esther scroll needs to be recognizable as a scroll of its own, for ritual purposes. Therefore if it is part of a larger scroll it is no good. Rava's statement legislates that to be recognizable it need only be written on parchment that is slightly shorter or longer than the parchment surrounding it. Rava's statement is obviously Aramaic, authoritative and a normative formulation. It is also analytic.

More interesting however, is that this Rava statement is structurally identical to the earlier Hebrew Rava statement. In fact, the introductory phrase of one is almost a translation of the other: לא אמרן אלא (lo 'amaran 'ela) and לא שנו אלא (lo shanu 'ela) mean basically the same thing.[69] Another interesting point is that throughout the Bavli,[70] the לא שנו phrase introduces Hebrew statements, while the לא אמרן mainly introduces Aramaic phrases. However just as we have seen in Bavli Megillah, quoted here, the statements "do" the same thing. If they do the same thing, the language is irrelevant. It seems to me that this casts a pall over the argument for language as taxonomy.

It should be noted though, that while this answer seems to be mistaken, the question itself is a strong one. Even if one accepts some form of source critical methodology, it is still not clear why statements by the same attributed Sages, which have the same function, are in different languages. The answer might come from the way language works in specific *sugyot* both intra- and intertextually.[71]

---

[69] Cf. the following string of statements from Bavli Succah 7a:

1   אמר רבא ואינה נתרת אלא בצורת הפתח
2   איכא דאמרי אמר רבא וניתרת נמי בצורת הפתח
3   איכא דאמרי אמר רבא וצריכא נמי צורת הפתח

All three statements have the same structure, but 1 is in Hebrew, while 2 and 3 are Aramaic. This bolsters Neusner thesis that chronological factors are mostly irrelevant as to the choice of language. On the other hand, his categories don't account for it either.

[70] For statistical purposes, there are 487 לא שנו statements and 144 לא אמרן statements.

[71] And see my discussion in chapter six of the *lo shanu* statements as a narrative line in b Gittin 34-35b.

Another general methodological problem is raised by these categories. Are they actually categories? The language of the categories is not the language of the texts. In fact it is, almost by definition, foreign to the texts. The taxonomist, as Neusner refers to himself in relation to his work, looks upon the objects that he wishes to differentiate and discern with the supposedly neutral eye of the scientist. The categories themselves are then, at the same time, a meta-language and a transparent language. In other words, the claim of any taxonomist, and the implicit claim of much of the work under consideration here, is that the categories are natural. It is merely a question of finding which categories the various statements fit. Categorization, it is claimed is a necessary first step in understanding.

This approach stumbles at the point when we examine individual statements and try to fit them into these categories. We immediately notice that the categorization itself is an argument, an interpretation rather than a neutral classification. This is evident in that most of the assignations to either category could be disputed. We already mentioned the problem of midrash/exegesis – it is analytic, not normative, and yet appears in both Hebrew and Aramaic. The לא שמע also did not fit clearly into either category. It seems to me that this is not coincidental, but a result of the fact that the methodology employed by Neusner is top down rather than bottom up. The categories do not emerge from the *sugyot*. Individual *sugyot*, according to Neusner, are not an important unit of meaning. The first unit of meaning is the book. The categories are then an impressionistic statement about the "book" as a whole. That is, oftentimes we find that named Sages from the same period speak both Hebrew and Aramaic. It seems that often the Hebrew statements are normative while the Aramaic statements are "explanatory" or analytic in some general sense. To adopt the words of other scholars, it seems that the Aramaic statements or anonymous phrases give the Talmud its sense of being the Talmud, they create the *sugyot*.

At this very general level, Neusner is not saying much which is radically different from the scholars we looked at in Chapter Two. Since he has flattened the historical component, however, Neusner's differentiation between Hebrew and Aramaic is not prescriptive. That is, knowing the difference in its general sense, we are no further along in an attempt to understand how to study the Bavli – if that means how one reads and understands a *sugya*. As a general, impressionistic rule, the language as taxonomy distinction is also highly unsatisfactory for Neusner's own purposes. If it is not hard and fast, it cannot explain what motivated a "framer" or a member of the "authorship" to choose one language over the other.

Even if we agree with some of his conclusions about the intelligibility of the Bavli, that the Bavli is not just a chaotic mass of accumulated source material, but is an edited work – it is not necessarily because we believe that Neusner has proven his case.[72] We have tried and failed to find a methodology of interpretation of *sugyot* in the large volume of Neusner's work. It seems that while starting from the whole allows him to ask new and interesting questions – what the significance of the Bavli's rhetoric is, for example – it does not adequately provide answers to either the old or new ones.

In the next chapter I examine the work of two scholars who would accept at least some of Neusner's premises about the historicity of the Bavli, while at the same time offering very different approaches to interpreting the Bavli.

---

[72] I find myself agreeing to a large extent with what Neusner calls his "fabricated null hypothesis." "[T]he Bavli is a quite orderly document, but my account of the principles of order errs; [Neusner has] identified false indicators and missed more telling ones therefore classifying the wrong data and ignoring more pertinent ones." (*Bavli's One Voice*, 189)

4

Talmud as Literature and Cultural Production

Introduction

In this chapter I review the work of Jonah Fraenkel and Daniel Boyarin on Talmudic Aggadah. There is much that these two scholars have in common. Both Fraenkel and Boyarin approach the Aggadic portions of the Talmud as literature. Both use literary-theoretical approaches to interpret this material. In an important sense, they followed Isaac Heinemann's[1] lead in taking the stories – fanciful, serious, surreal – of the Talmud as "seriously" as the legal material, in an effort to understand the "theological" or "cultural" world of the Sages.

While the scholars whose work we reviewed in Chapter II, used "literary tools" in the service of historical or redactional questions, Fraenkel and Boyarin are both interested in Talmud as literature per se – with all the baggage that that label brings to each of their theoretical perspectives. Both agree that the stories found in the Talmud are not resources for writing a history of those about whom the stories tell, yet both also agree that, if understood properly, the stories have something to say about the cultural milieu of their authors.

---

[1] Both Frankel and Boyarin acknowledge their debt to Heinemann. The title of Frankel's recent magnum opus *Darkei HaAggadah Ve'Hamidrash* quotes Heinemann's *Darkei Ha'Aggadah*. This is not incidental, as Frankel makes clear in his introduction that he is indebted to Heinemann:

"יודעי ספרות המדרש, המכירים את דרכו של היינמן, יבחינו בנקל עד כמה אני הולך בעקבותיו ובמה דורנו ייחד את עצמו בהבנת דרכי הדרשה." (p. א)

Boyarin, in *Intertextuality and the Reading of Midrash* (Indiana University Press, Bloomington, 1990), explicitly frames his project as a "new *Darkei HaAggadah*" (p.11).

Fraenkel and Boyarin both understand Talmudic literature through specific theoretical prisms which were regnant at critical times in their careers. For Fraenkel this is phenomenological criticism and New Criticism,[2] while for Boyarin this was post-structuralism and then New Historicism.

They differ at the points at which their theoretical frames part. Fraenkel sees each story as "hermetic," having a strong "internal" and "external" closure.[3] While individual stories might have originated in larger collections (קבצים), each is to be understood on its own.[4] Boyarin, on the other hand, sees the stories as part of larger cultural and textual webs, or "discursive formations." While there are important ways in which the stories are crafted units, on a more significant level of analysis he refuses the notion of a hermetically sealed text. The larger cultural frame resists closure locally. Therefore, part of Boyarin's project is the rethinking of the contexts of specific stories, and the relation between Aggadic and Halakhic literature in general. He places stories within the context of other Halakhic and Aggadic texts which were produced out of certain cultural tensions.

In this chapter I will first review Fraenkel's methodology, and his interpretation of specific stories. I will then review Boyarin's methodology. Finally I will look at a somewhat longer Aggadic *sugya* that both Boyarin and Fraenkel interpret. I will argue, at the end of this chapter, that Fraenkel errs in seeing the *ma'aseh* as hermetic and subsequently contextless. I will also argue that Boyarin errs in moving too quickly, or easily, from the local to the widest cultural intertext. The methodology that I develop and employ in the second half of this dissertation follows, in many ways, from both Fraenkel and Boyarin – despite the differences. This chapter then, provides an appropriate end point of this review and a starting point for the constructive project undertaken in the second part of this work.

Before we embark on this exercise I think it appropriate to connect back to the beginning of this spectrum. One indication of the breadth of vision of Avraham Weiss was that he articulated the very types of questions that Fraenkel, and especially Boyarin are asking. In outlining his understanding of the needs and goals of a program of Talmudic research, he says the following:

---

[2] See Jonah Fraenkel "She'elot hermeneutiyot beḥeker sippur-ha'aggadah," *Tarbiz*, 47(1978): 139 n. 1 and 142ff.
[3] "She'elot hermeneutiyot beḥeker sippur-ha'aggadah," pp. 157.
[4] "She'elot hermeneutiyot beḥeker sippur-ha'aggadah," pp. 157-159; *Darkei HaAggadah Ve'Hamidrash*, p. 161.

All-inclusive Talmudic research implies the clarification of all the spiritual currents in the *sugyot* and in all of the Talmud. That is, to clarify the cultural and human value of the Talmud in general and its importance in the development of Judaism and the Jewish people in particular. It is incumbent upon this type of research to look at and understand these currents through a speculum of the spirit of those days. Its function is to also examine the spiritual currents that preceded the Talmudic period. ...In addition to this it must pay attention to all the spiritual currents surrounding the Talmud, that is those currents in its area and surroundings, currents that accompanied it as it developed, and undoubtedly influenced in some manner its development. On the basis of these wide ranging studies, it will be possible to clear for the Talmud the space that it deserves in the history of human culture and literature, in general, and in our history in particular.[5]

Although Weiss did not pursue this line of research, the space in which contemporary theorists think about the cultural formations generated by Talmud was, in some sense, cleared by him. Perhaps this generation will be worthy to realize the possibilities of the research program that Weiss envisioned.

I. Jonah Fraenkel

For Fraenkel, the first, and possibly the most important, step in understanding Rabbinic literature, is the ability to identify its genre properly. In the words of Northrop Frye, one of the great literary theorists of this century:

The purpose of criticism by genre is not so much to classify as to clarify such traditions and affinities, thereby bringing out a large number of literary relationships that would not be noticed as long as there were no context established for them.[6]

---

[5]*The Talmud in its Development*, p. 14-15.

חקירת התלמוד כוללת אומרת בירור כל זרמי הרוח שבסוגיות ושבכל התלמוד כולו. היינו לברר את ערכו התרבותי והאנושי של התלמוד בכלל וחשיבתו בהתפתחות היהדות והיהודים בפרט. על חקירה כזו להתבונן ולהסתכל בזרמים הללו מתוך אספקלריה של רוח הימים ההם. תפקידה להעמיד על אבן הבוחן גם את הזרמים הרוחניים שקדמו לתקופת התלמוד. ...נוסף על כל זה עליה לשים גם לב לכל הזרמים הרוחניים שמסביב לתלמוד, היינו הזרמים שבקירבתו ובסביבתו, זרמים אשר לוו אותו בדרך התהוותו והשפיעו בל"ס באיזו מדה שהיא על התפתחותו. על יסוד בירורים מקיפים כאלה אפשר יהיה לפנות לתלמוד את המקום הראוי לו בקורות תרבות האנושית וספרותה בכלל ובדברי ימינו בפרט.

[6]Northrop Frye, *Anatomy of Criticism: Four Essays* (Princeton, New Jersey: Princeton University Press, 1957): 247-8. Jonathan Culler puts it in a similar fashion: "...what we speak of as conventions of a genre or an *ècriture* are essentially possibilities of meaning, ways of naturalizing the text and giving it a place in the world which our culture defines. To assimilate or interpret something is to bring it within the modes of order which culture makes available, and this is usually done by talking about it in a mode of discourse which a culture takes as natural." *Structuralist Poetics: Structuralism, Linguistics, and the Study of Literature* (Ithaca, New York: Cornell University Press, 1975): 137.

That is, in order to interpret a text, one needs to know the rules by which this text "operates." It is only by knowing those rules that one is able to enter the hermeneutic circle properly. At the point of entry, the reader or critic must know – or be able to establish – that the text under consideration is of a certain kind so as to be able to identify certain characteristics as either significant or coincidental.

This is not unlike the claim made by an early genre-critic about the book of Job. In Chapter 22 of Part III of *The Guide of the Perplexed*, Maimonides writes the following about the first chapter of the book of Job:

> Now according to both opinions, the one that considers that *[Job] has existed* and the one that considers that *he has not*, the prologue – I mean the discourse of *Satan*, that of God addressed to *Satan*, and the giving over [of Job to Satan] – is indubitably, in the view of everyone endowed with intellect, a parable.[7]

Only after establishing that Chapter One is a parable – that is, not an historical account – can Maimonides justify his interpretation of elements that, in an historical account, would be understood as contingent and, therefore, insignificant.

> The first thing you will consider is its dictum, *There was a man in the land of Uṣ* (Job 1:1), in which figures the equivocal word *Uṣ*. It is the name of an individual: *Uṣ his first born* (Gen. 22:21); and also the imperative of a verb meaning to reflect and meditate: *Uṣu `eṣah [take counsel together]* (Isaiah 8:10). It is as if [Scripture] said to you: Meditate and reflect on this parable, grasp its meaning, and see what the true opinion is.[8]

Once the reader (in this case Maimonides) knows that the book of Job is a work of fiction, that reader is aware/may claim that proper names occurring in the narrative may function both as a mere "tag" and as a literary signifier.[9] The name of a land in an historical account of a man who happened to live there, would not have additional literary significance. In a fictional account, however, it does.

Misidentifying the genre of Aggadic stories, or sage stories, according to Fraenkel, is the reason that scholars have thought to obtain historical information from these texts.[10] Whether or not some of the sage

---

[7] Moses Maimonides, *The Guide of the Perplexed*, translated with an introduction and notes by Shlomo Pines (Chicago: University of Chicago Press, 1963): 486.
[8] Ibid, 487. On Maimonides' hermeneutics see Shalom Rosenberg, "על פרשנות המקרא בספר המורה," in *Jerusalem Studies in Jewish Thought*, vol I (1981): 85-157.
[9] This is referred to in semiotic analysis as syllepsis. See Michael Riffaterre, *Fictional Truth* (Baltimore: Johns Hopkins University Press, 1990): 35-37.
[10] See Fraenkel's discussion of the Aggadah about the brothers Hyrcanus and Aristobulus, and its relation to Josephus. *Darkei HaAggadah Ve'Hamidrash*, 238.

Talmud as Literature and Cultural Production

stories were generated, at one time, by actual events, they are deliberate artistic creations, made "for the ideological-pedagogical needs of the authors in the Talmudic literature."[11]

> The Aggadic story, which tells of the days of the Mishnah and the Talmud, that is, of the days of the Sages themselves, is not an historical story, or a chronography but a literary creation which expresses the Sages' understanding of the religious reality in which man lives and which he creates with his actions.[12]

As a literary creation, the Aggadic story is set off from the world of what might be referred to as "historical reality." Though there are usually common reference points, and many Aggadic stories are written in a realistic rather than a surrealistic or supernatural mode, Aggadic stories are independent of that reality.

> The literary reality is not opposed to the normal reality, rather it is outside of it, and anyone who would want to explain [the literary reality] by comparison with and similarity to the normal reality is mistaken.[13]

Accepting Aristotle's division of literary works into three genres – epic, dramatic, and lyric – Fraenkel claims that the Sage stories are dramas. This distinction is made on the basis of the fact that the Aggadot, according to Fraenkel, are not interested in describing the world – people's appearances, landscapes, objects – as such. As opposed to the epic, the Sage stories only supply events. This is the characteristic of drama.[14] Additionally, Fraenkel maintains, the dramatic figure is the

---

[11] ...עיבוד מכוון של חומר, אשר אי פעם סיפר על מאורעות העבר, בשביל הצרכים החינוכיים- רעיוניים של המספרים בספרות התלמודית. *Darkei HaAggadah Ve'Hamidrash*: 238. Compare this statement to the following:
ייתכן מאד, שבזה קבענו עוד הבדל מהותי בין סיפור האגדה לבין טקסט היסטורי: טקסטים היסטוריים נרשמים כדי שיספרו לבאים את העבר כפי שהיה, ועצם הכתיבה בא 'למען יעמדו ימים רבים' כפי שהם. ... אין סיפור האגדה מעיד על רצון מודע לשמר את העבר, אלא על שאיפה לחנך את העם. "She'elot hermeneutiyot beḥeker sippur-ha'aggadah," 149 n. 33. This is a problematic distinction between historical and literary texts which I will return to.
[12] סיפור האגדה המספר על ימי המשנה והתלמוד, כלומר על ימי חז"ל עצמם, אינו סיפור היסטורי ולא כרונוגרפי אלא יצירה ספרותית המבטאת את תפיסת חז"ל על המציאות הדתית שבה חי האדם ואותה הוא יוצר במעשיו. *Darkei HaAggadah Ve'Hamidrash*, 242.
[13] המציאות הספרותית אינה מנוגדת למציאות הרגילה, אלא היא מחוץ לה, וכל מי שירצה לפרש אותה מתוך השוואה ודמיון למציאות הרגילה אינו אלא טועה. "She'elot hermeneutiyot beḥeker sippur-ha'aggadah," 145.
[14] *Darkei HaAggadah Ve'Hamidrash*, 240. See Richard Kalmin's very helpful review, "The Modern Study of Ancient Rabbinic Literature: Jonah Fraenkel's *Darkhei ha'aggadah vehamidrash*," *Prooftexts: A Journal of Jewish Literary History* vol. 14, 2 (1994): 189-204, especially his remarks about Fraenkel's claim that Aggadot are drama, 191-193.

most important figure in the eyes of the Sages, that is the figure of opposites and tensions.

Aggadic stories, as drama, have a number of characteristics which are important for Fraenkel. First, the stories are self-contained. This means that they can be, or must be understood in and of themselves, and that they have no continuation outside of themselves. Fraenkel writes of this in terms of internal and external closure.[15] This claim is embedded in Fraenkel's larger theoretical understanding of literature.

> The art of the story – as all art – creates works which are totally complete within themselves, and which following them, that is outside of them, nothing has happened, nothing needs to happen and in the future nothing needs to change at all.[16]

This means, first and foremost, that stories are outside of the flow of history. The participants in Aggadic stories are not connected to a historical chain of events.[17] Whereas a biblical author, who according to Fraenkel *is* interested in writing history, would mention David's lineage and accession as an important part of the confrontation between David and Michal the daughter of Saul – this type of information is irrelevant to the Aggadic writer.[18]

There is also another aspect of this external closure. For Fraenkel, there is no connection between any single Aggadic story, and any other Aggadic story – even about the same person.[19] This aspect of "external closure" is significant in that it makes a claim against the existence of an Aggadic *sugya*. That is, a series of Aggadot must not be interpreted as being in dialogic, or narrative, relation to each other. The series should be

---

[15] סגירות כלפי חוץ וסגירות כלפי פנים "She'elot hermeneutiyot beḥeker sippur-ha'aggadah," 157.

[16] אמנות הסיפור-כמו כל אמנות -יוצרת יצירות שהן שלמות לגמרי בתוך עצמן, ושאחריהן, כלומר מחוץ להן, לא קרה כלום, לא צריך לקרות כלום ובעתיד לא צריך להשתנות כלום. "She'elot hermeneutiyot beḥeker sippur-ha'aggadah," 158. Cf *Darkei HaAggadah Ve'Hamidrash*, 237-240.

[17] It should be noted here that the claim for the epistemological and rhetorical differentiation between history and literature, that Fraenkel is supporting, has been challenged by historians, legal theorists, and literary theorists. See, e.g., Hayden White, *Tropics of Discourse: Essays in Cultural Criticism* (Baltimore: Johns Hopkins University Press, 1978): 101-120; Robert Cover, *Narrative, Violence, and the Law: The Essays of Robert Cover*, Edited by Martha Minow, Michael Ryan, and Austin Sarat,(Ann Arbor: The University of Michigan Press, 1992): 95-103; Stephen Greenblatt, *Marvelous Possessions: The Wonder of the New World* (University of Chicago Press, 1991).

[18] Cf. e.g. David's statement in II Samuel 6:21-22, and especially the ending of the story, verse 23, with the Aggadic stories about David in e.g. b Ber. 3b-4a.

[19] "She'elot hermeneutiyot beḥeker sippur-ha'aggadah," 158.

Talmud as Literature and Cultural Production

seen as merely a collection or anthology – possibly around a central theme. This is a point that I will take up, and dispute, later in this section.

The other type of closure – "internal closure" – is "a pure literary artistic phenomenon."

> Its meaning is that every detail in a story is connected to every other, every part is planned in relation to the whole story, the beginning reflects the end and the end is understood from the beginning.[20]

The importance of this for interpretation is obvious. Starting with the structure of the story itself, and continuing with puns, wordplays, polysemy (both ironic and not) and allusions – every part of the story is significant.[21] The interpretation of an Aggadic story starts with a structural analysis. The structure fits and informs the content. This latter point is significant and needs some elaboration.

Fraenkel sees the chiastic structure[22] as typical of and fitting for Aggadic stories. That is, the significant moment of the story is the one that is centrally located. This, too, is the moment at which the hero of the Aggadah (typically a Sage) learns something significant, which forces him to change his understanding of that which preceded. The understanding at the end of the Aggadah, is exactly opposite that of the Aggadah's opening. This is the Aggadah's closure, and also its point. The heroes of the Aggadah, for Fraenkel, need to find their own way to the truth or the "proper understanding of the way of the world and the actions of people."[23] As opposed to the Biblical heroes, a Sage does not have prophetic vision to help him, his truths, therefore, are arrived at by reevaluating a situation that he thought he understood.[24] The chiasm reflects life.

In the same manner, the ambiguities of interpretation of verses, or the polysemy of words used in the Aggadic stories – whether ironic or not – reflect the ambiguities of life itself.

> This is one of the tasks that the Aggadic story tellers chose for themselves – they themselves felt the ambiguities of life and created

---

[20] הסגירות הפנימית היא תופעה ספרותית אמנותית מובהקת. משמעה הוא, שכל פרט בסיפור מתקשר אל חברו, כל חלק הוא כמתוכנן מבחינת כלל הסיפור, ההתחלה משקפת את הסוף והסוף מובן מתוך ההתחלה. "She'elot hermeneutiyot beḥeker sippur-ha'aggadah," 159.
[21] See Jonah Fraenkel, "Paranomasia in Aggadic Narratives," In *Studies in Hebrew Narrative Art Throughout the Ages*, Joseph Heinemann, Samuel Werses, ed. (Jerusalem: Magnes Press, 1978): 27-30.
[22] The classic chiastic structure is: A B C B_1 A_1.
[23] *Darkei HaAggadah Ve'Hamidrash*, 243.
[24] Ibid, 245-6.

in the Aggadic story the vessel with which they fulfill their religious obligation – uncovering the masked truth.[25]

In this way, the literary form and structure is an integral part of the meaning of the Aggadah.

Fraenkel's reading of an Aggadah, b Ber. 18b, serves as a focus for a discussion of his method and theory.[26]

---

[25] זהו אחד התפקידים שבחרו לעצמם מספרי האגדה – הם הם שהרגישו בדו-משמעות של החיים ויצרו בסיפור האגדה את הכלי שבו הם ממלאים את חובתם הדתית – לגלות את האמת המחופשת. בסיפור האגדה הסיטואציה האירונית נתונה בהתאם לנאמר: See also the following (267) לעיל: המציאות האנושית אינה מובנת בפשטות, אינה מובנת לעתים נכונה או מובנת בדרך חד-צדדית מוגבלת. (269)

[26] The translation is mine. I consulted the Soncino translation and Fraenkel's notes on his text in *Darkei HaAggadah Ve'Hamidrash*, 253-254.

Talmud as Literature and Cultural Production

Babylonian Talmud; Berachot 18b

בבלי ברכות יח ע"ב

תא שמע:
Come and hear:

דאבוה דשמואל
That the father of Samuel (*Avuha DiShmuel*)

הוו קא מפקדי גביה זוזי דיתמי
5 had money belonging to orphans deposited with him

כי נח נפשיה.
when he died.

לא הוה שמואל גביה.
And Samuel was not with him.

הוו קא קרו ליה
They called him,

בר אכיל זוזי דיתמי.
'The son of one who consumes the money of orphans'.

אזל אבתריה לחצר מות.
10 He went after him [his father] to the courtyard of death.

אמר להו אבא היכא.
He said to them: Where is *Abba* (father).

אמרו ליה אבא טובא איכא הכא.
They said to him: There are many fathers (*Abba tuva*) here.

אמר להו בעינא אבא בר אבא.
He said to them: I want *Abba bar Abba*.

אמרו ליה אבא בר אבא נמי טובא איכא הכא.
They said to him: There are many *Abba bar Abba*s.

אמר להו בעינא אבא בר אבא אבוה דשמואל
15 He said to them: I want Abba bar Abba the father of Samuel.

אמרו ליה סליק למתיבתא דרקיעא.
They said to him: He has gone up to the Academy of Heaven.

אדהכי חזייה ללוי דיתיב אבראי.
Meanwhile he saw Levi sitting outside.

אמר ליה אמאי יתבת אבראי
He said to him: Why are you sitting outside?

מאי טעמא לא סלקת?
Why have you not gone up [to the Academy of Heaven]?

אמר ליה, דאמרת לי, הואיל וכל הני שני
20 He said to him: For they said to me: Since all those years

לא אזלת למתיבתא דרבי אפס,
you did not go up to the Academy of R. Efes

ואחלישתיה לדעתיה,
and embarrassed him,

השתא נמי לא מעיילינן לך למתיבתא דרקיעא.
now we will not let you go up to the Academy of Heaven.

אדהכי והכי אתא אבוה.
Meanwhile his father came.

חזייה דהוה קא בכי ואחיך.	25 [Samuel] observed that he was both weeping and laughing.
אמר ליה אמאי קא בכית?	He said to him: Why are you weeping?
דלעגל קא אתית.	Because you are coming here soon.
ומאי טעמא אחיכת?	What is the reason you are laughing?
דחשיבת בהאי עלמא טובא.	Because you are highly esteemed in this world.
אמר ליה אי חשיבנא עיילוה ללוי.	30 He said to him: If I am esteemed let them take up Levi.
דברוה ללוי ועיילוהו.	They led Levi and took him up.
אמר ליה זוזי דיתמי היכא יתבי?	He said to him: Where is the money of the orphans?
באמתא דרחיא,	In the case of the millstones.
עילאי ותתאי דידן	[The money on the] top and the bottom is ours,
ומיצעי דיתמי.²	35 that in the middle is the orphans'.
אי גנובי גנבי, מגנבו מידן.	So that if thieves steal, they should steal ours,
אי אכלה ארעא אכלה מדידן.	if the earth damages [the money], it should damage ours.
²בדפוס נוסף: אמר ליה מאי טעמא עברת הכי? אמר ליה	¹ The printed editions have Samuel asking at this point: "Why did you do it like that?" as in lines 19 and 28.

"The story," writes Fraenkel, "opens with a 'dispute' about the understanding of reality."²⁷ Samuel's father dies while still in possession of the orphans' money. Samuel, not having been at his father's side at the time of his death, does not know anything of this affair. "They," that is, people in general accuse the father of having stolen the money.

At this point in the explication, Fraenkel has made one important textual choice, and is about to make another. In explaining בר אכיל זוזי דיתמי (line 9) as "The son of one who consumes the money of orphans," rather than "one who consumes the money of orphans"²⁸ –

---

²⁷ (254) הסיפור פותח ב'מחלוקת' על הבנת המציאות.
²⁸See Fraenkel, ibid., 254 note to line 3. In the endnote to this explanatory note, he states that this is the regular meaning of בר ..., citing b Pes. 49a, where there are three occurrences of בר in a compound form which accord with Fraenkel's interpretation here. However, there are actually many other occurrences of בר in compound form, which do not conform to this interpretation, but rather mean "one who [does/is something/someone]." This would translate here as: "One who consumes the money of orphans." That is Samuel is the one who consumes the orphans' money. The impact of the difference is obvious. The occurrences of בר in compound form which support this translation, in b Ber. and b Gittin alone, are: בר חיובא; בר טבילה; בר נטיעה; בר קטלא; בר מזבין תאני; בר איתויי ניטא; בר סמכא; בר היתירא, בר דויה.
Cf. Marcus Jastrow, *A Dictionary of the Targumim, the Talmud Babli and Yerushalmi, and the Midrashic Literature*, c.v. ברII: "The meaning of בר in compound

Talmud as Literature and Cultural Production

which is the other possibility – the focus of the story becomes Samuel's righteousness. The word בר in compound form, can be read either way. If we understood line 9 to mean "one who consumes the money of orphans," there would be a motive other than righteousness for Samuel to seek out his father and find the money. He would want to clear his own name. For the moment, we just point out that we must ask why Fraenkel made the choice that he did.

The second choice, based on a variant reading,[29] is interpreting lines 5 and 6 as one sentence, and line 7 as a separate sentence. The alternative would have been:

> 5   had money belonging to orphans deposited with him.
>   When he died, Samuel was not with him.

The manuscript reading adopted by Fraenkel,[30] has a *"vav"* at the beginning of line 7 (ולא הוה גביה שמואל) thus suggesting that this is a separate action. The printed versions lack the *"vav."* Fraenkel's interpretation lessens the significance of Samuel's not having been with his father at the father's time of death. It becomes a statement which explains some coming action (why he did not know the whereabouts of the money), rather than a statement about Samuel's relation with his father. As Fraenkel interprets the Aggadah:

> Samuel also had not heard anything from his father and he too has no knowledge of the place of the money, but he is sure that the money was not "eaten" rather, its whereabouts are just unknown. Of course it is not a surprise that Samuel recognizes the righteousness of his father, and in truth it is surprising to what extent the public is suspicious.[31]

In interpreting these opening lines, Fraenkel has set the stage – or shown how the Aggadah has set the stage – for the rest of the story. We are primed for the closure of line 37, when the truth emerges finally. Not

---

forms is generally the same as of בן a. בעל, e.g. בר אולפן *a scholar*..." For this form in Jewish Palestinian Aramaic, see Michael Sokoloff, *A Dictionary of Jewish Palestinian Aramaic of the Byzantine Period* (Ramat Gan, Israel: Bar Ilan University Press, 1992): 97-101. The Bialik-Ravnitsky translation in *Sefer Ha'aggada* (Tel Aviv: Dvir, 1987): 332, is a non-committal בן-אוכל.

[29]Fraenkel has adopted the version of MS Oxford 366.1. See *Darkhei HaAggadah Ve'Hamidrash*, 625 n. 101.

[30]On Fraenkel's use of manuscripts, and choice of versions as a part of his method, see Richard Kalmin, "The Modern Study of Ancient Rabbinic Literature: Yonah Fraenkel's *Darkhei ha'aggadah vehamidrash*," *Prooftexts: A Journal of Jewish Literary History* vol. 14, 2 (1994): 196.

[31]גם שמואל לא שמע דבר מאביו וגם הוא אין לו ידיעות על מקום הכסף אך הוא בטוח שהכסף לא נאכל אלא שלא ידוע איפה הוא. כמובן שאין זה פלא ששמואל מכיר את צדיקותו של אביו ואכן מפתיע הוא עד כמה שהציבור חושד. (254)

only did Samuel's father not "eat" the money of the orphans, but he used his own money to protect the orphans' money from being "eaten." Samuel's mission, which he chooses to accept, is to persuade the public of this truth.

Samuel's journey through the "courtyard of death" is, then, no different than any other course of action that a Sage might pursue. That is, the life of a Sage, for Fraenkel, is the struggle to do good. Sometimes the good itself is not obvious. The Sage in those situations must learn what the good is. The unique aspect of this story is that even when Samuel leaves the realm of good and evil – that is, this world – he is still involved in the struggle to do good. Moreover, in keeping with the non-prophetic character of the world of the Sages, he only gets information that he could have received in this world, if only his father had not died too early. He is not in search of any information which would place him out of the realm of good and evil.[32] Nor does he do anything which is dependent on knowledge from beyond this world. Even when he demands that Levi be taken up to the Academy (line 30), Fraenkel notes, he has no way of knowing whether or not his demand will be fulfilled. He also has no reaction at all to the news that he is going to die soon.

In the end, Samuel goes and returns as a person of this world. He accomplishes what he sets out to accomplish – to clear his father's name, and get the money to the orphans – and no more.

We see in Fraenkel's reading of this Aggadah a number of the central points of his method. First, he seeks the correct version of the story. Second, he divides the story into lines, or sentences. Third, he interprets according to a chiastic structure. In this case the outer closure (A-A$_1$) is lines 9 and 37. The focal point is the Levi episode (lines 18-30), which shows that even in the next world, Samuel the Sage and person of this world, does good.

This is, however, not the only possible reading of this Aggadah. I will offer an alternative reading which incorporates some of Fraenkel's method – attention to detail and structure of the story – while calling into question the external closure of this Aggadah, which is central to Fraenkel's theoretical understanding.

I would suggest that the opening line (4) provides the framework within which to read the Aggadah. It is something of a title, in the strong sense of that word. It is not merely a tag, but a direction for reading, a hermeneutic signpost. The line alerts us to two things. First, the Aggadah is about a father-son relationship. Second, in that relationship, the son is

---

[32]Fraenkel argues, quoting Wittgenstein from the Tractatus that "Free will is based on the fact that one cannot tell what will be in the future." *Darkhei HaAggadah Ve'Hamidrash*, 638 n. 68.

Talmud as Literature and Cultural Production

named while the father is named only in relation to the son. Samuel's father doesn't seem to have any independent existence, at least for Samuel whose point of view seems to dominate the narrative. By this last comment I mean that we are looking at the story from the place at which Samuel is standing, and then we travel with Samuel, after his father, to the courtyard of death.

Following this signpost we are sensitive to the situation in line 6. As suggested above, I would read lines 6 and 7 as one sentence rather than two.[33]

> When he died, Samuel was not with him.

This line reinforces the distance we sense in the title, with a geographic distance – which is itself a sign of filial distance. Reading this line strongly we understand that even at his father's death, Samuel was not present. The story does not provide any mitigating circumstances for Samuel's absence. We are not told that the death was sudden or tragic. We are also not told that Samuel returned for the funeral, but only when he had to put certain affairs in order.

We now come to the issue of Samuel's motives. While Fraenkel says that it "is not surprising that Samuel recognizes the righteousness of his father," I would suggest that actually Samuel knows nothing of the righteousness of his father. The first he finds out about the whole affair is when people accuse *him* of making off with the money. As mentioned above, this is the equally plausible reading of the phrase בר אכיל זוזי דיתמי on grammatical grounds[34]. It is also warranted on purely narrative grounds. There is no other motivation for Samuel to get involved.

Samuel's journey, is then a journey in which he learns who his father is, reestablishes the father-son relationship by learning *from* his father, and is moved by that understanding to recognize the importance of using his own prestige for the benefit of others, namely Levi.

When Samuel confronts whoever it is that is in charge of the courtyard of death, a verbal *pas de deux* ensues:

> He said to them: Where is *Abba* (father).
> They said to him: There are many fathers (*Abba tuva*) here.
> He said to them: I want *Abba bar Abba*.
> They said to him: There are many *Abba bar Abba*s.
> 15 He said to them: I want Abba bar Abba the father of Samuel.
> They said to him: He has gone up to the Academy of Heaven.

It is only after traversing the physical distance (from his place of residence to the courtyard of death), and the psychic distance (from the

---

[33]This is also the reading in *Sefer Ha'aggadah*, 332: כשמת לא היה שמואל אצלו.
[34]See note 23 above.

generic *Abba* to the naming of his father as his own father in line 15) that he is allowed to see his father. While waiting for his father to come down, he learns about Levi's situation. When his father does come down, he questions his father in the way a student would question a teacher: What is the reason that...? (מאי טעמא) Samuel questions his father twice in the version used by Fraenkel, and once more in the printed editions, before line 36. In this way he learns both of his father's righteousness (the reasons for putting the money where and how he did), and he initiates a son to father relationship by treating his father as teacher. When he asks that Levi be "taken up" to the Academy, he has shown that he has learned from his father and can follow in his footsteps.

The point of the Aggadah as I read it, is not that "a person of this world comes to the next world and with the help of the knowledge gained in the next world, he accomplishes his wishes in this world."[35] Rather, read in the context of the *sugya* of which it is a part, the point is that the courtyard of death, or the place at which death and life meet, is a place of learning for the living. Through that experience, the living learn from the dead. This reading is not a psychologized reading of the Aggadah, nor a denial of supernatural aspects of it. I would claim that this reading comes from looking at the Aggadah in its setting as part of a larger *sugya*.

The Aggadah is brought as a prooftext (line 3: תא שמע) in a discussion of whether or not the dead know about the living, and can convey that information to the living. The immediately preceding Aggadic prooftext, concerns a man who learned about upcoming climatological patterns from hanging out in the cemetery and listening to the dead speak to each other. The *sugya* as a whole, is generated by a larger discussion emanating from the Mishnah (Ber. 3:1) concerning the prayer obligations of a mourner on the day of death. The Aggadic *sugya* is generated in part by the halakhic *sugya* preceding it (b Ber 18a) which deals with various aspects of the day of death, and cemetery procedures. For Fraenkel, this setting is irrelevant for the understanding of the Aggadah, since all Aggadot have external closure. That is, as we mentioned above, they have no connection with any thing outside them.

I would strongly argue, however, that removing an Aggadah from its setting is not placing it in a vacuum, but giving it a new setting. In this case, the new setting that Fraenkel is giving this Aggadah is the collection of Sage stories. In that collection as a whole, the Sage is the righteous hero, and therefore the idea that the Sage might be the one

---

[35] איש העולם הזה בא לעולם הבא ובעזרת ידיעותיו מן העולם הבא הוא מבצע את מאוויו שבעולם הזה.
Darkhei HaAggadah Ve'Hamidrash, 255.

Talmud as Literature and Cultural Production   85

who needs to learn righteousness is not an option.³⁶ In the context of the *sugya* in b Ber. 18b, however, the question is precisely what the dead can or cannot teach the living.

This same entry point into the hermeneutic circle, seems to (pre)determine Fraenkel's reading of another Aggàdah. This one (b Ber. 3a), is cited by Fraenkel as "including within it the whole problematic of our subject in all its shades [of meaning]."³⁷ The "subject" is, specifically, the relation between the Sages and the "other world," and more generally, the figure of the Sage himself. The Aggadah concerns the meeting between R. Yosi and the prophet Elijah.³⁸

---

³⁶In his theoretical article "She'elot hermeneutiyot beḥeker sippur-ha'aggadah," (esp. 141) Fraenkel himself raises the question of where an interpreter enters the hermeneutic circle. He focuses on pious interpreters (specifically the Maharsha) who would gloss over seemingly problematic aspects of stories, since those aspects are not possible from where they enter the circle of interpretation. Fraenkel's own entrance into the hermeneutic circle is guided by his theoretical understanding of Aggadot, as well as the understanding what a Sage is – which itself is a result of constructing Aggadot collections and then constructing a universal definition of what a Sage is, rather than asking what this specific Sage character is doing.

Richard Kalmin raises some related concerns about the problem of Fraenkel's insistence on external closure in his review of *Darkhei HaAggadah Ve'Hamidrash*. See "The Modern Study of Ancient Rabbinic Literature: Yonah Fraenkel's *Darkhei ha'aggadah vehamidrash*," 197. I disagree with Kalmin, however, when he argues that while the Rabbinic authors might have distorted sources that dealt with earlier periods, this is not the case with regards to periods closer to their time. The point is the word distorted. According to Fraenkel, and I agree with him in this, the Rabbinic authors did not distort sources, as that would be dependent on their having made a claim to some historical truth. The sources that they might have used, whether for earlier periods or their own time, served merely as an impetus to the story which was *crafted* or *created* as art with a message. In this there is no logical reason to distinguish between early and late sources.

³⁷*Darkei HaAggadah Ve'Hamidrash*, 256.

³⁸The translation is based on the Soncino translation, though freely changed to preserve the literary qualities of the original.

בבלי ברכות ג ע"א | Babylonian Talmud; Berachot 3a

תניא	It has been taught:
אמר רבי יוסי	R. Yosi says,
פעם אחת הייתי מהלך בדרך	One time I was traveling on the road
ונכנסתי לחור בה אחת מחור בי ירושלים	5 and I entered into one of the ruins of Jerusalem
להתפלל	in order to pray.
בא אליהו זכור לטוב	Elijah, of blessed memory, came,
ושמר לי על הפתח (והמתין לי)	and guarded the door for me, and waited for me,
עד שסיימתי תפלתי	until I finished my prayer.
לאחר שסיימתי תפלתי אמר לי	10 After I finished my prayer, he said to me:
שלום עליך רבי	Peace be with you my master!
ואמרתי לו שלום עליך רבי ומורי	And I said to him: Peace be with you my master and teacher!
ואמר לי בני מפני מה נכנסת לחורבה זו	And he said to me: My son, why did you go into this ruin?
אמרתי לו להתפלל	I said to him: To pray.
ואמר לי היה לך להתפלל בדרך	15 And he said to me: You ought to have prayed on the road.
ואמרתי לו מתיירא הייתי שמא יפסיקו בי עוברי דרכים	And I said to him: I feared lest passer-by might interrupt me.
ואמר לי היה לך להתפלל תפלה קצרה	And he said to me: You ought to have said an abbreviated prayer.
באותה שעה למדתי ממנו שלשה דברים	At that moment I learned from him three things:
למדתי שאין נכנסין לחורבה	-One must not go into a ruin,
ולמדתי שמתפללין בדרך	20 -One must say the prayer on the road,
ולמדתי שהמתפלל בדרך	-And if one does say his prayer on the road,
מתפלל תפלה קצרה	he says an abbreviated prayer.
ואמר לי	And he said to me:
בני מה קול שמעת בחורבה זו	My son, what sound did you hear in this ruin?
ואמרתי לו	25 I said to him:
שמעתי בת קול שמנהמת כיונה	I heard a divine voice, cooing like a dove,
ואומרת אוי לבנים	and saying: Woe to the children!
שבעונותיהם החרבתי את ביתי	For on account of their sins I destroyed my house
ושרפתי את היכלי והגליתים לבין האומות	and burnt my Temple, and exiled them among the nations!

Talmud as Literature and Cultural Production

ואמר לי חייך וחיי ראשך	30	And he said to me: By your life and by your head!
לא שעה זו בלבד אומרת כך		Not in this moment alone does it exclaim thus,
אלא בכל יום ויום שלש פעמים אומרת כך		But three times every day does it exclaim thus.
ולא זו בלבד אלא בשעה שישראל נכנסין		And not only this, but whenever Israel go into
לבתי כנסיות ולבתי מדרשות		the synagogues and study houses
ועונין יהא שמיה הגדול מבורך	35	and responds: May His great name be blessed!
הקדוש ברוך הוא מנענע ראשו ואומר		the Holy One of Blessing, shakes his head, and says:
אשרי המלך שמקלסין אותו בביתו כך		Happy is the king who is thus praised in his house!
מה לו לאב		What is there for the father
שהגלה את בניו		who had to banish his children?!
ואוי להם לבנים	40	And woe to the children
שגלו מעל שולחן אביהם:		who were banished from the table of their father.

Fraenkel interprets this Aggadah as follows:

> R. Yosi acts at first according to his feelings, when he enters the ruin to mourn Jerusalem in privacy and there he merits the revelation of a divine voice. Afterwards he meets Elijah who is disguised as a "Rabbi" and he learns from him the law [*halakhah*] that one shouldn't enter a ruin to pray, and in a totally free manner he accepts upon himself this law [*halakhah*]. [He does] this even though he could have inwardly scorned this "Rabbi" who, seemingly, did not know what great revelation he had in the ruin. As reward for the freely made decision to give up the divine voice, Elijah "reveals" himself to him and teaches him secrets from Heaven – why it is better not to enter a ruin to pray, but it is better to go to the synagogues to pray with the community.[39]

For Fraenkel, the point of this Aggadah is that, despite the connection with the supernatural – in the person of the prophet Elijah – the Sage does not lose his free will. Moreover, all the actions that the Sage – here R. Yosi – takes, are taken freely, as a result of his own free choice. What the storyteller has succeeded in doing, according to Fraenkel, is the description of a world which is not realistic, and the

---

[39] *Darkei HaAggadah Ve'Hamidrash*, 256.

כאן עושה ר' יוסי בתחילה לפי רגשותיו בהכנסו לחורבה להתאבל ביחידות על ירושלים ושם הוא זוכה לגילוי בת-קול. אח"כ הוא פוגש באליהו המחופש ל'רבי' ולומד ממנו הלכה שאין להכנס לחורבה להתפלל, ובאופן חפשי לנמרי הוא מקבל על עצמו הלכה זאת, וזאת אע"פ שהיה יכול ללעוג בלבו ל'רבי' שאינו יודע לכאורה איזה גילוי גדול היה לו בחורבה. בתור שכר על החלטתו החפשית לוותר על בת קול, 'מתגלה' אליו אליהו ומלמדו סודות מן השמים מדוע מוטב לא להכנס להתפלל בחורבה אלא משובח יותר ללכת לבתי כנסיות להתפלל עם הציבור.

presentation of a dramatic hero (the Sage) who still, even in, or in connection with, that world, freely determines his path in his religious life. The overriding concern of these Aggadot is the free will of the Sages.

I would claim, however, that there is a very different possible reading of this Aggadah – when it is interpreted in its context. The immediate context of this Aggadah, is the *sugya* in which it occurs, which is generated by a statement in M Ber. 1:1 about the proper time for reading the evening *Shma* prayer. The immediately preceding part of the *sugya* claims that the Mishnah (or actually R. Eliezer in the Mishnah) articulated the appropriate times for reading the *Shma* in terms of the "watches of the night," in order to teach something about the affairs of heaven.

דתניא	For it has been taught:
רבי אליעזר אומר שלש משמרות הוי הלילה	R. Eliezer says: The night is three watches,
ועל כל משמר ומשמר יושב הקדוש ברוך הוא	and at each watch, the Holy One of Blessing sits
ושואג כארי	and roars like a lion.
שנאמר,	For it is written:
ה' ממרום ישאג	*The Lord roars from on high,*
וממעון קדשו יתן קולו	*He makes His voice heard from His holy dwelling;*
שאוג ישאג על נוהו (ירמיהו כה:ל)	*roaring He does roar over His [earthly] abode.* (Jer. 25:30)

This picture of God roaring at each watch, a militant picture of a vengeful God is modified radically only a few lines later:

אמר רב יצחק בר שמואל משמיה דרב	R. Isaac b. Samuel says in the name of Rab:
שלש משמרות הוי הלילה	The night is three watches,
ועל כל משמר ומשמר יושב הקדוש ברוך הוא	and at each watch, the Holy One of Blessing sits
ושואג כארי	and roars like a lion
ואומר אוי לי שהחרבתי את ביתי	and says: Woe to me, for I have destroyed My house
ושרפתי את היכלי	and burnt My temple
והגליתים לבין אומות העולם:	and exiled them among the nations of the world.

The vengeful God portrayed in the statement attributed to R. Eliezer, is here portrayed as a mourning God. A God who, possibly, can do nothing about the destroyed Temple and exiled people except mourn and wail. This statement directly precedes the Aggadah of R. Yosi and Elijah. Moreover it shares language and concerns with it. Both speak of three times, God's statement in both is the same. I would suggest that this setting informs the meaning of the Aggadah of R. Yosi and Elijah in a very significant way.

When R. Yosi enters "one of the ruins of Jerusalem" I would suggest that, in light of the lines that immediately precede it, any of the ruins of Jerusalem synecdochically stand in for the one ruin of Jerusalem – the Temple. The Aggadah's concern is whether and how one might pray outside the Temple when the Temple itself lays in ruins. In this reading, the moment when R. Yosi chooses to accept of his own free will the teaching of Elijah-as-Rabbi, instead of sneeringly accepting the divine voice, is not the central moment.

The critical moment of the Aggadah is that R. Yosi did not hear the divine voice, or did not recognize its significance until Elijah pointed it out to him. R. Yosi could not, on his own, make a connection between the mourning God and his own prayers. R. Yosi was still tied up in the conception of God that posited a Temple, and prayers that were answered – perhaps by a God that roared out the defeat of the oppressors as in the Jeremiah verses according to R. Eliezer. Elijah needed to teach R. Yosi that the voice he heard, is actually connected to his prayer. This was the response of the God of the destroyed Temple.

Elijah's "legal" teachings, in this understanding, take on another level of meaning. It is possible to pray in less than optimal circumstances. The destruction of the Temple is not the end of prayer, though it might necessitate its redefinition.

Whether or not this is the "correct" reading, I would claim that this reading does point out the problem of divorcing an Aggadah from its context. Again as in the story of Samuel and his father, we see that taking the Aggadah out of its context, is actually putting it into a new context. This new context – the collection of Sage stories – informs the meaning of Aggadah. Parts of the Aggadah that would be highlighted or informed by its context, are missed when it is seen as just another Sage story, or a story about a Sage and the supernatural.

This review of Jonah Fraenkel's interpretive methodology highlighted its theoretical basis and its practical application. It was in the practical application that the method faltered, and the theory was found wanting. I argued that framing Aggadot as hermetic units ignored the decisive part context plays in generating meaning – and it is from within the context of a *sugya* that Aggadot are interpreted.

II. Daniel Boyarin

Daniel Boyarin, in his book *Carnal Israel*,[40] argues for three different points. First he claims that a main difference between "rabbinic Judaism"

---

[40]*Carnal Israel: Reading Sex in Talmudic Culture*, (Berkeley: University of California Press, 1993). A clear and concise summary of Boyarin's understanding of New Historicism – in relation to Aggadic accounts of the martyrdom of Rabbi Akiva –

and "Greek speaking Jewish formations, including much of Christianity," were their respective "representations and discourses of the body and sexuality."[41] His second claim is for a way of reading Talmudic texts which falls within the parameters of the methodology known as New Historicism. Boyarin affiliates his own four cubits of New Historicism with what Stephen Greenblatt calls "cultural poetics."[42] Finally, Boyarin argues for a "feminist restructuring of sex and gender in very late antiquity – that is, in our own time."[43] Boyarin sees this work as "the search for male opposition, within the Talmud itself, however rudimentary, to the dominant, androcentric discourse."[44] He states that his "goals are both redemptive and cultural-critical, and in some ways the Talmudic culture that I hope to partly describe is both my own and not my own."[45]

For the purposes of this chapter, it is Boyarin's second claim which is primary. While the three aspects of Boyarin's project are necessarily intertwined, the core of the book is a certain way of reading Talmudic texts. It is this method of reading that interests me. I will claim that while the method itself is sound, on the whole, Boyarin's application of it is flawed. This, naturally, affects the substantive arguments that he is making, and I will note that.[46]

Boyarin's interpretive method, or "practice" is situated in what has come to be known as the New Historicism. New Historicism is one of the results of the reaction in literary theory and historiography against the "old historicism" and New Criticism. Post-structuralist and deconstructionist criticism reacted against the New Critical claim to a

---

may be found in his article in Hebrew "Hamidrash ve'Hama'aseh – 'Al haḤeker haHistory shel Safrut Ḥazal," in Shamma Friedman, ed., *Saul Lieberman Memorial Volume*, (New York and Jerusalem: Jewish Theological Seminary of America, 1993): 114-117. The theory of midrash that Boyarin presupposes in *Carnal Israel*, is worked out in *Intertextuality and the Reading of Midrash*, (Bloomington: Indiana University Press, 1990), though in that work the theoretical conceptualization borrows from Michael Riffaterre ("ungrammaticalities") and Wolfgang Iser ("gaps") (xi). The differentiation between an allegorical and a midrashic reading, which is so important for *Carnal Israel*, is articulated in the discussion of *mashal* in Chapter Five, and the move towards New Historicism is obvious in Chapter Seven, which is a version of the article in the *Saul Lieberman Memorial Volume*.
[41]*Carnal Israel*, 5.
[42]Ibid., 9-13.
[43]Ibid., ix.
[44]Ibid., 228.
[45]Ibid., 230.
[46]For a review of *Carnal Israel* in which the history of sexuality aspects of the work are critiqued more seriously, see Michael Satlow, "They Abused Him Like A Woman – Homoeroticism, Gender Blurring and the Rabbis in Late-Antiquity," *Journal of the History of Sexuality*, 5:1 (July 1994).

stable and objective meaning of any literary work. That is, they denied the stability of meaning in general, and the ability to identify the one correct meaning of any specific poem, story, etc. For the same reason, deconstructionists questioned the notion of genre, the rigid differentiation between types of writing. This was striking at the heart of the New Critical enterprise, as we saw above with Fraenkel's work.[47] The New Critics claimed that one could never know how to interpret a text without first establishing its poetic parameters – that is, the way in which it should be read as a result of the type of writing (history, poetry, law) to which it belonged. The deconstructionists countered by essentially agreeing with the New Critical claim, and then going on to show that no parameter, such as a genre, could totally define any written work. The writing would, if pressed hard enough, subvert any category it was put into. All writing then was text, that is, signs to be interpreted, rather than "a poem" or "a book," with a given boundary and poetics.

At the same time Marxist literary critics (influenced by the work of Michel Foucault) challenged the New Critical practice of privileging texts that were considered "works of art," by separating them from the material circumstances[48] that brought about their production. That is, according to the Marxist critics, the New Critical claim that a work of art is a hermetically sealed object, obfuscates the relations of power that bring about its creation. Cutting a literary work off from the material conditions of the society in which it was produced, serves only to hide the "real" currency of societal relations – power rather than genius. The Marxist critics claim that the category of "(great) work of art" itself is a result of the relations of power in society. These texts then, must be read as representative of, and as reproducing the political, social and class arrangements of the mainstream society ("the hegemonic discourse") – or as, to some small measure, subverting those arrangements.

These theoretical currents impacted on the practice and writing of history (the "old historicism") in two ways. First, the idea that literary works were transparent, and therefore could be used as windows into the past, or as a clear background for the events of the past[49] was challenged by the new understanding of the radical instability of meaning. If we can't say what a text of Antiquity means, how can we draw any conclusions about what it says about a specific time and place?

---

[47]73.
[48]Economic realities, structural hierarchies, the means of production and access to them.
[49]Cf. "*Hamidrash ve'Hama'aseh*," 114, discussing Alon and Safrai on the martyrdom of Rabbi Akiva.

Second, the practice of historical *writing* was also called into question. Initially, historiographers, influenced by structuralism, claimed that the writing of history itself is not a unique act ("telling it as it was"). Rather, writing of history, is like other narrative writing, and needs to be seen as any other literary representation rather than a unique form of truth telling.[50] Subsequently, post-structuralists, under the influence of Derridean "negative hermeneutics" challenged the concept of a coherent narrative itself. The underlying necessity of narrative for history writing – the demand for causal explanation – was itself called into doubt. It was unclear (so the post-structuralists argued) whether narrative described causal relations or created them.[51]

In the next stage, the deconstructionist critics came under fire from the Marxists[52] and the emerging post-colonial critics. These latter argued that since the deconstructionists had cut out any ground on which they might stand – since all "ground" inevitably ends up as deconstructed bits of dust in the wind – their tools merely served to frustrate any oppositional critical project. At the same time, the deconstructionists accused the Marxists of succumbing to the same sin (hubris?) as the New Critics – claiming that the Marxist framing of a text could successfully "saturate" it, so that a single stable interpretation could be reached.

New Historicism emerged, as a literary approach or theory, out of many of these concerns.[53] Before we explore Boyarin's understanding

---

[50] "On analysis, every mimesis can be shown to be distorted and can serve, therefore, as an occasion for yet another description of the same phenomenon, one claiming to be more realistic, more 'faithful to the facts.'" Hayden White, *Tropics of Discourse: Essays in Cultural Criticism*, (Baltimore and London: Johns Hopkins University Press, 1978): 5.

[51] "Cause, in particular, which can be seen as merely the product of narrative structures once the world is considered as a text, is a trap, always to be questioned." Hans Kellner, "Narrativity in History: Post-Structuralism and Since," in *History and Theory: Studies in the Philosophy of History*, 26 (1987):5. This article is an excellent survey of the issues leading up to and into New Historicism.

[52] E.g. "In much deconstructive theory, the view that interpretation consists in an abyssal spiral of ironies, each ironizing the other to infinity, is commonly coupled with a political quietism or reformism. If political practice takes place only within a context of interpretation, and if that context is notoriously ambiguous and unstable, then action itself is likely to be problematic and unpredictable." Terry Eagleton, *Ideology: An Introduction*, (Verso, London, 1991): 40.

[53] As has been often noted, many of those centrally identified with New Historicism (e.g. Stephen Greenblatt), have disowned the term or the affiliation. See H. Aram Veeser's excellent discussion in "The New Historicism," in H. Aram Veeser, ed., *The New Historicism Reader*, (New York, London: Routledge, 1994) esp. 7-12.

Talmud as Literature and Cultural Production

and application of New Historicism, I will rejoin the world of Rabbinics, and situate the study of Rabbinic texts within these conflicting claims.

Many of these contradictory trends were also present in the study of Rabbinic literature. We already saw that Fraenkel critiqued the "old historicist" use of Aggadah as a resource, from a New Critical perspective. From a different direction, Neusner raised serious doubts about the authenticity of any attributions in Rabbinic literature, and therefore the possibility of using that literature as a historical resource.[54] It is at this point that the New Historicists, and Boyarin among them, join the fray.[55]

The New Historicists, like the "old historicists," believe that one can write history using literary texts. The central and overarching point of difference between the two groups, is the question of what *kind* of history can be written. New Historicists claim that the only history that can be written is the "history of ideas," or the "history of discursive processes and social sites, of communal mechanisms and institutions."[56] This Foucauldian formulation is used in order to differentiate the new history of ideas from the old history of ideas. In the new history of ideas, the texts in which the ideas are embedded are not seen as separate from the societal processes out of which they are produced. The texts therefore are legitimate objects of study as products of those ideas. As Boyarin puts it:

> I propose that the older insight that there is a connection between the genres of rabbinic textuality and also between them and a society can be preserved when we understand literature as discourse – as discourse in the Foucauldian sense... This notion of literature as a process integrally connected with other social processes is a very powerful one for the study of Talmudic texts. ... If we can no longer write biographies of Rabbis, which can then be used to explain (even

---

[54]See the discussion of Neusner and historiography in Chapter III. Cf David Goodblatt's defense of Talmudic History, and specifically his response to Neusner's criticisms, in his article "Towards the Rehabilitation of Talmudic History," in B. M. Bokser, ed., *History of Judaism: The Next Ten Years*, (Chicago: 1981): 31-44. "In short, the impossibility of rabbinic biography does not entail the impossibility of Talmudic history." (34) See also the discussion of the relation between texts, realia, and "reality," in Miriam Beth Peskowitz, "'The Work of Her Hands': Gendering Everyday Life in Roman-Period Judaism in Palestine (70-250 CE), Using Textile Production as a Case," (Ph.D. diss., Duke University, 1993), 39-44.

[55]From here on in, at least in the body of the text, I will write as if Boyarin represents New Historicism as a whole, although, essentially, no one does. For an overview of the various New Historicist positions, and their common themes see Veeser above note 53.

[56]The former formulation is from *"Hamidrash ve'Hama'aseh,"* 114. ההיסטוריה העיקרית שניתן ללמוד אותה מטקסטים ספרותיים, היא ההיסטוריה של האידיאות. The latter is from *Carnal Israel*, 12.

partially) their halakhic interventions..., we can, it seems, use both halakha and aggada together to write a history of discursive processes and social sites, of communal mechanisms and institutions.[57]

Boyarin sees the New Historicism as a way of utilizing Rabbinic literature as a whole, and to claim that this whole can be informative about a society, while sidestepping the pitfalls that earlier attempts of this kind fell into. New Historicism attempts to sidestep these pitfalls by not privileging literary texts, but seeing them, rather as "one practice among many by which a culture organizes its production of meaning and values, and structures itself."[58]

This leads to the principles that are more or less shared by all those within the New Historicist orbit. The following is Boyarin's formulation:

1. The study of a literary work cannot be pursued in isolation from the other concurrent socio-cultural practices.
2. So-called high culture has no essential privilege over "popular" and "mass" culture, nor do the latter more truly reflect society than the former. These very distinctions are a cultural practice and an ideological intervention that must be examined.
3. Some kind of materialism must be assumed (not necessarily Marxian).
4. Much of the rigid barrier between the current humanities and social sciences must be dismantled.[59]

The first two of these principles establish a level playing field for all documents and artifacts to be considered historical, whether they are literary texts, paintings of grand masters, or shopping lists and doodlings. They are all "socio-cultural practices," and therefore reflect to the same degree the cultural tensions and processes of a given society. The high culture-low culture distinction is rejected on both the Marxist and deconstructionist grounds we mentioned above.

The third principle assumes that there is a connection between all types of production (including literary production) and the relations of power and economics in a society. It is also assumed that the economic model might be imposed beyond the literal marketplace. One can speak of an economy of sexuality, etc. This being the case, it is argued, insight into the material conditions of society by way of, for example, a private communication between a person and her physician, can afford important insight into a literary production.

---

[57]*Carnal Israel*, 11-12.
[58]Ibid.
[59]Ibid., 12-13.

These three principles allow for New Historicism's most distinctive trait – the introduction of documentary material into the historical discussion as affording an insight that is unavailable through the literary material. In Boyarin's words:

> A founding assumption of the practice of new historicism... [is] that the document, proclamation, deed, diary or private letter provides access in some sense to a processed, more transparent version of the discursive practices of the period and can then serve as an explanatory context for the "text."[60]

When dealing with the field of Talmudic literature, however, there is virtually no documentary evidence outside of the literary. That is, we have almost no diaries, private letters, etc. from this period. All of the texts that we have are of the same status – they are all to the same degree literary, and essentially part of the same corpus. The only differences that exist are between genres of writing: midrashic texts and halakhic texts.

For this reason Boyarin modifies the New Historicist method by using writings of different types to shed light on each other. Since the tensions that are produced by a culture are found, by New Historicist definition,[61] in the culture's literary productions, those different productions can be analyzed to reveal those tensions. Here again there is an intersection with a theme common to most of the Talmudists that we have seen. The first reading of a text – *sugya*, midrash, etc. – is to find the tensions, ungrammaticalities, or *deḥukim*.[62] The difference is, of course, in the way those tensions are understood, or read.

> My practice here will be to look at texts as (necessarily failed) attempts to propose utopian solutions to cultural tensions. The tensions are what interest me, so using the sensibilities and even techniques of the various hermeneutics of suspicion[63], I hope that by observing the

---

[60]Ibid., 13.

[61]Or, some might say, by axiom.

[62]"The method of reading employed in this book often involves the identification of a point of tension or conflict between the voices of the texts that the Talmud quotes and the ideological interests of the redactors." *Carnal Israel*, 115.

[63]E.g. Elisabeth Schüssler Fiorenza: "A *hermeneutics of suspicion* seeks to explore the liberating or oppressive values and visions inscribed in the text by identifying the androcentric-patriarchal character and dynamics of the text and its interpretations. Since biblical texts are written in androcentric language within patriarchal cultures, a hermeneutics of suspicion does not start with the assumption that the Martha and Mary story is a feminist liberating text just because its central characters are women. Rather it seeks to investigate *how and why* the text constructs the story of these two women as it does." Elisabeth Schüssler Fiorenza, *But She Said: Feminist Practices of Biblical Interpretation*, (Boston: Beacon Press, 1992): 57. And see the rest of the discussion there 57-62.

effects of the energy expended by the culture in attempting to suppress or (put more positively) deal with the tensions, the underlying strains and pressures can be brought to light.[64]

The existence of the tensions in the texts are evidence that the solutions of the harmonized text haven't obviated the problems. In order to obtain insight into the tensions underlying the text he is focused on, Boyarin proposes bringing together texts of different genres – halakhah and aggadah, Talmud and midrash – which share the same theme or "cultural problematic." Boyarin assumes "that both the halakha and the aggada represent attempts to work out the same cultural, political, social, ideological, and religious problems."[65] These varying texts can then be grouped together in such a way that they offer insight into the range of cultural solutions to specific tensions. Boyarin calls these groupings "discursive formations."

Thus, in general, one might characterize Boyarin's interpretive method as follows: First, one reads a text to find the tensions in the text. This reading "respects the literariness of literary texts (that is, as texts that are marked by rhetorical complexity and for which that surface formal feature is significant for their interpretation)."[66] In other words, in this reading one is looking for metaphors, wordplays, puns, repetitions, structural forms, syntactical and grammatical anomalies, and so forth.

Second, one identifies the intertexts of this specific text, in order to identify/create a grouping of texts ("discursive formation") which might yield insight into the cultural problematics underlying the tensions in the initial text (or all of the texts in the discursive formation). At the point of defining the cultural tensions, Boyarin employs the "hermeneutic principle of charity." This is the principle that "one would [not] want to begin with premises that ascribe the worst possible motives to *any* group of people."[67]

It is the second step which is problematic. When does one abandon the rhetorical structure of one text in order to insert it into another "formation?" How does one identify a "discursive formation?" These

---

This hermeneutics of suspicion, *mutatis mutandis*, might easily be applied to Talmudic texts.
[64]*Carnal Israel*, 15.
[65]Ibid.
[66]Ibid., 13.
[67]Ibid., 118 n. 9. Boyarin refers to his whole enterprise at times as "generous critique," which is "a mode of analysis that is not apologetic and yet maximizes our understanding of the needs and drives that motivated a certain group of people to make the cultural 'decisions' they made." 229. The line between generous critique and apologetics, of course, is in the eye of the beholder.

Talmud as Literature and Cultural Production 97

questions can be better addressed through an analysis of Boyarin's practice rather than his theory. Therefore, I will now analyze Boyarin's reading of texts that he has grouped in a chapter that he calls "Lusting After Learning." Fraenkel has also interpreted these texts,[68] and I will address their two readings, which are at times similar and at times radically different. A central concern in this analysis will be the efficacy of using the concepts "discursive formulation" (Boyarin), or "collection" (קובץ) (Fraenkel) as framing devices for the texts discussed. I will then propose the use of the concept of *sugya*, as an alternative to these.

III. Boyarin, Fraenkel (and me)

There is a long series of stories[69] in b Ketuboth 62a-63b[70], which follows a *halakhic* discussion about the length of time a scholar is

---

[68]Jonah Fraenkel, *Iyunim Be'Olamo HaRuḥani Shel Sippur HaAggadah*, (Hakibbutz Hameuchad Publishing House Ltd., 1981): 99-115.

[69]The use of the expression "long series of stories" is an attempt at a neutral ground between Fraenkel's קובץ של סיפורים (collection of stories) ("*Iyyunim*," 98) and Boyarin's "discursive formation," of which, in any event, this is just a part. I will propose a third way to look at these stories – as a *sugya*. One need also seriously take into account Eli Yassif's suggestion of a "story cycle" (מחזור סיפורים), which has a central theme that is achieved as a result of the "accumulative meanings and impressions of all the stories taken together." The meaning of this cycle (b Ket. 62a-63b) according to Yassif, "is the tension between a scholar who knows that learning Torah is the purpose of his life... and the suffering and hardship of his family as a result of their abandonment for the sake of the Torah." המתיחות בין תלמיד חכם היודע שלימוד תורה היא תכלית חייו, ... לבין ענוותה) (ומצוקתה של משפחתו בגלל הזנחתה למען לימוד התורה. (This general understanding is not far from either Fraenkel's or Boyarin's.) Yassif points out that none of the stories in the cycle except the Akiva story, offer a solution, and that each story by itself is a slice of "reality," while the cumulative effect of the whole raises the stories to a more encompassing and abstract level of understanding. This is another nuanced reading which situates the tensions in the text at b Ket. 62b-63a itself – a point I will return to later. See Eli Yassif, "*Maḥzor HaSippurim BeAggadat Ḥazal*," *Meḥkarei Yerushalayim BeSifrut Ivrit* 12 (1990): 133. Another reading of the series of stories as a connected series is that of Shulamith Weller, "*Kovetz Sippurim BeSugyat Ketubot Daf 62b-63a*," in Meir Ayali, editor, *Tura: Studies in Jewish Thought: Simon Greenberg Jubilee Volume* (Tel Aviv: Hakibbutz Hameuchad Publishing House, 1989): 95-108. Weller follows Fraenkel to a large degree, but works out the implications of reading the "collection" as a *sugya*. I don't agree with her final analysis, as will be apparent later on, but her assumption that it is a *sugya* is important. She also does an excellent job in highlighting the differences between the versions of some of the stories, especially the Akiva stories in Ketuboth and Nedarim. However, I seriously part company with Weller in her attempt to identify the original source of each story. See esp. 96-101. The differences between the "versions" that Weller herself points to, seem to me to vastly override the much smaller similarities, which makes the discussion of an "original version" beside the point. [Cf. Fraenkel's comment on the version of II

98   Rereading Talmud

permitted to leave his wife/home in order to study. The stories are part
of a *sugya* generated by M Ket. 5:7:

> If one takes a vow not to sleep with his wife;
> Bet Shammai say two weeks, and Bet Hillel one week.
> The students may go away from their homes for study of Torah without
>   permission for thirty days,
> and laborers for one week.
> The "season" [required frequency of intercourse] which is mentioned in
>   the Torah: for the *tayyalin*,[71] it is every day; for laborers, twice a
>   week; for donkey drivers, once a week;
> for camel drivers, once in thirty days; for sailors, once in six months; these
>   are the words of Rabbi Eliezer.[72]

There is an obligation incumbent upon the husband, and inscribed in the
ketubah agreement, to have sexual intercourse with his wife at regular
intervals. If he abrogates this obligation, he is forced to divorce her, and
pay her the divorce settlement. This Mishnah is setting out the

---

in p Bikkurim 2:3, 65c: .(ושונה לנמרי) סיפור מקביל "a parallel story but completely
different." (*Iyyunim*, 170)]
[70]The text of b Ket. 62a-63b in Hebrew and English is in the appendix. For the
apparatus I relied on Rabbi Moshe Hirshler, ed., מסכת כתובות עם שינויי נוסחאות מכתבי
היד של התלמוד ועם השוואות להבאות מהגמרא בחז"ל, גאונים וראשונים (ירושלים: מכון
התלמוד הישראלי השלם, תשל"ב). The abbreviations in the apparatus are as follows: מ –
MS Munich 95 (the MS of the complete Bavli); ר¹ – Vatican 113; ר² – Vatican 130; ר³
– Vatican 487; ל – MS Leiden; לפ – MS Leningrad-Firkowitz 187; ה – all eds. of
Hagadot Hatalmud. For a description of the MSS, see Hirshler, 65-72. The
division into lines is mine, based on the Shamma Friedman paradigm (see above
Chapter I part 3). The Hebrew and English line numbers are the same.
    The reader might want to skim through the whole text before proceeding.
The translation in the appendix is mine, though I consulted both the Soncino
English translation (by Rabbi Dr. S. Daiches and Rev. Dr. Israel W. Slotki), and
Fraenkel's Hebrew translation in *Iyyunim*. The translations of the *sugya*, quoted in
the body of this chapter are from *Carnal Israel*. The translation in the appendix,
therefore, differs at times from the translations quoted in the chapter. At
significant points, this discrepancy is noted in the chapter.
[71]"This is a difficult term that means something like idlers; it may mean those
who spend all of their time in study." *Carnal Israel*, 143 n. 18. Albeck in his
comment to M Ket. 5:6 translates as idlers. The Bavli Ket. 62a, offers 1) those who
study with a teacher in town and therefore sleep at home; 2) the spoiled, fat
scholars of the Land of Israel who eat and drink enough to have the energy to
have intercourse every night (Rashi).
[72]
משנה בתובות ה:ו
המדיר את אשתו מתשמיש המטה,
בית שמאי אומרים אומרים שתי שבתות. בית הלל אומרים שבת אחת.
התלמידים יוצאין לתלמוד תורה שלא ברשות שלשים יום.
הפועלים שבת אחת.
העונה האמורה בתורה-הטיילין בכל יום, הפועלים שתים בשבת, החמרים אחת בשבת, הגמלים
אחת לשלשים יום, הספנים אחת לששה חדשים, דברי רבי אליעזר.

parameters of that obligation, and negotiating the conflicts between that obligation and various other obligations, or necessities. The one that becomes of primary concern for the *sugya* b Ket. 62b-63a, is the conflict with the study house. How long might a husband leave his wife to study Torah?

The series consists of seven stories whose most obvious common denominator is that they are all about men who leave their wives to study Torah in an academy. Boyarin and Fraenkel both analyze (some of) these texts at length, though neither analyzes all of them.[73] Boyarin at times relies on Fraenkel's analysis and at times differs from him. Neither Boyarin nor Fraenkel are interested in the stories as a *sugya*.. Fraenkel frames these stories as about "the scholar and his wife" (תלמיד חכם ואשתו) – the dramatic choice that a scholar must make between investing all his energy in his study, and devotion to his wife. When the balance is not kept – tragedy strikes.

Boyarin frames these stories as part of a larger cultural tension around the desire for study and the obligation to procreate, or "[t]he absolute and contradictory demands of marriage and commitment to study of Torah."[74] Rather than equal poles, for the sages, the pull of the study hall was far greater. As per his methodology, Boyarin looks to many different texts to illuminate these cultural tensions.

My method in this section will be to present the texts as Boyarin does, presenting Boyarin's reading of the texts along with Fraenkel's when that is appropriate. At the end of this presentation, I will read Boyarin's reading, that is, I will interrogate the choices that Boyarin made when constructing this discursive formation. I will then analyze Fraenkel's reading. At the end I will sketch an alternate reading.

Boyarin opens the space of this discursive formation by first quoting a text that represents the internal conflict between study and marriage, and then one which represents the idealized solution. Boyarin reads a statement by Ben Azzai in T Yev. 8:4, as "the perfect representation" of this internal conflict.

---

[73]Boyarin reads the stories that I have numbered I, II, IV, VI and VII though he reads VI (the romance of Akiba and the daughter of Kalba Sabua) as interchangeable with b. Ned. 50a. Fraenkel reads I, II, IV, V, and VI, though he reads the version of IV as found only in a manuscript version of Genesis Rabbah *Piska* 95 (Vatican 30 [noted as א in the Theodor-Albeck apparatus]): 1232. Boyarin sees the two versions of IV as embodying opposing ideologies, while Fraenkel sees b. Ned. 50a as a "differing parallel" (מקבילה שונה).

[74]*Carnal Israel*, 134. The fact that the understanding of the texts which Boyarin comes to is not that different than Fraenkel's – though Boyarin does frame the texts eventually within the discussion of celibacy or "married monks" – or from Yassif's (above n.1), might be cause for reflection.

> Ben Azzai says, anyone who does not engage in procreation is a murderer and diminishes the Divine Image, for it says, *One who spills blood of a human, for the sake of the human his blood will be spilt, for in the image of God, He made the human, and as for you, be fruitful and multiply.*
> Rabbi Elazar ben Azariah said to him, "Ben Azzai, words are fine when accompanied by practice. There are those who interpret well and behave well, and those who behave well but do not interpret well. You interpret well, but do not behave well."
> Ben Azzai said to them, "what shall I do? My soul desires Torah, Let the world continue by the efforts of others!"[75]

This text, according to Boyarin, "personifies" in Ben Azzai the radical conflict between procreation and study. Lust in this case, comes out on the side of Torah. Ben Azzai's desire to study is called חשק, an erotic desire. The conflict is then between two poles, both of which are eroticized, while Torah study is the one more lusted after. Situating this discussion as analogous to early Christian valorization of chastity and virginity, Boyarin claims that the "extravagant praise of the married state, which occurs over and over in rabbinic texts, is a marker not of how happily married the Rabbis were but of how much pressure against marrying there was in their world."[76]

The idealized solution to the conflict, or in Boyarin's words, the "Babylonian attempt at a utopian resolution and justification for the local practice,"[77] is introduced here in the story of the romance of Akiva and the daughter of Kalba Sabua. The story is introduced as it appears in b Ned. 50a:[78]

---

[75]The translations, except where otherwise noted, are from *Carnal Israel*.

תוספתא יבמות ח:ד (צוק' 249-250)

בן עזאי אומר, כל מי שאינו עוסק בפו"ר הרי זה שופך דמים ומבטל את הדמות שנאמר "כי בצלם אלהים עשה את האדם וכתיב ואתם פרו ורבו וגו'":
אמר לו ר"א בן עזריה, נאין דברים כשהן יוצאין מפי עושיהן.
יש נאה דורש ואין נאה מקיים נאה מקיים ואין נאה דורש.
בן עזאי נאה דורש ואין נאה מקיים.
אמר לו מה אעשה חשקה נפשי בתורה ויתקיים העולם באחרים:

[76]*Carnal Israel*, 136.
[77]Ibid., 150.
[78]

בבלי נדרים נ ע"א

רבי עקיבא איתקדשת ליה ברתיה דכלבא שבוע.
שמע כלבא שבוע אדרה הנאה מכל נכסיה.
אזלא ואיתנסיבה ליה בסיתוא.
הוה גנו בי תיבנא. הוה קא מנקיט ליה תיבנא מן מזייה.
אמר לה, אי הואי לי, רמינא ליך ירושלים דדהבא.'
אתא אליהו, אידמי להון כאנשא, וקא קרי אבבא.
אמר להו, 'הבו לי פורתא דתיבנא-דילדת אתתי, ולית לי מידעם לאנוחה.'
אמר לה רבי עקיבא לאנתתיה, חזי גברא דאפילו תיבנא לא אית ליה.
אמרה ליה, 'זיל הוי בי רב.'

[Rabbi Akiva was the shepherd of Kalba Sabua.]⁷⁹
The daughter of Kalba Sabua became engaged to Rabbi Akiva.
Kalba Sabua heard and cut her off from any of his property.
She went and married him in the winter.
They used to lie in the hay-barn, and he would take hay out of her hair.
He said to her, "Were I only able, I would give you a 'Jerusalem of Gold!'"
Elijah the Prophet came and appeared to them as a person crying out at the door.
He said, "Give me some of your hay, for my wife is giving birth and I have nothing for her to lie down on."
Rabbi Akiva said to his wife, "You see, there is someone who doesn't even have hay."
She said to him, "Go and sit in the House of Study."
He went for twelve years and studied with Rabbi Eliezer and Rabbi Yehoshua.
At the end of twelve years, he came home.
He heard from behind his house, a certain rogue saying to his wife, "Your father treated you suitably. First of all, he [Rabbi Akiva] is not of your kind, and moreover he has left you a grass widow all of these years."
She said to him, "If he were to follow my wishes, he would remain for another twelve years."

אזל תרתי סרי שנין קמי דרבי אליעזר ורבי יהושע.
למישלם תרתי סרי שנין קא אתא לביתיה.
שמע מן אחורי ביתיה דקאמר לה חד רשע לדביתהו, שפיר עביד ליך אבוך, חדא דלא דמי ליך,
ועוד [שבקך] ארמלות חיות כולהון שנין.'
אמרה ליה, 'אי צאית לדילי להוי תרתי סרי שנין אחרנייתא.'
אמר, הואיל ויהבת לי רשותא איהדר לאחורי.
הדר אזל הוה תרתי סרי שני אחרנייתא. אתא בעשרין וארבעה אלפין זוגי תלמידי.
נפוק כולי עלמא לאפיה, ואף היא קמת למיפק לאפיה.
אמר לה ההוא רשיעא, 'ואת להיכא?'
אמרה ליה, "יודע צדיק נפש בהמתו."
אתת לאיתחזויי ליה, קא מדחן לה רבנן.
אמר להון, 'הניחו לה, שלי ושלכם שלה הוא.'
שמע כלבא שבוע, אתא ואיתשיל על נידריה ואשתרי ואשתרי.
מן שית מילי איעתר רבי עקיבא מן כלבא שבוע..

---

⁷⁹Boyarin inexplicably adds this first line to the b Ned. story. It appears in b Ket. yet it is none of the MSS of b Ned. nor is it added on to the b Ned. text in any of the later Midrashic compilations (e.g. Yalkut Shimoni Proverbs, #948). this is only the most explicit way in which Boyarin seems to read the two stories as if they are one and the same. This first line is very significant for Boyarin since he claims "the entire story of the romance of Rabbi Akiva and Rachel is generated by one root metaphor: Akiva as the shepherd and Rachel as a ewe." (*Carnal Israel*, 151) Bialik-Ravnitzky also have the b Ned. version with the first line of the b Ket. version. They cite it to both places. *Sefer Ha'aggada*, 179. (My thanks to Ari Elon for pointing this out to me.)

There is a very interesting version of the story in the medieval collection *Midrash HaGadol* (ed. Margaliot 68-70) to Exodus. It is in Hebrew rather than Aramaic, and substitutes Proverbs 14:1 חכמות נשים בנתה ביתה for Proverbs 12:9. The midrash there also weaves together many of the Akiva Midrashim into one whole semi-coherent narrative.

> He said, "Since she has given me permission, I will go back."
> He went for another twelve years. He came with twenty four thousand pairs of disciples.
> Everyone came out to receive him, and she also came out to meet him.
> That rogue said to her, "Where do you think you are going?"
> She said, "'The righteous man senses the need of his animal[80].' [Prov. 12:10]"
> She came to show herself to him.
> The Rabbis were pushing her aside.
> He said to them, "Leave her be. That which is mine and that which is yours is really hers!"
> Kalba Sabua went and asked to be relived of his vow, and he was released.
> In six ways Rabbi Akiva became wealthy from the property of Kalba Sabua.

Boyarin doesn't read this story at this time. He just introduces it to generate the questions: "Why is this story told about Rabbi Akiva? What is the cultural work that is done by making the hero of the 'romance' specifically a great scholar and martyr and more specifically Rabbi Akiva?"[81]

The second text Boyarin gathers into this "discursive formation" is from b Kid. 29b. This is a *halakhic* text which explicitly considers the conflict between marriage and studying Torah. The discussion here, however, is from the point of view of priorities, rather than exclusive and oppositional choices.

> The sages have taught: On studying Torah and marrying a woman? He should study Torah and then marry,
> but if he cannot manage without a wife, he should marry and then study Torah.
> Said Rav Yehudah that Shmuel said, "The *halakhah* is that he should marry and then study Torah."
> Rabbi Yoḥanan said, "A millstone around his neck and he will study Torah!?"
> And they do not disagree; that is for us and that is for them.
> [...]
> Rav Huna [the Babylonian] said[82], "Anyone who is twenty years old and not married, all of his days are sinful."
> Can you really think that he is sinful? Rather I will say, "All of his days are in thoughts of sin."

---

[80]Boyarin translates this as "pet," as he thinks beast would be "misleading in its connotation." (*Carnal Israel*, 137 n.8). This might be true, but so would "pet." It seems to me that animal has the middle ground – charitable but not apologetic.
[81]*Carnal Israel*, 138.
[82]The translation should actually be "Rav Huna [the Babylonian], following his reasoning (לטעמיה), said." Boyarin however, doesn't quote the original Rav Huna statement, which this statement is purportedly following – nor does he note the ellipse.

Talmud as Literature and Cultural Production

> Rava said, and thus also the One of the House of Ishmael teaches, "Until the twentieth year, the Holiness, May it be blessed, waits for the man; when will he marry. When he is twenty and unmarried, He says, 'Blast his bones!'"
>
> Rav Ḥisda said, "I am preferable to my fellows, for I married at sixteen and if I had married at fourteen, I could have said to Satan, 'An arrow in your eyes!'"[83]

Boyarin sees in this text a difference in practice and ideology between the Palestinian and Babylonian Rabbinic community. This is first codified in the statement that Rav Yehudah attributes to Shmuel – one of the two "founders" of the Babylonian community – that the law is that one must marry first and then study. The Palestinian Rav Yoḥanan strongly disagrees.

This dispute, for Boyarin, is not merely about the obligation to start a family. It is about the place of sexuality in a scholar's life. Rav Ḥisda's statement is understood by Boyarin as commentary on the statement of Rav Yoḥanan. According to this understanding, there is a need to recognize that sexual activity is a necessary part of life. "The Babylonian rabbinic community strongly encodes its own self-perception that adult males cannot live without sex, and therefore the young scholar should marry and then study."[84]

The next text that Boyarin reads as part of this "discursive formation," is a discussion of, or commentary on, M Ket. 5:6 (b Ket. 61b-62a):

> **The students may go away from their homes for study of Torah without permission for thirty days and laborers for one week.**
> With permission how much? As much as he wants.
> But what is the correct behavior?

---

[83] קידושין כט ע"ב

תנו רבנן, ללמוד תורה ולישא אשה-ילמוד תורה ואח"כ ישא אשה
ואם א"א לו בלא אשה, ישא אשה ואח"כ ילמוד תורה.
אמר רב יהודה אמר שמואל, הלכה נשא אשה ואח"כ ילמוד תורה.
רבי יוחנן אמר, ריחיים בצוארו ויעסוק בתורה?
ולא פליגי הא לן הא להו.
[...]
רב הונא לטעמיה,
דאמר, בן עשרים שנה ולא נשא אשה כל ימיו בעבירה.
בעבירה סלקא דעתך? אלא אימא כל ימיו בהרהור עבירה.
אמר רבא, וכן תנא דבי ר' ישמעאל, עד כ' יושב הקדוש ברוך הוא ומצפה לאדם מתי
ישא אשה כיון שהגיע כ' ולא נשא אומר תיפח עצמותיו.
אמר רב חסדא, האי דעדיפנא מחבראי דנסיבנא בשיתסר, ואי הוה נסיבנא בארביסר הוה
אמינא לשטן גירא בעיניך.

[84]*Carnal Israel*, 141.

> Rav said, one month here [studying] and one month at home, for it says, "in the matter of the labor brigades, one goes and one comes month by month for the months of the year." (I Chron. 27:1)
> Rabbi Yoḥanan says, one month here and two at home, for it says, "One month they will be in Lebanon and two months at home." (I Kings 5:28)[85]

This discussion is setting up outside limits for absences, sanctioned (by the wife) and unsanctioned. This itself is interesting as the Mishnah doesn't make that distinction. The Talmud establishes "if not a strictly legalistic proscription, a strong moral one on being away from home for longer than thirty days."[86] Boyarin then brings into the discussion, the *halakhic* text that immediately precedes the series of stories at the heart of the "discursive formation."

> ...These are the words of Rabbi Eliezer.
>
> Rabbi Bruna said that Rav said, The halakhah is accordance with the view of Rabbi Eliezer.
> Rabbi Ada b. Ahvah said[87], Those are only the words of Rabbi Eliezer,
> but the Sages hold that the students [may] leave, for [the purpose of] Torah study, for two or three years without [receiving] permission [from their wives].
> 5 Rava said that our Rabbis have relied on [the ruling] of Rabbi Ada b. Ahvah, and indeed practice in accordance with his view.[88]

---

[85]
כתובות דף סא ע"ב – סב ע"א
התלמידים יוצאין לתלמוד וכו':
ברשות כמה? כמה דבעי.
אורחא דמילתא כמה?
אמר רב, חדש כאן וחדש בבית, שנאמר "לכל דבר המחלוקות הבאה והיוצאת חדש בחדש לכל חדשי השנה." (דה"א כז:ם)
ורבי יוחנן אמר, חדש כאן ושנים בביתו, שנאמר "חדש יהיו בלבנון שנים חדשים בביתו."
(מלכים א ה:כח)

[86]ibid., 144.

[87]Boyarin has: "Rav Ada the son of Ahva said that Rav said." This is the version of our printed editions, but is not attested in any of the MSS. The surprising thing about this, is that Boyarin cites this as a "dissenting tradition of what Rav had to say." (146) And further remarks about Rav Ada's tradition: "...it is nevertheless remarkable that this tradition became accepted as authoritative in spite of the fact that it contradicts another tradition of Rav's own view." (146) The two conflicting versions of Rav's own view heighten the cultural tension that Boyarin is describing. It doesn't, however seem to have textual support in this instance. (Which also seems to me unnecessary for the larger claim...)

[88]Or: "act accordingly [at risk of] their lives." The Hebrew בנפשייהו literally means 'in their souls' or "in their/them selves". However, the meaning of "[at risk of] their lives" [as attested, e.g. b Yev. 64 b. Cf. Rashi there: בנפשה – בסכנת נפש (at the danger to his life)] needs to be at least in the background. I think that the immediately following story – especially the use of the term נח נפשיה in line 11 (and 22, and 25) to mean he died – draws out this meaning, which is why I

As Boyarin points out, these two texts are contradictory. Whereas the former text prescribes limits on the time that men may leave *even with permission*, the latter text follows Ada b. Ahvah's opinion that essentially sets no limits at all. "The Talmudic commentary on this Mishnah is revealing in the manner in which it vacillates and contradicts itself. Thus, close reading of the text will provide us with symptomatic evidence of the unresolvability of the cultural problem of tension between marriage and Torah-study with the Babylonian rabbinic system."[89] In other words, to use language that we are familiar with from the previous chapters, the ungrammaticalities, or *dehukim*, in the text serve as hermeneutic indices which point to a deeper problem. That problem is the tension between marriage and study of Torah.

Boyarin now moves to the analysis of several of the stories in the series that immediately follows this text. The first story is the story of Rav Rehume.

> Thus R. Rehume, who was a disciple of[90] Rava's in Mehoza.
> He would regularly visit his wife[91] on the Eve of every Yom Kippur.
> One day his studies[92] absorbed him.
> His wife was waiting for him: Now he will come. Now he will come.
> 10   He did not come. She became upset.[93] A tear fell from her eye.
> He was sitting on the roof, the roof collapsed under him, he died.

This short story is both aesthetically and emotionally powerful. The compressed form – short verbal phrases[94] – heightens the drama,

---

translated accordingly. Noting the ambiguity of the word בנפשייהו here, supports Boyarin's reading of the following story of R. Rehume as "a strong condemnation of the practice at the same time that it is overtly supporting it." *Carnal Israel*, 148.

The Hebrew version of this text, and the whole sugya b Ket. 62b-63a, is in the appendix to this chapter.
[89]*Carnal Israel*, 143.
[90]lit.: was usually found in front of Rava...
[91]Fraenkel (98) translates this as "his house" (לביתו). The Aramaic literally means "his house," though it is a common euphemism for wife. It is in fact used that way throughout the stories here, and in line 9, Fraenkel also translates "his wife." The difference is that the word in line 9 (דביתהו) literally means "of their house," therefore more explicitly referring to his wife. Although, Fraenkel interprets ביתו in the Hananiah b. Hachinai story in Gen. Rabbah #95 as "his wife," (*Iyyunim*, 105 and 170; see above note 73) Fraenkel's translation also highlights the dialectic that Fraenkel reads in the story between his house, and the house of study (בי רב).
On the connection between house and wife see M Yoma 1:1 and b Shabbat 118b.
[92]lit.: tradition
[93]lit.: her mind/thought/knowledge was weakened.
[94]For this reason I preferred the more awkward "who was frequenting [the school] of Rava in Mehoza." to translate line 6, since this preserves the verbal form of הוה שכיח קמיה.

tensions and ironies of the story. I will point out some of the more salient features of the story, which Fraenkel, Boyarin and others[95] have interpreted.

The story contains a number of puns and word plays which serve to destabilize any obvious meaning. The name Reḥume can mean "lover" in Aramaic. Boyarin reads Reḥume as meaning lover in an ironic or poignant way or, possibly, "Rav Reḥume is indeed a lover, a lover of Torah. That is, we would have here actuated once again a version of the topos that we saw above with regard to Ben-Azzai of the life of a Torah-student as erotic abandonment to Torah, such that the wife becomes a rival to the beloved Torah."[96]

Fraenkel points out the irony in the first two lines of the story. The scene is set as if there was no problem. R. Reḥume learned at the academy of Rava. However, the second line pushes the normalcy of the scene to an ironic or sarcastic point. His normal schedule was to come home *regularly* every year. The *regularity* of annual visits strikes a deeply ironic chord, especially on a background in which we know little about where Reḥume lived. He might have lived in Meḥoza. That is, there is no attempt on the part of the narrator to explain the annual visits as a result of distance.[97]

The ironic reading is reinforced by the next line: "*One day* his studies absorbed him." This reinforces the claim to *regularity* which is anything but *regular*. This line might be read: "It just happened that on one of those days when he was supposed to go home...." Standing outside the story, the reader knows that *those days* occur only once a year.

Two word plays and a chiastic structure are the further elements of the Aggadah according to Fraenkel's reading. The word "absorbed" (משכתיה) in line 8, and "waiting" (מסכיא) in line 9, are phonetically similar. The similarity then stresses the tension of the two words and the two characters. The scholar to the Academy, and the wife to her husband/family.

In the exact center of the Aggadah is the phrase: "He did not come." (לא אתא) This phrase is a Janus element. It summarizes all that has come before, and generates what will come after. It provides, in a manner of speaking, the causal relationship between the two halves of the Aggadah.

This is immediately followed by the play on the words "fell" (אחית) in line 10, and "collapsed" (אפחית) in line 11. They are "structurally" the same. That is, they both describe the same movement (downwards), and

---

[95]See the articles mentioned above note 69.
[96]*Carnal Israel*, 147.
[97]*Iyyunim*, 101.

they are phonetically close – one letter apart. The structure and the puns create the literary equation, for Fraenkel, that Reḥume was "absorbed" by his Torah – to the exclusion of his wife – *therefore* the roof "collapsed" and he died.

Fraenkel and Boyarin both read the story as inviting identification with the wife. Fraenkel stresses "the ancient and eternal motif of Jewish literature through all the generations,"[98] of the abandoned woman's tears. While Boyarin stresses the erotic pull of the Torah as oppositional to the (erotic) pull of the wife, both Boyarin and Fraenkel read the Aggadah as a cautionary tale. The problem is only when the balance between academy and "home"[99] is skewed. The use of this story as "support" for Ada b. Ahvah's statement is itself mired in ambiguity. As Boyarin says:

> ... the way that the entire story is presented provides rather a strong condemnation of the practice at the same time that it is overtly supporting it. We will find this strain between overt support and covert contestation in other texts as well.[100]

For Boyarin this tension is indicative of the cultural tension which is at the heart of this discursive formation: studying Torah vs. married life. For Fraenkel, when read correctly, the Aggadah leaves one with the message that a balance need be struck between the legitimate desire of the scholar to study Torah, and the legitimate needs of the wife for her husband.

The second story (lines 16-23):

> Yehuda, the son of R. Hiyya was the son in law of R. Yannai.
> He went and sat in the academy,
> Every Friday at twilight he would return to his house,
> and when he would come, they would see in front of him a pillar of fire.
> 20 One day he became engrossed[101] in his study,[102] and did not come.
> As soon as they did not see the sign [the pillar of fire], R. Yannai said to them: Turn over his bed,
> for were Yehuda alive he would not fail to fulfill his sexual obligation.
> And it was "...like an error from the mouth of a ruler..." (Ecclesiastes 10:5), and he died.

---

[98]Ibid.
[99]This polar tension is stressed later on when the Academy is referred to as בֵּי רַב (house of the master), while the wife in the Aggadot is referred to as דביתהו (of his house).
[100]*Carnal Israel*, 148.
[101]This is the same word (משכחיה) as in line 8 which Boyarin translates as "absorbed."
[102]lit: tradition.

Boyarin follows Fraenkel's understanding of this story in most of its details. The tension in this story, according to this interpretation, is between the scholar's willingness to fulfill his obligation to study Torah, and his willingness – or here, his reluctance – to fulfill his obligation to sleep with his wife. The symbol of the "pillar of fire," "the very sign that led the Jews in the Wilderness and brought them to the promised Land,"[103] indicates the sacredness of marital sex. Fraenkel suggests that it also might be indicative of the internal struggle in Yehudah between these two obligations. Boyarin notes that the phallic form and erotic nature of the pillar of fire underscore the tension between two sacred erotic poles. What is clear to both Boyarin and Fraenkel is that the pillar of fire moves the story away from a conflict between the sacred and the secular, and into the heart of a conflict between sacred and sacred. The tension is between study and the fulfillment of the commandment of marital sex.[104]

Fraenkel understands that the connection between this story and the previous one is the focus of both on the home. In both, according to Fraenkel, the detailed picture is of the home deserted by the sage. "Furthermore, the home is the essence and it is the point around which the narrative revolves. Since the member of the study hall doesn't understand this, he doesn't have 'permission' to sit in the study hall, and he must die."[105]

Boyarin adds that "[this] story, like the previous one, remains an eloquent testimony to the unworkability of the utopian solution of the halakhah requiring the husband who studies to nevertheless come home regularly."[106] I would just note here, as an aside to be returned to later, that the prevalence and thematization of death in these stories has not been adequately dealt with, as yet.

---

[103] *Carnal Israel*, 150.
[104] Fraenkel's interpretation is actually much more involved. He points to the fact that (in line 17) Yehudah *sits* in the academy while (in line 18) he *comes* home. That is, the focus of Yehudah's life is the academy while the home is secondary. Fraenkel also makes an interesting claim that there is a total disjunction between the way in which the members of the household perceive the events (i.e. Pillar of fire – a holy man is coming. Yehudah isn't coming home – he must have died, that is the only thing that could have kept him away.), and the way that they "really" happen in the academy (i.e. Pillar of fire – struggle between sacred and sacred. Yehudah isn't coming home – his sin, that is, his refusal to fulfill his obligation, is punished by death.). Weller disagrees with this last claim ("*Kovetz Sippurim ...*," 96 and n. 3).
[105] *Iyyunim*, 104.

יתר על כן, הבית הוא העיקר והוא הציר שעליו סובבת העלילה. מכיון שבן בית המדרש אינו מבין זאת, אין לו "רשות" לשבת בבית המדרש, והוא חייב למות.

[106] *Carnal Israel*, 150.

Talmud as Literature and Cultural Production 109

Neither Boyarin nor Fraenkel interpret the next story in the series in b Ket. Fraenkel introduces the story that I numbered IV (in a different version), which Boyarin gets back to later. Boyarin now returns to the Akiva "romance" with the surprising statement that "[a]t this point in the text of the Babylonian Talmud, the story of Rabbi Akiva and his romance with Rachel is produced."[107] His statement is surprising for two reasons. First, there are two stories between the one we just saw and the Rabbi Akiva story. Second, it is not even clear that the story is about Rachel – her name is not mentioned once in the story. This latter is a point of analysis that Boyarin deals with. The former, however, like the additional first line in the story in b Nedarim, is stated without comment or explanation.

The reason that Boyarin introduces the Akiva story now is that, for him, it is "the ultimate Babylonian attempt at a utopian resolution and justification for the local practice,... of husbands spending enormous quantities of time away from home to study Torah."[108] The Akiva story is produced, in essence, in order to, or out of a cultural need to mediate the tragic tensions that appear in the two stories just read. Whilst these previous stories demonstrated the impossibility of the halakhic demand to both study Torah and also to regularly be a part of a home or marriage, the Akiva romance provides the cultural ground for the support of this enterprise by the wife of the sage herself. In other words, the solution would be to validate the experience of the deserted wife, as an important and vital spiritual practice to the point that she would willingly support the husband's endeavor – as "Rachel" does with Akiva.[109]

The story as it appears in b Ket. (VI) follows:

> R. Akiva was a shepherd of Ben Kalba Sabua.
> [The latter's] daughter saw him as modest and noble.
> 65 She said to him: Were I to betroth you, would you go to study at an academy?
> He said to her: Yes.
> She betrothed [herself] to him in secret and sent him away.
> Her father heard, drove her from his house, and forbade her by a vow to have any benefit from his estate.

---

[107]Ibid.
[108]Ibid.
[109]It is interesting to note that Fraenkel reads the Akiva story in exactly the same way as Boyarin, except that he judges the "solution" positively. That is, he assigns positive valence to the idea that a woman would spend all her life in misery supporting her husband in exchange for the acknowledgment that she has a share in his study. Cf. *Iyyunim*, 113: "It is obvious to the narrator that the study of Torah and greatness in Torah are the thing that the woman wants for her husband."

	He went and stayed at the academy twelve years.
70	When he came back, he brought twelve thousand students with him.
	He heard an old man saying to her: For how long are you to conduct yourself as in living widowhood.
	She said to him: If he would listen to me, he would stay another twelve years.
	He [R. Akiva] said: I am acting with permission.
	Again he went, and stayed at the academy another twelve years.
75	When he came back, he brought twenty four thousand students with him.
	His wife heard. She was going out to meet him.
	Neighbors said to her: Borrow clothes, dress and cover yourself.
	She said: "A righteous man knows the needs of his beast." (Proverbs 12:10)
	When she drew near him, she fell on her face, and kissed his feet.
80	His attendants were pushing her aside.
	He said to them: Leave her! Mine and yours are hers.
	Her father heard that a great man had come to town.
	He said: I will go to him, perhaps he will invalidate my vow.
	He came to him.
85	He [R. Akiva] said to him: With the knowledge that he was a great man, would you have made your vow?
	He said to him: Rabbi, even one chapter, even one halakhah.
	He said to him: I am he.
	He fell upon his face and kissed his feet and gave him half his wealth.
	R. Akiva's daughter acted the same way towards Ben Azzai.
90	This is what people say: "Ewe follows ewe; a daughter's acts are like those of her mother."

Fraenkel reads a movement in the story from one unequal relationship to another. (For Fraenkel, the story ends at line 88. 89-90 aren't part of the story.) In the beginning of the story, Kalba Sabua's daughter is wealthy while Akiva is a simple shepherd. She is the active participant in the relationship. She sees him, evaluates him, betroths him, and sends him off to learn while he is silent. By the end of the story, Akiva is respected, has a massive following of people who obey him (81, 82-86), and is ultimately wealthy while she is poverty stricken and powerless (79,80). Akiva commands, is magnanimous (81) and reprieves/forgives (85-87) while she is silent (79-81).

The story is structured around three meetings between Akiva and the daughter of Kalba Sabua. In the first meeting they are betrothed, though not married.[110] The second meeting almost happens. It accomplishes its purpose, with the help of the old man as a foil – Akiva gets permission to study for another twelve years – without necessitating a real meeting. This meeting which was not a meeting, also mirrors the state of their relationship – married yet not married. Fraenkel also suggests that if the meeting were to really have happened, Akiva might

---

[110]Rabbinic marriage is divided into two parts: 1. betrothal (קידושין) and 2. marriage (נישואין).

not have returned. The third meeting happens with a bang. Both Akiva and the daughter of Kalba Sabua are intent on having the meeting. Akiva comes to town with an enormous entourage and procession that could not be missed. At the same time, the daughter of Kalba Sabua is intent on meeting him – she literally throws herself at his feet (79).

The romantic climax, and the dramatic shift takes place between lines 78 and 81. In response to their concern about her lack of proper clothes, she answers her neighbors that "A righteous man knows the soul of his beast." Fraenkel understands this as her saying that no matter the external differences between them ("man" – "beast"), they are one in soul. At their meeting Akiva reverses even this external hierarchy by saying "Mine and yours are hers." Akiva and his thousands of students are now the ones with nothing, while this impoverished woman actually has everything.

Boyarin's reading of the story, while ideologically very different is also very much the same. It might be useful to cite his approach to the story.

> Close reading of the story will show how it performs as narrative its ideological and cultural function of female subjugation and how its deployment of the romance genre is crucial as well. The key to my reading is the name, Rachel, which the tradition has universally (and with good textual warrant, as we will see) assigned to Rabbi Akiva's wife. This name, while quite common for Hebrew women, is also the usual word for ewe. The entire story of the romance of Rabbi Akiva and Rachel is generated by one root metaphor: Akiva as the shepherd and Rachel as a ewe. Rabbi Akiva's relationship with his wife is figured in several ways as the relationship of a shepherd to a beloved ewe-lamb; the very site of their erotic idyll is a barn. Rachel's declaration that the "righteous [shepherd] knows the soul [desire] of his animal" is, in fact, the key moment in the story.[111]

This ideological and cultural function is exactly the reading that Fraenkel proposed.[112] That is, the valorization of the woman who renounces her own "rights" for the sake of her husband's Torah study. The cultural tension between marriage and lust for learning is solved by the right woman. If she goes along with her own status as ewe – that is, subservient though neither denigrated nor despised – she is rewarded with great prestige. Boyarin claims that this is the way in which the Akiva and Rachel romance is historical.

> Our romantic historical fiction is a historical document in precisely this sense. The romance of Rabbi Akiva and Rachel is foundational for the two-edged sword of European Jewish patriarchal culture, which

---

[111]*Carnal Israel*, 151.
[112]Ibid., 153 and n. 34.

often gave women much power and prestige in the "secular" realm while denying them participation in the religious sphere.¹¹³

Boyarin reads the last story in the series in b Ket., the story which immediately follows the Akiva-Rachel story, as evidence of the "cracks just under the surface of the utopian solution" proposed by Akiva as "married monk," and a mark of "[t]he amount of conflict that the new social practice engendered...."¹¹⁴

> R. Yosef the son of Rava [was] sent [by] his father to the House of Study to study with Rabbi Joseph.
> They set for him six years of study [i.e., he had been married and it was decided that he would be away from home for six years].
> After three years, on the Eve of Yom Kippur,
> He said: I will go and visit my wife¹¹⁵.
> 95 His father heard, and went out to him with a weapon.
> He said to him: "Your remembered your whore?"
> (Another version: You remembered your dove.)
> They fought, and neither of them got to eat the final meal¹¹⁶ before the fast.

Rava's appearance as a central character in this story, contributes to the sense of the extensive conflict that this innovation roused in Babylonia – since Rava was Babylonian and had come down in favor of the practice earlier in the series, b Ket. 62b (line 5). Boyarin stresses that "[r]epresenting the strife as between Rava and his own son makes that conflict vividly real."¹¹⁷

Before we move on to two versions of the fourth story, which Boyarin sees as proof of the Palestinian-Babylonian opposition over the "married monk" phenomenon, I just want to note a couple of things about the story we just read. There are a number of ways in which this story seems to pick up on some of the motifs and language of several of the other stories. First, it shares with the Rav Reḥume story the fact that it occurs on the eve of Yom Kippur. Second, it shares with the third story,¹¹⁸ the story neither Boyarin nor Fraenkel analyzes, the language of פסקו ליה – they decided for him – which initiates the departure to the Academy. It also shares with the third story the usage of the term "whore." It shares with the Akiva story being "sent away" to study (67

---

¹¹³Ibid., 155.
¹¹⁴*Carnal Israel*, 155.
¹¹⁵lit.: the people of my house. The translation "my wife" in this instance may not be warranted since the Aramaic is more explicitly referring to "the people of my house." Rava in the story, however, obviously understands that the intent of the visit is to see the wife.
¹¹⁶lit.: 'separated'
¹¹⁷Ibid., 156
¹¹⁸which we have not analyzed – see the appendix.

Talmud as Literature and Cultural Production

and 91). At the same time it breaks the mold of the other stories in terms of the time (six years as opposed to three) and directions (they אזל [go away] to the House of Study: 17 36, 42, 51; and אתי [come back] home: 7, 18, 36, 43, 52 70, 75; while Rabbi Joseph אזיל s home: 94). I will try to tie some of these threads together when I argue that the stories here comprise a *sugya*.

Boyarin puts his thesis of a "Babylonian solution" to the test by comparing the Ḥanina b. Ḥakinai story in b Ket. (IV in my numbering) and the story in Genesis Rabbah[119]. Boyarin's claim that the two versions are evidence "that the practice of marrying and leaving one's wife for extended periods was much more heavily stigmatized in Palestine than in Babylonia," rests on his framing of the two stories. He claims that it is an "evident fact that we have the *same* story in front of us in two versions." It is, for Boyarin, this fact that "enables us to perceive the different cultural work that each version is doing, thus providing for differences between the two cultures that produced them."[120]

Fraenkel analyses the story in Genesis Rabbah extensively. When however, he compares that story with the one in b Ket., he refers to the b Ket. story as "a completely new story about Ḥanina b. Ḥakinai."[121] We need to ask, then, if the stories are actually the same. Furthermore, if they are the same, do they perform the cultural work that Boyarin claims they do? In order to simplify comparison, I will follow Boyarin's lead by presenting the stories side by side.

b Ketuboth	Genesis Rabbah
R. Ḥanina b. Ḥakinai was going to the academy towards the end of R. Shim'on b. Yoḥai's wedding.	Ḥananiah the son of Ḥakinai and Rabbi Shimon the son of Yoḥai went to study Torah with Rabbi Akiva in Bnei Berak.
He said to him: Wait for me until I can come with you. He did not wait for him.	
He went and stayed at the academy twelve years.	They were there for thirteen years.

---

[119]Piska 95, ed. Theodor-Albeck: 1232.
[120]Ibid., 156-157. Emphasis in the original.
[121]*Iyyunim*, 108.

	Rabbi Shimon the son of Yoḥai used to send letters to his wife, and used to know what was happening to his family.
	Hananiah the son of Ḥakinai did not send letters to his wife and did not know what was happening to his family.
	His wife sent to him, "Your daughter is grown; come and find her a match."
	Rabbi Akiva perceived with the Holy Spirit and said, "Anyone who has a grown daughter should go and find her a match."
By the time he returned the streets of the town were changed, and he didn't know how to go to his home.	
He went and sat on the river bank.	What did he do? He went and sat by the well. He heard the voices of water-drawers saying, "daughter of Ḥakinai fill your pitcher and ascend."
He heard that they were calling to one girl: Daughter of Ḥakinai! Daughter of Ḥakinai! fill up your pitcher and let us go.'	
He said: Infer from this — this girl is ours. He went after her.	She went, and he went after her, until he came into his house.
His wife was sitting and sifting flour.	
He lifted up her eye, she saw him, her heart was overjoyed, her spirit fled.	Just as his wife saw him her soul left her.
He said before Him: Master of the universe, this poor woman, is this her reward?	[There are those who say that it returned.]
He prayed for mercy for her, and she revived.	

Boyarin reads the Palestinian version (Gen. Rabbah[122]) as a condemnation of the practice of extended leavetaking after marriage,

---

[122]

בראשית רבא צה בכי"ו (ת-א 1232)
ויאמר ישראל אל יוסף אמתה הפעם [אחרי ראותי את פניך כי עדך חי]:(בראשית מו:ל)

חניה בן חכיניי ור' שמעון בן יוחיי הלכו ללמד תורה אצל ר'עקיבה בבני ברק, עשו שם שלש עשרה שנה.
ר' שמעון בן יוחיי הוה משלח כתבין לביתיה והוה ידע מה בביתיה.
חניה בן חכיניי לא הוה משלח כתבין לביתיה ולא הוה ידע מה בביתיה.
שלחה אשתו ואמרה לו, "בתך בגרה בא והשיאה."

Talmud as Literature and Cultural Production   115

while the Babylonian version (b Ket.) ameliorates this harsh criticism in rewriting the story. In the Palestinian version, Ḥanina b. Ḥakinai is not accorded the title "Rabbi," he has no knowledge whatsoever of his family, and is finally forced to leave the study hall and attend to his familial responsibilities – after ignoring the plea of his wife – by none other than Rabbi Akiva. Once he gets home, he bursts into his house without warning[123], thereby killing his wife. In this version of the story the husband and wife never make contact – she dies as soon as she sees him. The literary equation of the story is that his lack of connection with his wife killed her.

In the Babylonian "rewriting", according to Boyarin, the critique is muted.

> We are not told that he did not contact his family, or that he only decided to go home when forced to either by the wife or by the teacher. When his wife dies, he is horrified and intervenes with heaven to restore her to life.[124]

Even the miraculous ending to the Babylonian story – which is a gloss in the Palestinian story – "only emphasizes the failed utopian resolution of the story even more." For Boyarin, the story seems to be saying that only a miracle can juggle the contradictory absolute demands of marriage and study. By contrast, the Palestinian community seems to have understood both the importance of ascetic practice, and the untenability of imposing such a practice on a wife.[125]

Fraenkel, as we mentioned above, reads the two versions, as two completely different stories.[126] The Gen. Rabbah version contrasts the figure of Rabbi Shimon b. Yoḥai – the sage who knows how to maintain a balance between home and study hall – with Ḥanina – who doesn't. Rabbi Shimon b. Yoḥai maintains a constant connection with his

---

צפה ר' עקיבה ברוח בקודש, אמ' "כל מי שיש לו בת בוגרת ילך וישיאה."
מה עבד? אזל למליתה, שמע קלהן דמלווחיה אמרן "בתו שלחכיניי מלי קולחיך וסוק ליך."
הוות מהלכה והוא מהלך בתרה עד זמן דעלת לביתיה.
לא הספיקה ביתו לראותו עד שיצאתה נשמתה.
ואית דאמרן חרת.

[123]This – the danger of bursting into a house without warning, after being away for an extended period – is the explicit frame of the story in Gen. Rabbah (and Lev. Rabbah). The lemma that the story is "commenting" on is the verse from Genesis (46:30) in which Jacob tells Joseph that he can die now after seeing him. Following the story is a statement by Rabbi Simon b. Yoḥai to the effect that one of the things that God hates and he also doesn't like is "one who enters his house suddenly, and all the more so, one who enters the house of his fellow suddenly." הנכנס לביתו פתאום וקל וחומר לבית חבירו (Genesis Rabbah, ed. Theodor-Albeck, 1232)
[124]*Carnal Israel*, 158.
[125]Ibid., 159.
[126]*Iyyunim*, 105-108.

household, and is aware of what is happening there, while Ḥanina is totally absorbed in the study hall, at the expense of his house/family. At the same time it is Rabbi Shimon b. Yoḥai who is famous as a scholar, while Ḥanina is lost to obscurity. The point of the story, according to Fraenkel, "is that the house of study does not want to maintain a person who ignores his own house."[127]

The Babylonian version is more "optimistic." In this story, Ḥanina returns home on his own, without the prodding of a teacher, and his plea for his wife's life shows that he was aware of her sufferings all these lonely years. As a result of his long absence, his connection to his home might have been totally severed (he no longer knew how to go home). However the surviving "connection" – his daughter – leads him home, and his prayer – which shows that he understands his wife's suffering – insures that the return home is successful.

I agree with Fraenkel that the Babylonian version is very different – "a completely new story." I also tend to agree with his reading of the Palestinian version, to the extent that the thrust of that story is the comparison of Ḥanina and Shimon b. Yoḥai. Since Shimon b. Yoḥai seems to have successfully negotiated the balance between the two houses – home and study hall – that story doesn't seem to be doing the cultural work that Boyarin claims for it. One can stay away for extended periods of time – one just has to "reach out and touch someone..."

If we look at the white spaces, the absences, in the comparison of the two stories, we find that they are about different things. In the Babylonian story, Shimon b. Yoḥai gets short shrift – if anything it might signify Ḥanina's bypassing the wedding to go to the academy. The bulk of the Palestinian story – comparison of the two scholars away from home – is not a part of the Babylonian version, nor is its absence missed. The climax of both stories, the return home, means very different things in the two different stories. Here, however, I take leave of Fraenkel's optimistic reading. As is his way, he reads the story in isolation. It is in context however, in which the meaning is produced.

This story shares significant language and form with the story before and after it. The lines in the Babylonian Ḥanina story that are not in the Palestinian story, and are puzzling by themselves are:

> By the time he returned the streets of the town were changed, and he didn't know how to go to his home.
> He went and sat on the river bank.
> 45 He heard that they were calling to one girl: Daughter of Hakinai! Daughter of Hakinai!
> He said: Infer from this – this girl is ours. He went after her.

---

[127] שבית המדרש אינו רוצה לקיים בו את מי שמתעלם מן הבית ... Ibid., 106.

Talmud as Literature and Cultural Production

The phrase, "By the time he returned," (עד דאתא) occurs in the previous story also (36). There, the whole phrase is:

> By the time he returned his wife was sterile.

In both stories this phrase is immediately preceded by the line (36, 42):

> He went and stayed at the academy twelve years.

As has been noted several times already, the word used for wife and house are exactly the same. We could translate line 43 as: He didn't know how to get to his wife. This move, though, seems to confuse rather than clarify. That is, unless we push the structural similarities between the stories. Not knowing how to get to his wife, in this context, is the same as being sterile. This reading of not being able to get to his wife, is reinforced by the fact that the word translated as "girl" (רביתא) in lines 45 and 46, is used earlier (25) to refer to a (potential) wife. The scene at the river then, at least has the subtext of Ḥanina's not knowing who his wife is.[128] Until this point in the story, no daughter was mentioned. Fraenkel has noted that the "daughter" is referred to as "daughter of Ḥakinai," and not "daughter of Ḥanina." I would claim that this ambiguity (at the least) makes sense in the light of the previous and the following stories – which are about the failure of the scholar to reproduce. The endings of III and IV are also very similar in language.[129] This makes sense if we understand the equation of sterility and death as the inability to reproduce. The ending of V is about a different *type* of failure of reproduction (the scholar doesn't know he has reproduced and is not recognized as the father/his paternity is challenged [60]), but in the end it is the same.

Reading Boyarin Against the Grain

It should be noted that Boyarin introduced the romance of Akiva and the daughter of Kalba Sabua – the text which he considers as the most significant – right after the Ben Azzai text (T Yev. 8:4) – even though he read it after the second story in the series in b Ket. The effect of introducing the story earlier is that it becomes part of the discursive formation, as the groundwork of the cultural tension is first laid out. Further, Boyarin uses the version of the story that is in b Ned. 50a. He claims that the differences between the stories are "irrelevant for my

---

[128] It is also noteworthy that there is none of this ambiguity in the Genesis Rabbah story.
[129] In fact, one MSS (Munich) uses the same exact phrase in lines 37 and 49 (see the Hebrew text). This suggests that at least one scrib(e)(al tradition) read the stories in dialogue with each other.

reading here."[130] This raises a methodological question. If the other stories (in the b Ket. 62a-63b series), amongst which the Akiva story is found are important to the understanding of the Akiva story – why not read the story as it is in b Ket., where it shares language and themes with those other stories? I will also argue that the differences between the stories are not irrelevant.

Boyarin claims that the questions that this story generates – "Why is this story told about Rabbi Akiva? What is the cultural work that is done by making the hero of the 'romance' specifically a great scholar and martyr and more specifically Rabbi Akiva?" – can only be answered by placing the story in the discursive formation we have just seen. At the same time, however, removing the story from the b Ket. context, hampers the reader's ability to see the series in b Ket. as intratextually connected – or even as its own discursive formation.

I say "removing the story" from its context, since Boyarin treats the two stories as one. This, effectively, places both the b Ket. context and the b Ned. context in brackets. It doesn't consider the possibility that the language of the b Ket. story is connected to the series in b Ket., while the language in b Ned. is connected to the context there, which is poverty.

Boyarin's "close reading" of the story is also problematic. The identification of Akiva as a shepherd occurs only in b Ket. The barn as a site of their erotic idyll occurs only in b Ned. (In fact, if Fraenkel is right, there is no erotic relationship between Akiva and his wife in the b Ket. story until perhaps the very end.) The saying which alludes to the name Rachel, only occurs in b Ket. Akiva's love for "Rachel" is expressed by his wish to get her a "Jerusalem of Gold" only in b Ned. In b Ket. he is silent for the first half of the story. In b Ket. she is active at the beginning and he is active at the end, whereas in b Ned. she is not active at all. This is very prominent in the climactic scene in both stories – the ultimate meeting. In the b Ket. version:

> His wife heard. She was going out to meet him. ...
> When she drew near him, she fell on her face, and kissed his feet.

She is the one who is acting. Whereas in the version in b Ned.:

> Everyone came out to receive him, and she also came out to meet him.
> ...
> She came to show herself to [lit. to be seen by] him.

She only goes along in the wake of "everyone."[131] Also, in b Ket. she actively betroths him, while in b Ned. she is passively betrothed to him.

---

[130] Ibid., 150 n.28.
[131] Weller catalogues nine differences between the two stories. "*Kovetz Sippurim,*" 104-105.

The only real similarity between the two stories is the scene of the final meeting. She quotes the verse "A righteous man knows the needs [soul] of his beast," and he says, "Leave her! Mine and yours are hers." Even these lines, however, have different meanings in the different settings. The story in b Ned. is about poverty and wealth, about ownership. In the climactic moment of the story, Akiva teaches his students about what real ownership and wealth is, just as Elijah had taught him. In contrast, the b Ket. story is about Torah study (her betrothing him is conditioned upon it), modesty and honor. In the climactic moment of the story, Akiva teaches his students about what real Torah, and honor are.

When the Akiva stories are read apart from each other, the shepherd-ewe/Akiva-Rachel line is weakened. The biggest problem with Boyarin's reading of the missing name Rachel as the key to this story, however, is that it misses one point that is driven home by all the stories in b Ket. 62b-63a – the women are *not* named. They are defined by their relationship to men, by their silence, by their absence with all manner of life and death consequences. When the stories in b Ket. 62b-63a – including the Akiva story – are read as a *sugya*, there is a progressive movement towards the woman's complete acquiescence in her own irrelevance in relation to the locus of significance in the male world – the academy. One of the axes on which this turns is that women are *not* named.

When the series of Aggadot in b Ket. is read as a *sugya*, the narrative that it generates is about the scholarly fantasy of a male study house that is self-sufficient to such extent that (male) scholarly reproduction which does not require women fulfills the true reproductive role. There is also a recognition that this fantasy is a fantasy. A full reading is beyond the scope of this chapter, so I will just sketch the outline of such a reading in order to make the point that the first locus of interpretation needs to be the *sugya* – the immediate context.

There is a progression from I to VI which involves both erasing the role of women, and reproduction. The woman is always the locus of death, in that she is the opposite of the study hall, and the end of the scholarly line, if she is not impregnated by the scholar's leaving the study hall. Each successive story plays out the inability of the specific sage to reproduce in the study hall. The closest that the sage gets is in V, where the meeting of father and son is in the study hall – it still, however, misfires. And it is the woman who points that out (60).

Then comes the Akiva story. This is the fantasy in all its glory – Akiva gives birth to twenty four thousand students/children with the full complicity of his wife, who has totally erased herself. She is penniless, childless, voiceless, and yes, nameless. The final act is between

Akiva and his father-in-law who make up and "marry their fortunes." Meanwhile, Akiva's wife has disappeared – at the moment when he ostensibly gives her ownership to all that is his.

The denouement (VII) both reinforces the fantasy while reintroducing reality. This story serves as a subversive closure to the *sugya*. We noted above the way that it shares language and structure with the other Aggadot. At the same time, it switches the directions and, by doing so, the valences of the actions in the other Aggadot. The young R. Joseph goes home (אזל) the way everyone else goes to the study hall. This validation of the wife brings Rava out in full armor, blocking the way back to the house/wife. It is in that twilight of the Eve of Yom Kippur that the battle rages endlessly on.

The point of this interpretive sketch is not to provide the last word on what the Aggadic *sugya* of b Ket. 62b-63a means. It is rather to point towards the interpretive directions that could not be taken as a result of either moving too quickly away from the immediate context (in the case of Boyarin[132]), or ignoring that context (in the case of Fraenkel).

Conclusions

The discursive formation that Boyarin assembled here is an excellent example of reading together texts that are usually seen as from different genres. The texts that are central to this formation are T Yevamot 8:4[133], b Nedarim 50a, b Kiddushin 29b, M Ketuboth 5:6, b Ketuboth 62b-63a, and Sifri Numbers 99. They include halakhah (M Ket. 5:6 and b Kid. 29b), Aggadah (b Ned. 50a, b Ket. 62b-63a) and Midrash (Sifri Numbers 99 and T Yev. 8:4), and some of the texts could be categorized in more than one of these genres. They also stem from different parts of the corpus of rabbinic literature – Mishnah, Tosefta, Midrash, Talmud.

The central methodological point – that texts of rabbinic literature, which are usually understood as being of different genres, might profitably be read together, is a strong one. It is very convincing that texts that grew out of a particular cultural formation, deal with similar issues. The question that remains is: how does one decide what constitutes the frame of a specific text. This is a question that arises specifically out of the practice of cultural poetics. In the use of cultural poetics or New Historicism in the study of Elizabethan drama, for

---

[132]Boyarin's reading doesn't end here, it continues with a midrash from Sifri Numbers which is read to back up the anti-celibacy polemic that Boyarin understands as happening in Palestine. That part of the chapter doesn't add anything *methodologically*, to the argument so I am skipping it for the purposes of the present chapter.

[133]Mistakenly identified in *Carnal Israel* on page 134 as 8:7.

example, there are many "non-canonical" historical sources to utilize – diaries, memos, private letters, etc. The practice of cultural poetics is then to "deconstruct" the given hierarchy between the high-cultural and low-cultural, or the historical and non-historical. Equal weight is given to both. At the same time, the boundaries of both letter and play (for example) are already pre-established, as it were. The introduction of the "non-canonical" literary production (the letter) alters the way we had viewed the workings of the culture as represented by the "canonical" literary production (the play).

In the case of rabbinic literature, however, there is no readily available hierarchy to deconstruct, as many of the definitions and boundaries of the materials are essentially contested. To claim that *an* Aggadah or *a* midrash is a separate literary work which can be juxtaposed with other separate literary works (in the same way that a play and a letter might be) is a contested, rather than a simple move. When dealing with "canonical" or "received" literary productions, the first step, I would argue, needs to be the delineation of the boundaries of the texts that are part of a discursive formation. It is the calling into question of the interpretive frame that achieves significant results in the work of the New Historicists. That can be accomplished by first interpreting within the *sugya*, for example, and then bringing other texts into the discursive space.

On the other hand, the New Critical practice of Jonah Fraenkel, errs on the side of isolationism. Texts are not impermeable and hermetic. Removing them from their context doesn't leave them context free, but rather puts them into a new context – even if that context might be the collection of all "Sage Stories." This new context – whatever it is – informs the meaning of the specific story. This was the case with the Aggadot that we read with Fraenkel in the first part of the chapter, and also with the Aggadic *sugya* in b Ket. The narrowing vision of the hermetic Aggadah precludes the possibility of essential ties to Aggadot (or anything else) fore and aft.

With this chapter I close the arc that started with Avraham Weiss. We walked through the door that he opened with his articulation of the concept of "literary formulation" (קביעה ספרותית) of Talmudic statements. While his interest was redactional/historical, the very act of distancing the statement from a speaker, and treating it as literature was revolutionary. In different ways, Halivni and Friedman pushed the question further. Though both were still interested in the history of the text, the questions they asked were based on literary phenomena. Friedman especially opened up a whole new vista, with the stress he placed on the structure of *sugyot*.

Neusner's radical skepticism of history, and iconoclastic view of literature and literary production, challenged the questions we were attempting to formulate. Unfortunately, in his discussion of literary theory, the bark of his outrage is much louder than the bite of his theoretical understanding.

As we have just seen, Fraenkel abandoned the historical quest, and adopted New Critical hermeneutics. Boyarin attempts to get back to history, obliquely – the history of ideas as represented in cultural practices and literary production.

In the second half of this dissertation, I will attempt to articulate a methodology for reading *sugyot* which learns from, but avoids some of the pitfalls of the methodologies I have reviewed. The theoretical core of the methodology will be an attempt to articulate a poetics of the *sugya* – that is, *sugyaetics*.

Talmud as Literature and Cultural Production

Appendix: b Ketuboth 62b-63a

כתובות ס"ב ע"ב – ס"ג ע"א

הספנים אחת לששה חדשים דברי ר' אליעזר:

אמר רב ברונא אמר רב הלכה כר' אליעזר[134].
אמר רב אדא בר אהבה[135]: זו דברי ר' אליעזר,
אבל חכמים אומרים התלמידים, יוצאין לת"ח ב ו ג' שנים שלא ברשות.
אמר רבא סמכו רבנן אדרב אדא בר אהבה, ועבדי עובדא בנפשייהו.   5
כי הא דרב רחומי. הוה שכיח קמיה דרבא במחוזא[136].   I
הוה רגיל דאתי[137] לביתיה כל מעלי יומא דכיפורי.
יומא חד משכתיה שמעתא.
הוה קא מסכיא[138] דביתהו: השתא אתי? השתא אתי?
לא אתא. חלש דעתה. אחית דמעתא מעינה.   10
הוה יתיב באיגרא, אפחית איגרא מתותיה, ונח נפשיה[139].

עונה של תלמידי חכמים אימת?
אמר רב יהודה אמר שמואל[140]: מע"ש לע"ש.
"אשר פריו יתן בעתו" (תהילים א:ג)[141].
אמר רב יהודה, ואיתימא רב נחמן: זה המשמש מטתו מע"ש לע"ש.   15
יהודה בריה דר' חייא חתניה דר' ינאי הוה.   II
אזיל ויתיב בבי רב,
וכל בי שמשי הוה אתי[142] לביתיה,
וכי הוה אתי הוו[143] קא חזי קמיה עמודא דנורא,
יומא חד משכתיה שמעתא ולא אתא[144].   20
כיון דלא חזי ההוא סימנא, אמר להו רבי ינאי: כפו מטתו.
שאלמלא יהודה קיים לא ביטל עונתו.
הואי "כשגגה שיוצא מלפני השליט," (קהלת י:ה)[145] ונח נפשיה דיהודה[146].

רבי איעסק ליה לבריה בי רבי חייא,   III

---

[134] **דפוס**: כר"א
[135] **דפוס**: אהבה אמר רב
[136] במחוזא] ליתא מ
[137] **דפוס**: דהוה אתי
[138] קא מסכיא] ע"פ רבד
[139] ש: הוה יתבה – מתותחה ונח נפשה
[140] אמר רב יהודה אמר שמואל: חסר מ
[141] והיה כעץ שתול על פלגי מים אשר פריו יתן בעתו ועלהו לא יבול וכל אשר יעשה יצליח.
[142] ר'ל : הוה אזיל
[143] **דפוס**: הוה קא חזי
[144] ולא אתא] מ ר' ל ח
[145] יש רעה ראיתי תחת השמש כשגגה שיצא מלפני השליט.
[146] דיהודה] ליתא דפוס

25 כי מטא למיכתב כתובה, נח נפשה דרביתא,
    אמר רבי: דילמא¹⁴⁷ ח"ו פסולא איכא, יתבו ועיינו במשפחות.
    רבי אתי משפטיה בן אביטל, ורבי חייא אתי משמעי אחי דוד.
    אמר ר': אי לאו דהוה מילתא לא הוה שכיבא.¹⁴⁸
    אזיל איעסק ליה לבריה בי ר' יוסי בן זמרא.
30 פסקו ליח תרתי סרי שנין למיזל בבי רב.
    אחלפוה קמיה, אמר להו: ניהוו שית שנין.
    הדור¹⁴⁹ אחלפוה קמיה, אמר להו: איכניס והדר איזיל.
    הוה קא מכסיף מאבוה, אמר ליה: בני, דעת קונך יש בך.
    מעיקרא כתיב, "תביאמו ותטעמו," (שמות טו:יז)
35 ולבסוף כתיב, "ועשו לי מקדש ושכנתי בתוכם." (שם כה:ח)
    אזיל¹⁵⁰ יתיב תרתי סרי שני בבי רב, עד דאתא איעקרא דביתהו.
    אמר רבי: היכי נעביד? נגרשה, יאמרו ענייה זו לשוא שימרה.
    ניניסיב איתתא אחריתי, יאמרו 'זו אשתו וזו זונתו,'
    בעי עלה רחמי ואיתסיאת.

IV 40 רבי חנינא¹⁵¹ בן חכינאי הוה קאזיל לבי רב בשילהי הלוליה דר"ש בן יוחי.¹⁵²
    אמר ליה: איעכב לי עד דאתי בהדך. לא איעכבא ליה.
    אזל יתיב תרי סרי שני בבי רב.
    עד דאתי אישתנו שבילי דמתא, ולא ידע למיזל לביתיה.
    אזל יתיב אגודא דנהרא.
45 שמע להחיא ריביתא דהוו קרו לה בת חכינאי בת חכינאי מלי קולתך ותא ניזיל.¹⁵³
    אמר שמע מינה האי ריביתא דידן. אזל בתרה.
    הוה יתיבא דביתהו קא נהלה קמחא.
    דל עינה, חזיתיה, סוי לבה פרח רוחה.
    אמר לפניו: רבונו של עולם ענייה זו זה שכרה?¹⁵⁴
50 בעא רחמי עלה וחייה.

V   רבי חמא בר ביסא אזל איתיב תריסר שנין בבי רב.¹⁵⁵
    כי אתא, אמר לא איעביד כדעביד בן חכינאי.
    על יתיב במדרשא. שלח לביתיה.
    אתא ר' אושעיא בריה, יתיב קמיה.
55 הוה קא משאיל ליה שמעתא,
    חזא דקא מתחדדי שמעתיה, חלש דעתיה,

---

¹⁴⁷דילמא] מ רב⁵ הל⁵ שמא ר
¹⁴⁸ר⁵ ל⁵⁰ ה (עם שניים), ליתא מ דפוס
¹⁴⁹הדור] ליתא דפוס
¹⁵⁰ר: אזיל נסבא והדר אזיל
¹⁵¹דפוס: חנניה
¹⁵²דפוס: יוחאי
¹⁵³מלי ... ניזיל] ליתא רב⁵
¹⁵⁴מ: ענייה זו לשוא שימרה
¹⁵⁵רב⁵מ: אזיל יתיב תרי סרי שני בבי מדרשא דפוס

Talmud as Literature and Cultural Production 125

	אמר, אי הואי הכא הוה לי זרע כי האי.
	על לביתיה, על בריה, קם מקמיה.[156]
	הוא סבר למשאליה שמעתתא קא בעי.
60	אמרה ליה דביתהו: מי איכא אבא דקאים מקמי ינוקיה?[157]
	קרי עליה רמי בר חמא: "החוט המשולש לא במהרה ינתק." (קהלת ד:יב)
	זה ר' אושעיא בנו של רבי חמא בר ביסא.
VI	ר"ע רעיא דבן כלבא שבוע הוה.
	חזיתיה ברתיה דהוה צניע ומעלי.
65	אמרה ליה: אי מקדשנא לך אזלת לבי רב?
	אמר לה: אין.
	איקדשא ליה בצינעה ושדרתיה.
	שמע אבוה, אפקה מביתיה, אדרה הנאה מנכסיה.
	אזל יתיב[158] תרי סרי שנין בבי רב.
70	כי אתא, אייתי בהדיה תרי סרי אלפי תלמידי.
	שמעיה לההוא סבא דקאמר לה: עד כמה[159] קא מדברת אלמנות חיים?
	אמרה ליה: אי לדידי ציית, יתיב תרי סרי שני אחריני.
	אמר: ברשות קא עבידנא.
	הדר אזיל ויתיב תרי סרי שני אחריני בבי רב.
75	כי אתא, אייתי בהדיה עשרין וארבעה אלפי תלמידי.
	שמעה דביתהו. הות קא נפקא לאפיה.
	אמרו לה שיבבתא: שאילי מאני לבוש ואיכסאי.
	אמרה להו: "יודע צדיק נפש בהמתו." (משלי יב: ט)
	כי מטיא לגביה, נפלה על אפה, קא מנשקא ליה לכרעיה.
80	הוו קא מדחפי לה שמעיה.
	אמר להו: שבקוה, שלי ושלכם שלה הוא.
	שמע אבוה דאתא גברא רבה למתא.
	אמר: איזיל לגביה אפשר דמפר לי[160] גדראי.
	אתא לגביה.
85	אמר ליה: אדעתא דגברא רבה מי נדרת?
	אמר ליה: אפילו פרק אחד ואפי' הלכה אחת.
	אמר ליה: אנא הוא.
	נפל על אפיה ונשקיה על כרעיה, ויהיב ליה פלגא ממוניה.
	ברתיה דר"ע עבדא ליה לבן עזאי הכי.
90	והיינו דאמרי אישי "רחילא בתר רחילא אזלא"[161], כעובדי אמה כך עובדי ברתא."
VII	רב יוסף בריה דרבא שדריה אבוהי לבי רב לקמיה דרב יוסף.
	פסקו ליה שית שני.

---

[156] **דפוס**: קמיה
[157] **ל**ב"**ם**, אבא דקאים מקמיה ברא **דפוס**
[158] **דפוס**: יתיב
[159] עד כמה] ליתא ם ר'
[160] לי] ם רב', ליתא דפוס
[161] רחילא...אזלא] ם ר' ליתא

כי הוה תלת שני מטא מעלי יומא דכפורי.
אמר איזיל ואיחזינהו לאינשי ביתי.
שמע אבוהי שקל מנא ונפק לאפיה.
אמו ליה: זונתך מכרת.
איכא דאמרי[162]: יונתך מכרת.
איטרוד, לא מר איפסיק ולא מר איפסיק.

95

---

[162] מ רב¹, דאמרי אמר לה דפוס

B. Ketuboth 62b

[The time for conjugal relations prescribed by the Torah[145], for] sailors is once every six months; these are the words of R. Eliezer.[146]

R. Bruna said in the name of Rav, The law (*halakhah*) is according to R. Eliezer.
R. Ada b. Ahavah said, This is the opinion of R. Eliezer,
but Sages say: The students [may] leave, for [the purpose of] Torah study, for two or three years without [receiving] permission [from their wives].

5   Rava said: Rabanan relied on [the ruling] of R. Ada b. Ahavah, and act accordingly [at risk of] their lives[147].

I   Thus R. Rahumi, who was frequenting [the school] of[148] Rava in Mehoza.
It was his habit to return to his home on the Eve of every Yom Kippur.
One day he was drawn by the teaching[149].
His wife was anticipating [his arrival]: Is he coming now? Is he coming now?

10 He did not come. She became depressed.[150] A tear fell from her eye.
He was sitting on the roof, the roof collapsed beneath him, he died.

What is the time prescribed by the Torah for conjugal relations, for scholars?
R. Yehuda said in the name of Shmuel: From Sabbath eve to Sabbath eve.
"[He is like a tree planted beside streams of water,] which yields its fruit in season," (Psalms 1:3)

15 R. Yehuda, and perhaps R. Nahman, said, This is the one who [only] has conjugal relations[151] from Sabbath eve to Sabbath eve.

II Yehuda, the son of R. Hiyya was the son in law of R. Yannai.
He went and stayed in the academy,
and every twilight[152] he would return to his house,
and when he would come, they would see a pillar of fire before him.

20 One day he was drawn by the teaching[153], and he didn't come.
Since they did not see that sign, R. Yannai said to them: Turn over his bed, for if Yehuda was alive he would not have neglected his appointed time.
It was "...as an error committed by a ruler..." (Ecclesiastes 10:5), and he died.

III Rabbi was engaged in [marrying] his son to the family of R. Hiyya,
25 when the *ketuba* was about to be written, the girl died,

---

[145]cf. Exodus 21:10
[146]M. Ketuboth 5:6
[147]lit.: in their lives
[148]lit.: was usually found in front of Rava...
[149]lit.: tradition
[150]lit.: her mind/thought/knowledge was weakened.
[151]lit.: services his bed
[152]i.e. every Friday evening just before Shabbat
[153]lit.: tradition

Rabbi said: Perhaps, God forbid, there is a disqualification [in the marriage]? They sat and checked the [lineage of the] families.

Rabbi came from Shephatiah the son of Avital, and R. Hiyya came from Shim'i the brother of David[154].

Rabbi said: If there had not been a problem she would not have died.

He went and was engaged in [marrying] his son to the family of R. Yose b. Zimra.

30 They decided that he[155] would go for twelve years to the academy.

They passed her before him, he said to them: Let it be six years.

Again they led her before him, he said to them: I will marry[156] her and then go.

He felt ashamed before his father. He said to him: My son, you have the mind of your creator,

At first it is written, "You will bring them and plant them [in Your own mountain]" (Exodus 15:17)

35 At the end it is written, "And let them make me a sanctuary that I may dwell among them." (Exodus 25:8)

He went and stayed at the academy twelve years. By the time he returned his wife was sterile.

Rabbi said: What shall we do? Were we to [order him to] divorce her, they would say 'This poor woman waited in vain.'

Were we to [order him to] marry another woman, they would say 'This is his wife and this is his prostitute.'

He prayed for mercy for her, and she recovered.

40 **IV** R. Hanina b. Hakinai was going to the academy towards the end of R. Shim'on b. Yohai's wedding.

He said to him: Wait for me until I can come with you. He did not wait for him.

He went and stayed at the academy twelve years.

By the time he returned the streets of the town were changed, and he didn't know how to go to his home.

He went and sat on the river bank.

45 He heard that they were calling to one girl: Daughter of Hakinai! Daughter of Hakinai! fill up your pitcher and let us go.'

He said: Infer from this – this girl is ours. He went after her.

His wife was sitting and sifting flour.

He lifted up her eye, she saw him, her heart was overjoyed, her spirit fled.

He said before Him: Master of the universe, this poor woman, is this her reward?

50 He prayed for mercy for her, and she revived.

V R. Hama b. Bisa went and stayed at the academy twelve years.

When he returned he said, I will not act as b. Hakinai did.

He entered and sat in the house of study. He sent [a message] to his house.

His son, R. Oshaia, came, sat down before him,

---

[154]Rabbi therefore was from Davidic lineage as Avital was one of David's wives while R. Hiyya wasn't. This was the disqualification. (Rashi)

[155]i.e. the son

[156]lit.: bring in

Talmud as Literature and Cultural Production

55 and was asking him about a teaching[157].
He [R. Hama] saw that he [R. Oshaia] was very sharp in his study. He became depressed.
He said: Had I been here, I would have had a child[158] like this.
He entered his house, his son entered, he stood up before him.
He [R. Hama] thought that he wanted to ask him [more] legal questions.
60 His wife said to him: Is there one who stands before his baby?
Rami b. Hama applied to him [the verse]: "A threefold cord is not readily broken." (Ecclesiastes 4:12)
This is R. Oshaia, son of R. Hama, son of Bisa.

VI R. Akiva was a shepherd of Ben Kalba Sabua.
[The latter's] daughter saw him as modest and noble.
65 She said to him: Were I to betroth you, would you go to study at an academy?
He said to her: Yes.
She betrothed [herself] to him in secret and sent him away.
Her father heard, drove her from his house, and forbade her by a vow to have any benefit from his estate.
He went and stayed at the academy twelve years.
70 When he came back, he brought twelve thousand students with him.
He heard an old man saying to her: For how long are you to conduct yourself as in living widowhood.
She said to him: If he would listen to me, he would stay another twelve years.
He [R. Akiva] said: I am acting with permission.
Again he went, and stayed at the academy another twelve years.
75 When he came back, he brought twenty four thousand students with him.
His wife heard. She was going out to meet him.
Neighbors said to her: Borrow clothes, dress and cover yourself.
She said: "A righteous man knows the needs of his beast." (Proverbs 12:10)
When she drew near him, she fell on her face, and kissed his feet.
80 His attendants were pushing her aside.
He said to them: Leave her! Mine and yours are hers.
Her father heard that a great man had come to town.
He said: I will got to him, perhaps he will invalidate my vow.
He came to him.
85 He [R. Akiva] said to him: With the knowledge that he was a great man, would you have made your vow?
He said to him: Rabbi, even one chapter, even one halakhah.
He said to him: I am he.
He fell upon his face and kissed his feet and gave him half his wealth.
R. Akiva's daughter acted the same way towards Ben Azai.
90 This is what people say: "Ewe follows ewe; a daughter's acts are like those of her mother."

VII R. Yosef the son of Rava [was] sent [by] his father to the academy under R. Yosef.
They decided [that he would stay] six years.

---

[157]or: tradition
[158]lit.: seed

When he was there three years, Yom Kippur was approaching.
  He said: I will go and see my family[159].
95 His father heard, took a weapon, and went out to him.
  He said to him: You remembered your prostitute.
  (Another version: You remembered your dove.)
  They quarreled, and neither ate the last meal[160] before Yom Kippur.

---

[159]lit.: the people of my house
[160]lit.: 'separated'

5

Towards a Poetics of *Sugyot* or Sugyaetics

Introduction

In this chapter I articulate an interpretive methodology called sugyaetics – that is the analysis of the poetics of the sugya. In the following chapters I apply this method to *sugyot* from b Gittin.

This method consists of three types of analysis. First, reading the *sugya* against its grain, asking what the various rhetorical moves do, rather than acquiescing to their own claims as questions and answers. Second a structural analysis of the *sugya* to identify the recurrent forms, tropes and images in the *sugya*. Third, an intertextual analysis which situates the sugya within its literary and cultural universe. These analytical frames are all governed by an understanding of *sugya* as narrative. Not only (though also) in the sense that it claims to be narrative by seemingly having a beginning, middle and end to its dialogic structure; but more so in identifying the narrative that is grounded in its recurrent forms, tropes and images. It also partakes of larger and smaller cultural narratives – for example those about the relationship between men, women, and law, and a narrative of origins which makes each specific moment of legal "history" intelligible. Finally a *sugya* generates narratives which become the subsequent *halakhic* tradition.

In order to unpack this method, and then apply it, it is first necessary to locate *sugyaetics*, as a reading practice, in a theoretical understanding of reading and interpretation. In what follows I argue for the importance of reading contextually and then intertextually. After strongly locating textual meaning in a textual universe – rather than as a mediation between a textual universe and "reality" – I interrogate the possible relationship of text and reality. To this end I discuss the idea of textual representation, and the idea of law and/as narrative (leaning heavily on Robert Cover's work). This is at least partially by way of arguing for the importance of starting any understanding of Talmud with the *sugya*. At the end of the theoretical argument I explicate the method itself.

Reading and Context

The last several decades of literary theory have brought into sharp relief the activity of interpretation or the practice of reading. Moving away from a concept of a text which has one objective meaning that may be uncovered by the reader as archaeologist, recent theorists have embraced the idea that meaning is a function of context. That is, any unit of meaning – word, sentence, story, etc. – "means" only within a certain frame. Within a different frame that very same unit "means" something else. This context is, first, the local literary context: the sentence in which a word appears, for example. One has no way of knowing how to read (in all senses of this word) the phoneme "wind" without a sentence or other specific context.

The context in which a *sentence* appears also defines its meaning. In the following example Maimonides accurately reproduces a Talmudic saying, but by imbedding it in another literary and philosophical/cultural context he changes its meaning radically. This challenges the claim that by simply identifying a statement as not originally of its present context, that one can divine its original meaning.

Maimonides, in the first part of *The Guide to the Perplexed* attempts to explain, or explain away, certain terms which appear in the Bible and which seem to impute to God human actions or emotions. These anthropomorphic or anthropopathic terms would trouble the reader who has also "studied the sciences of the philosophers and come to know what they signify."[1] Some of the chapters in this first part deal with specific words or phrases – the so-called "lexicographical chapters."[2] In others, Maimonides sets out the principles of his theory of Biblical interpretation. The following is from one of the theory chapters:

> You know their dictum that refers in inclusive fashion to all the kinds of interpretation connected with this subject, namely, their saying: *The Torah speaketh in the language of the sons of man*. The meaning of this is that everything that all men are capable of understanding and representing to themselves at first thought has been ascribed to Him as necessarily belonging to God, may He be

---

[1] Introduction. *The Guide of the Perplexed*, translated with an introduction and notes by Shlomo Pines (Chicago: University of Chicago Press, 1963): 5.
[2] Leo Strauss, "How To Begin To Study *The Guide of the Perplexed*," in *The Guide of the Perplexed*, translated with an introduction and notes by Shlomo Pines (Chicago: University of Chicago Press, 1963): xxiv-xxv.

> exalted. Hence attributes indicating corporeality have been predicated of Him in order to indicate that He, may He be exalted, exists, inasmuch as the multitude cannot at first conceive of any existence save that of a body alone; thus that which is neither a body nor existent in a body does not exist in their opinion. (I:26)[3]

The principle that Maimonides is explaining here is that Biblical expressions that seem to indicate to the philosophical reader that God is corporeal, do not really mean that. These anthropomorphic expressions are used to indicate to the untutored masses that God *exists*. These untutored masses, not having the benefit of philosophical edification, cannot conceive of God existing in any way that is dissimilar to the way in which any other object exists. For this reason the Bible is written in a language which accords with the "imagination of the multitude," rather than the truth of the philosophers.[4] This, Maimonides claims, is what is explicitly meant by the dictum: *The Torah speaketh in the language of the sons of man.*

The statement: "the Torah speaketh in the language of the sons of man," appears many times in the Bavli.[5] Maimonides quotes it accurately (in Hebrew,[6] not in Arabic), and yet, if we were only to have the Maimonidean evidence for the existence of this phrase, we would not be able to reconstruct any "original" meaning for it. I quote one occurrence of the phrase in b Ket. 67b:[7]

Our Rabbis taught:

> *To lend* (Deut. 15:8) refers to a man who has no means and is unwilling to receive his maintenance [from the poor funds] to whom [the allowance] must be given as a loan and then presented to him as a gift.

---

[3] Ibid. 56.
[4] For a succinct description of Maimonides' reliance on reason at the expense of "literal meaning," see Marvin Fox, *Interpreting Maimonides: Studies in Methodology, Metaphysics, and Moral Philosophy* (Chicago: The University of Chicago Press, 1990): 40-42.
[5] In his translation, Pines refers to b Yebamoth 71a, and b Baba Metziah 31b, though I cannot fathom his reasons. In all of its appearances, the phrase has the same hermeneutic function (which we describe below).
[6] דברה תורה כלשון בני אדם.
[7]

בבלי כתובות סז ע"ב

תנו רבנן

"העבט," (דברים ט״ו:ח) זה שאין לו ואינו רוצה להתפרנס,
שנותנין לו לשום הלואה וחוזרין ונותנין לו לשום מתנה
"תעביטנו," (דברים ט״ו:ח) זה שיש לו ואינו רוצה להתפרנס,
שנותנין לו לשום מתנה, וחוזרין ונפרעין הימנו לאחר מיתה, דברי ר' יהודה.
וחכמים אומרים, יש לו ואינו רוצה להתפרנס, אין נזקקין לו.
ואלא מה אני מקיים תעביטנו? "דברה תורה כלשון בני אדם."

> *Though shalt lend him* (ibid.) refers to a man who has the means and does not wish to maintain himself [at his own expense]
> to whom [the allowance] is given as a gift and repayment is claimed from his [estate] after his death, so R. Judah.
> The Sages however, said: If he has the means and does not wish to maintain himself [at his own expense] no one need feel any concern about him.
> To what, however is the text *Though shalt lend him* to be applied?
> The Torah spoke in the language of the sons of man.[8]

This unit is found in a larger *sugya* whose general theme is the obligation to support the poor. The more specific question under consideration is the extent to which one needs to support a poor person. A seeming ungrammaticality in a verse is exploited to construct the unit's answers. The verse, Deuteronomy 15:8, can be translated as follows:

> Rather you must open your hand and lend him sufficient for whatever he needs.[9]

In the statement attributed to R. Judah, however, the repetition of the verb *lend* in the Hebrew (העבט תעביטנו – lend you shall lend) is exploited to mean that there are two different types of lending situations. In the first, a person of no means does not want to be supported by the communal fund. In the second, a person of means does not wish to maintain himself. R. Judah mandates that both are supported though under different conditions. Sages however, take issue with the second case. According to their understanding, if one can support oneself but refuses to do so, it is not incumbent upon the community to support one. The question is then asked: to what end do the Sages then interpret the doubling of the verb *to lend*? The answer is that they hold that there is no ungrammaticality, for such is the "language of the sons of man." In other words, the doubling of the verb "to lend" has no special significance in this situation – it is a stylistic device. The Torah wrote as people write – employing stylistic devices. Therefore, Sages would say, one should not subject this "extra" phrase to a midrashic reading since it is not extra at all.

As is seen from this example – and all other occurrences of the phrase are similar in form[10] – *The Torah speaketh in the language of the sons of man* is a hermeneutic principle, but, at least Talmudically, it is not invoked in cases of, nor does it refer to the interpretation of

---

[8] The translation is the Soncino translation of Rabbi Dr. S. Daiches except for the last line which Daiches paraphrases as: "The Torah employs ordinary phraseology." The phrase is translated accurately there in the notes. (412 n.5)
[9] NJPS. כי פתח תפתח את ידך לו והעבט תעביטנו די מחסרו אשר יחסר לו.
[10] Cf. b Git. 41b; Kid. 17b; Baba Metziah 31b, 94b; San. 56a, 64b, 85b, 90b; Mak. 12a; A. Z. 27a; Zeb. 108b; Arachin 3a; Krithut 11a; Nidah 32b, 44a.

anthropopathic or anthropomorphic phrases of the Bible. The Talmudic function of this principle is to limit the applicability of the midrashic reading practice in instances of the doubling of verbs. The "general rule" that one might[11] draw from this principle is that certain stylistic devices of the biblical text are not to be counted as redundancies, and therefore are not to be read midrashically.[12]

Maimonides reads this principle as a Rabbinic validation of a specific philosophical reading of Torah. That is, Maimonides imputes to the phrase the general rule that all anthropomorphic or anthropopathic terms in the Torah are not to be taken as literal. ("You know their dictum that refers *in inclusive fashion to all the kinds of interpretation connected with this subject...*") It is not however, the language of the phrase that has changed, but its context. This example also points to the importance of the cultural context of interpretation. It was the neo-Aristotelean philosophical discourse of the early Middle Ages that naturalized this recontextualization of the phrase.

The ability to define the context, or at least one context, of a statement or phrase, is the important first step in understanding a local meaning. Although one cannot support the absolute statement: "sentence X means Y," one might be able to support the claim that "sentence X means Y in context Z."

Reading Intertextually

Another aspect of the problem of interpretation is what I referred to above in Riffaterre's terminology as the "poeticity" of words. While ancient and medieval philosophers have deplored the polysemy of language, and have attempted to articulate or invoke external criteria (external to the reading process, that is) to stabilize meaning, modern theorists have embraced this polysemy. From Saussure's denaturalization of the connection between a word or sign and its signified,[13] the practice of reading has been seen as one of the maneuvering, by the reader or interpreter, of signs and signifieds into relation with each other. A word/phrase/unit of meaning, then, is not only informed by the local context in which it is found. It is also involved

---

[11] This "general rule" is, of course, both unstated and contested in Talmud – it is only a general rule for those who invoke it, i.e. Sages in this case.
[12] See the recent discussion by Jay M. Harris, *How Do We Know This: Midrash and the Fragmentation of Modern Judaism* (Albany: State University of New York Press, 1995): 33-43.
[13] Saussure, Ferdinand de, *Saussure's First Course of Lectures on General Linguistics (1907) : From The Notebooks of Albert Riedlinger*, French text edited by Eisuke Komatsu ; English [ed. and] translation by George Wolf (Tarrytown, N.Y.: Pergamon, 1996).

in an intertextual relationship, that is, it is informed by other texts which supply it with a larger context. It is this "ultimate word game" which defines what it is to perceive a text as literary.[14]

The intertextual relationship, sometimes called the semiotic relationship, is the understanding that when a text refers beyond itself, it is referring first and foremost to other texts. Words or phrases in literary texts are signs which refer to "preexistent word groups." These preexistent word groups, or intertexts – which might be sentences or books, text or a part of language – determine the production, or inform the meaning of signs in the text.[15] The specific word or phrase in the text being read might or might not appear in the intertext. The intertext might be triggered by a specific meaning or nuance of a word in the text.[16] Two texts might be helpful here.

The first text is a stanza from a song written by Bruce Springsteen. In this first person ballad of urban despair titled "For You,"[17] the "narrator" of the song says the following:

> You were not quite half so proud when I found you broken on the beach
> Remember how I poured salt on your tongue and hung just out of reach
> And the band they played the homecoming theme as I caressed your cheek
> They ragged, jagged melody she still clings to me like a leach
> 5 But that medal you wore on your chest always got in the way
> Like a little girl with a trophy so soft to buy her way
> We were both hitchhikers but you had your ear tuned to the roar
> Of some metal-tempered engine on an alien, distant shore
> So you left to find a better reason than the one we were living for
> 10 And it's not that nursery mouth I came back for
> It's not the way you're stretched out on the floor
> `Cause I've broken all your windows and I've rammed through all your doors
> And who am I to ask you to lick my sores? And you should know that's true
> I came for you, for you, I came for you, but you did not need my urgency
> 15 I came for you, for you, I came for you, but your life was one long emergency

---

[14] Michael Riffaterre, *The Semiotics of Poetry* (Bloomington: Indiana University Press, 1984): 42.

[15] Michael Riffaterre, *Fictional Truth* (Baltimore: Johns Hopkins University Press, 1990): 23, 128, 130.

[16] "The sememe of the kernel word functions like an encyclopedia of representations related to the meaning of that word. Their actualization has the effect of saturating the derivative verbal sequence with that meaning, overtly confirming what could have been gathered from a single word." *The Semiotics of Poetry*, 26. Cf. *Fictional Truth*, 129.

[17] Bruce Springsteen, *Greetings From Asbury Park N.J.*, CBS PCT 31903 (1973).

Through most of the verse, the narrator is apparently speaking to a woman who he once was attached to in some way, and is currently unattainable. It is this "unattainability," and the subsequent despair, which sets the tone for the song as a whole. However, line 12 seems to break the narrative line. It is not clear who the "you" is in this line. No one aside from the woman has been introduced – but what does the narrator mean by "your windows" and "your doors?" Whose windows? Why windows? A house hasn't been mentioned.[18] This is what Riffaterre calls an "ungrammaticality." A syntactical or grammatical problem, or a break in the narrative. Anything that disrupts the mimetic or representational understanding of the text is an ungrammaticality. It operates as a hermeneutic index, pointing to the possibility for a semiotic or intertextual reading.

I suggest that the following intertext informs this line, and allows us to reread the whole song. The following stanza is from Bob Dylan's famous song "The Times They Are A-changin'."[19]

> Come senators, congressmen
> Please heed the call,
> Don't stand in the doorway
> Don't block up the hall.
> 5 For he that gets hurt
> Will be he who has stalled
> There's a battle
> Outside and its raging.
> It'll soon shake your windows
> 10 And rattle your walls
> For the times they are a-changin'.

The battle that Dylan sings about optimistically, or at least expectantly, is one that harbors change – and, we assume, change for the better. In Springsteen's song the battle is over and nothing has changed. If at all, the change has been for the worse. The "homecoming theme" and the romanticized remembrance of life before the battle, have given way to a broken life and broken dreams. The unattainable "you" of the song is not only the woman, but the utopian politics that Dylan sings of. "For You" is now saying that not only is the personal, political, but both the political and the personal are scenes of desperation and futility.[20]

---

[18] A floor was mentioned in the previous line – but that floor doesn't seem to have any specific place to which it is attached. The important part of that line is "that way you stretched out...".
[19] "The Times They Are A-Changin'," Warner Bros. Inc. (1963, 1964).
[20] Recognizing this political intertext reframes some earlier lines that I did not quote. Lines such as: "Wounded deep in battle," and "get your carpetbaggers off my back," whose political resonances are highlighted.

Boyarin, in *Intertextuality and the Reading of Midrash*, argues that intertextuality is an integral part of the midrashic reading practice.[21] The next text example will support this claim and serve to further illuminate the intertextual relationship. The text is a midrashic comment (Genesis Rabbah 19:9) on the Garden of Eden story, specifically generated by Gen. 3:9: "The Lord God called out to the man and said to him, "Where are you?" (NJPS).

1. The Lord God called out to the man and said to him, "Where are you? (איכה)" (Gen. 3:9)
2. R. Abahu in the name of R.Hanina said: It is written, 'But they, to a man (כאדם), have transgressed the Covenant.' (Hosea 6:7)
3. [Read, rather] they, like the first man ("Adam"), (כאדם הראשון).
4. Just as I brought the first man into the Garden of Eden, and commanded him, and he transgressed my command,
5. and I sentenced him with banishment (שלוחין), and with driving out (גרושין), and I wailed over him "Alas!" (Lamentations 1:1).
6. I brought the first man into the Garden of Eden, for it is written "and He placed him in the garden of Eden." (Gen. 2:15)
7. and commanded him, [for it is written] "And the Lord God commanded the man." (2:17)
8. and he transgressed my command, [for it is written] "Did you eat of the tree from which I had forbidden you to eat?" (3:11)
9. And I sentenced him with banishment (שלוחין), [for it is written] "So the Lord God banished him from the Garden of Eden." (3:23)
10. And I sentenced him with driving out (גרושין), [for it is written] "He drove the man out." (3:24)
11. And I wailed over him *Eichah* [Lamentations], [Lamentations],[for it is written] "and [God] said to him 'where are you?'" – it is the same spelling as *Eichah* [the first mournful word of Lamentations].
12. So too with his [Adam's] children.
13. I brought them into the Land of Israel, and I commanded them, and they transgressed my commands, and I sentenced them with banishment (שלוחין), and with driving out (גרושין), and I wailed over them *Eichah* [Lamentations].
14. I brought them into the Land of Israel, [for it is written] "I brought you to this country of farm land..." (Jer. 2:7).
15. And I commanded them, [for it is written] "You shall command the Israelites..." (Exodus 27:20).
16. And they transgressed my commands, "All Israel has violated Your teaching..." (Dan. 9:11).

---

[21](Bloomington: Indiana University Press, 1990). Cf. *inter alia*: "...the fundamental moment of all of these midrashic forms is precisely the very cocitation of several verses. This analysis also makes clear the function of those midrashic texts which are *only* quotations strung together... . These would be, on my theory, the very ideal type of midrash." (29 and n.24) "...*all* of the generic patterns of midrash have this function of exposing creating intertextual hermeneutic relations between different biblical texts." (31)

Towards a Poetics of Sugyot *or Sugyaetics*

17. And I sentenced them with banishment (שלוחין), "Dismiss them from my presence and let them go forth." (Jer. 15:1)
18. And with driving out/divorce (גרושין), "I will drive them out of my house." (Hosea 9:15)
19. And I wailed over them *Eichah* [Lamentations], "Alas! Lonely sits [the city...]." (Lam. 1:1)[22]

The midrash is addressing two ungrammaticalities. One in the verse in Genesis, and the other in the verse in Hosea. The initial textual problem which generated the midrash seems to have been the effort to understand how God could be asking Adam "Where are you?" How could God not know where Adam was? The ultimate solution of the midrashist (11) is that God was not looking for Adam, he was lamenting for Adam. The midrashist gets from here to there by way of an intertextual reading practice.

The second ungrammaticality is the ambiguity of the word כאדם in the verse from Hosea (2). This ambiguity or ungrammaticality is reflected in the various translations. The translation above is rendered according to the NJPS. RSV has "But at Adam they transgressed the covenant." The LXX translates "as a man."[23] The midrashist "solves" both problems by reading intertextually. That is, by juxtaposing the two verses and letting their contexts be informed by, and inform each other.

Reading the Hosea verse as meaning "they, like the first man ("Adam"), (כאדם הראשון)," opens both narratives to a larger frame. They

---

[22]The translation is mine, the verse translations are NJPS. See ed. Theodor-Albeck, 178-9 for variants.

ויקרא ה' אלהים אל האדם ויאמר לו איכה. (בר' נ:ט)
א"ר אבהו בשם ר' יוסי בר' חנינא כתיב (הושע ו:ז) והמה כאדם עברו ברית.
המה כאדם הראשון.
מה אדם הראשון הכנסתיו לתוך גן עדן וצייתיו ועבר על צוויי,
ודנתי אותו בשלוחין ובגרושין, וקוננתי עליו איכה.   5
'הכנסתיו לתוך ג"ע,' שנאמר, ויניחהו בגן עדן. (דר' ב:טו)
'וצייתיו,' שנאמר, ויצו ה' אלהים על האדם. (בר' ב:ח)
'ועבר על הצווי,' שנאמר, המן העץ אשר צויתיך לבלתי אכל ממנו אכלת. (בר' נ:יא)
'ודנתי אותו בשלוחין,' שנאמר וישלחהו ה' אלהים מגן עדן. (בר' נ:כג)
'ודנתי אותו בגרושין,' דכתיב וינרש את האדם. (בר' נ:כד)   10
'קוננתי עליו איכה,' שנאמר ויקרא ה' אלהים אל האדם ויאמר לו אֶיְכָה. (בר' נ:ט)-אֵיכָה כתיב.
אף בניו-
הכנסתים לא"י וצייתים ועברו על הצווי ודנתי אותם בשלוחין ובגרושין וקוננתי עליהם איכה.
הכנסתים לא"י שנאמר (ירמיה ב) ואביא אתכם אל ארץ הכרמל.
צויתים שנאמר (שמות כו) ואתה תצוה את בני ישראל.   15
עברו על צווי שנאמר (דניאל ט) וכל ישראל עברו תורתך.
דנתי אותם בשלוחין שנאמר (ירמיה ט"ו) שלח מעל פני ויצאו.
דנתי אותם בגרושין שנאמר (הושע ח) מביתי אגרשם.
קוננתי עליהם איכה שנאמר (איכה א) איכה ישבה:

[23]*hōs anthrōpos.* The sense is "a mortal" as opposed to those who might attain *epignōsin theou* in the previous verse.

(the Israelites or Jews of Hosea) are enacting the narrative of Adam. At the same time, that narrative of origins acquires cosmic status. It is the ultimate repetition compulsion of the Jewish people. What is that original narrative?

4. Just as I brought the first man into the Garden of Eden, and commanded him, and he transgressed my command,
5. and I sentenced him with banishment (שלוחין), and with driving out (גרושין), and I wailed over him "Alas!" (Lamentations 1:1).

God brought Adam into the Garden of Eden, as God also brought the Jewish people into the Land of Israel. Adam transgressed the Covenant – God's commandment not to eat from the tree – as the Jewish people transgressed the commandments. Therefore God sent Adam out and banished him, as God also did to the Jewish people. God, then is not asking after Adam, God is lamenting Adam.

This last move (11) involves another intertextual reading. God is obviously not looking for Adam (as the midrashist has established by "common sense" and the Hosea verse). What then does איכה mean? The midrashist suggests an orthographic intertext. איכה is the first word of the Book of Lamentations, and its name in Rabbinic literature. In addition to naming the Book of Lamentations, the word איכה also has the iconic impact of mourning and exile. The impact of this intertextual reading is to understand the Eden story as the original exilic moment.[24]

This midrash points up the way in which intertextuality both transgresses and reinforces local contexts. While the intertext of Genesis 3:9, for the midrashist, is in Hosea – a seemingly unconnected text – the intertextual reading ultimately informs the meaning of the local context, the Eden story. Without a local context, there would be no sense that the original verse was ungrammatical. Once a local context is claimed, the textual universe of the specific text needs to be examined. While claiming a local context is not as great a problem for poetry or biblical literature, it is a major concern in studying *sugyot*.

Another result of this understanding of text is that reading is not merely a linear process. It is often fractured and interrupted by intertexts and by what might be called intratexts – or what Riffaterre refers to as a subtext. This is the repetition of certain images, phrases, symbols or signs

---

[24]There is another intertext, triggered by the repetition of שילוחין and גירושין, in lines 5 and 12, which strengthens the exilic connection. This is Deut. 24:1: וכתב לה ספר כריתות ונתן בידה ושלחה מביתו (...and he writes her a bill of divorcement, hands it to her, and sends her away from his house. NJPS) This verse is explicit in Jeremiah's and Isaiah's discussions of exile and, following them, midrashic discussions. See my own discussion of this intertext to the laws of divorce in the next chapter.

which call attention to themselves and serve as a "guide" to the reader in interpreting the text.[25] It is the ungrammaticalities in the text that often point to the subtext.[26] If we take the *sugya* we looked at in the last chapter (b Ketuboth 62b-63a) as an example, there were certain specific phrases whose repetition created the *sugya's* narrative subtext. The two most prominent ones were: "twelve years" (and by extension, "twelve") (ll. 30, 42, 51, 69, 70, 74, 75), and the phrases denoting the going to the Academy and the coming home to his wife (ll. 7, 18, 19, 30, 37, 40, 42, 43, 51, 52, 69, 70, 74, 75). All the actions in the *sugya* occur in relation to these phrases – and it is the repetition of these phrases that connects the reader from one to the next, and highlights the changes between one point and the next.

"Representation" and "Reality"

The idea that texts exist primarily in a textual universe also challenges assumptions that texts are "windows" into a historic "reality."[27] The personalities, institutions, objects and the relations between all of them are products of the texts, as much as (or more than) they are the found elements of a world which generates those texts. The text is more of a barrier between the reader and any world "behind" the text, than it is a window.[28] This is the main point of contention between the new and old historicists.

In *A History of the Jewish People*, a textbook of Jewish history, we read the following account in the chapter "The Jews in the Land of Israel (70-335 CE)," written by Shmuel Safrai a leading Israeli historian of the "old school."[29]

> The most prominent figure of the Jabneh era in the first third of the second century was R. Akiva ben Joseph. He was the son of poor parents and lived as a shepherd. Only as an adult did he begin to take an interest in the study of the Torah, to which he devoted himself while making a bare living from casual labor. In his interpretation of the Scriptures, in *aggadah* and in *halakhah* he always probed for the deeper meaning, on the assumption that the Torah does not "speak in the language of men." ...He was executed in the course of the persecution of Jewish leaders after the revolt. R.

---

[25]*Fictional Truth* 26-27.
[26]Ibid. 75-76.
[27]Cf. the discussion of this question in Chapter Four.
[28]"The hallmark of the 'linguistic revolution' of the twentieth century, from Saussure and Wittgenstein to contemporary literary theory, is the recognition that meaning is not simply something 'expressed' or 'reflected' in language: it is actually *produced*." Eagleton, *Literary Theory*, 60.
[29]Although this is a textbook, it is a summary of the work that Safrai published in many articles and in his book *Rabbi Akiva ben Joseph: His Life and Works* (Jerusalem: 1970). Safrai is standing in here for the "Old Historicists" in general.

> Akiva's confidence, steadfastness and fervor during his imprisonment, torture and execution made him the exemplar of one of the most harrowing and inspiring chapters of Jewish martyrology.[30]

Almost every line in this description is taken from a different source in Rabbinic literature.[31] Some of these sources are contradictory in many of their particulars.[32] The method of the "old historicists" was to attempt to extract a kernel of truth from among the many different stories, or to verify which of the versions was the correct one. This approach, however, ignores the literary nature of the sources. We saw in the previous chapter that the Akiva story in b Ket. is part of a highly edited *sugya*. (As is the similar, thought different story in b Ned.) Even the descriptions of Akiva's martyrdom appear in different, highly literary versions.

This is not to say that these stories are not in some way connected to "reality." It is not however a reality that is behind the text, but, rather, a cultural construction of the text. We saw in the previous chapter the way in which the Akiva story in b Ket. was part of the cultural construction of the study house, as a totally male domain – in which men even reproduced.

Daniel Boyarin has persuasively argued that while one can't learn the history of Akiva from the traditions about Akiva's martyrdom, one can learn about the way in which martyrdom was represented.[33] The most famous sources of "R. Akiva's confidence, steadfastness and fervor

---

[30](Cambridge, MA: Harvard University Press, 1976): 328.

[31]E.g.: "lived as a shepherd" – b Ket. 62b. "Only as an adult did he begin to take an interest in the study of the Torah," in b Ket. 62b and b Ned. 50 it seems that he was a young man – though no age is given), Abot deRabbi Nathan (ARN) 6 he is forty. "to which he devoted himself while making a bare living from casual labor," ARN 6.

[32]In the sources quoted in the previous note, he is a shepherd in Ket. and it is unclear what he did for a living before learning Torah in ARN and Ned. In Ket. and Ned. Akiva's wife has a role in his starting to study Torah, in ARN she is not mentioned, and he decides to study because of an entirely different reason. Some of the contradictions between the Akiva stories were already noted by the medieval commentaries who attempted to harmonize them. See Tosafot b Ket. 62b s.v. דהוה צניע ומעלי. Most of the Akiva traditions are brought together by Bialik-Ravnitzky, *Sefer Ha'aggada*, 178-183. "Akiva" never explicitly says the Torah does *not* speak in the language of man, and "he" is only, possibly, implicated in one of the disputes using that phrase.

[33]"המדרש והמעשה-על החקר ההיסטורי של ספרות חז"ל," in *Saul Lieberman Memorial Volume*, ed. Shamma Friedman (New York and Jerusalem: Jewish Theological Seminary of America, 1993): 114-116. התחיה שלי כאן היא, שאע"פ שאין אנו יכולים לשחזר מציאות מסוימת שמתוכה נאמרה דרשתו של ר' עקיבא, אנו יכולים לזהות בה רגע היסטורי מכריע בתולדות האידיאות של היהדות, היינו יצירת המושג של מות על קידוש השם כערך חיובי וביטוי לאהבת האדם בישראל לקונו. (115)

during his imprisonment, torture and execution..." (b Ber. 62b and p Sotah 5:7) mark a change in the representation of martyrdom. In the p Sotah text for the first time, martyrdom is a desidarata. Akiva at the moment of his death realizes how he is to fulfill the commandment to love God with all his soul. The authors of this text construct with this story a commandment to martyrdom, and note the passing to a new cultural understanding of martyrdom. The b Ket. story already takes this commandment to martyrdom for granted.

The distinction between representation and reality is especially important at sites that are at the center of cultural conflict. One of the most prominent of these is gender. Simone de Beauvoir's statement "One is not born a woman; one becomes one,"[34] generated a discussion which introduced a distinction between sex and gender into the analysis of the representations of men and women. In the classical formula: sex is to nature as gender is to culture. That is, while the physiological differences between men and women are in some sense, scientific fact, any statement beyond the basic physiological or biological description is a product of a specific cultural moment.[35] The impact of this on the analysis of texts, especially where gender issues are central, is significant. The relationship between text and the "reality" beyond that text is almost reversed. As Thomas Laqueur writes in his study of the representation of (physiological) sex in medical literature:

> Sex, like being human, is contextual. Attempts to isolate it from its discursive, socially determined milieu are as doomed to failure as the *philosophe*'s search for a truly wild child or the modern anthropologist's efforts to filter out the cultural so as to leave a residue of essential humanity. ...the private enclosed stable body that seems to lie at the basis of modern notions of sexual difference is also the product of particular, historical, cultural moments. It too like opposite sexes, comes into and out of focus. ... *Not only do attitudes toward sexual difference "generate and structure literary texts;" texts generate sexual difference.* (emphasis added)[36]

---

[34]*The Second Sex*, trans. E. M. Parshley (New York: Vintage, 1973): 301. Quoted in Toril Moi, *Sexual/Textual Politics: Feminist Literary Theory* (London: Methuen & Co., 1985): 92.

[35]In a more explicitly political formulation, and in an anthropological context: "Just as we have no apparent cause to look for physiological facts when we attempt to understand the more familiar inequalities in human social life – such things as leadership, racial prejudice, prestige, or social class – so to it seems that we would do well to think of biological sex, like biological race, as an excuse rather than a cause for any sexism we observe." M. Z. Rosaldo, "The Use and Abuse of Anthropology: Reflections on Feminism and Cross-cultural Understanding," *Signs: Journal of Women in Culture and Society*, 5,3 (1980): 400.

[36]*Making Sex: Body and Gender From the Greeks to Freud* (Cambridge, Massachusetts: Harvard University Press, 1990): 17.

As Laqueur notes, even something as seemingly stable and natural as the modern notion of body is actually a result of the cultural and textual practices of a specific historical moment. This is not to deny that there is a body that can be empirically discovered. Rather it is to say that what is said about that body is part of the political and cultural discourse of that specific moment.[37] This is also, and, perhaps, even more so the case when discussing the differences *between* bodies.

Since gender is a *product* of cultural practices, among which are the production of texts, questions about "the status of women" in Rabbinic literature are misplaced.[38] These questions about the status of women suppose that an entity called "women" exists independently of the texts, identical to itself through time. The questions that I will ask have to do with the *construction* of gender and gender differences in these texts. That is, how are men and women *represented* in these texts – by themselves and in relation to each other – without assuming that these representations are grounded in a historical "reality."

This also entails the employment of a hermeneutics of suspicion. Texts written by a specific group of elite males (the Rabbinic Class) cannot be taken at face value when they describe the experiences, or activities of women, and even men who are not of the Rabbinic Class. The way in which those experiences are framed must be interrogated, and problematized, that is, questions must be raised about the transparency of their cultural assumptions.

Narrative

Narrative is the organization of events over a spectrum of time. It denotes a movement from the previous moment to the present moment

---

[37]Cf. Jonathan Z. Smith's remarks on the politics of difference in zoology in "What a Difference a Difference Makes," in Jacob Neusner and Ernest S. Frerichs eds., *"To See Ourselves as Others See Us: Christians, Jews, "Others" in Late Antiquity* (Chico, California: Scholars Press, 1985): "Difference is... most often, something in which one has a stake."(4) "Note that such taxonomic distinctions [i.e. 'parasitism', 'benefit', 'symbiosis', 'commensalism'], by virtue of their concern for matters of association, are explicitly political. The definitions are based on hierarchical distinctions of subordination and superordination, on mapping structures of benefits and reciprocity." (9) "A 'theory of the other' must take the form of a relational theory of reciprocity. 'Otherness,' whether of Scotsmen or lice, is a preeminently political category." (10)

[38]For a cogent critique of the "status of women in Rabbinic literature" type of studies see Miriam Beth Peskowitz, "'The Work of Her Hands': Gendering Everyday Life in Roman-Period Judaism in Palestine (70-250 CE), Using Textile Production as a Case," (Ph.D. diss., Duke University, 1993), 18-38.

to the coming moment.³⁹ It is this "sense of an Ending,"⁴⁰ or seemingly human tendency towards concordance, or organization along a time spectrum that moves one to speak of *sugya* as narrative in this widest sense of the term.⁴¹ The narrative of the *sugya* (as opposed to narrative in which the *sugya* is embedded, or the narratives it generates) is the movement from one line or phrase to another in the *sugya*. It is not the movement that is urged by the explicit rhetoric of the *sugya* – question, answer, prooftext, etc. – but, rather, the movement that is marked by ungrammaticalities, and lexical or symbolic similarities.⁴² The narrative of the *sugya* is not its linear reading.⁴³

---

³⁹"...what is ultimately at stake in the case of the structural identity of the narrative function as well as in that of the truth claim of every narrative work, is the temporal character of human experience." Paul Ricoeur, *Time and Narrative, Vol. 1*, trans. Kathleen McLaughlin and David Pellauer (Chicago: The University of Chicago Press, 1984): 3.

⁴⁰The phrase is, of course, taken from Frank Kermode's book of the same name *The Sense of an Ending: Studies in the Theory of Fiction*, (London: Oxford University Press, 1967). Cf. his remark there: "Men, like poets, rush 'into the middest,' *in medias res* , when they are born; they also die *in mediis rebus*, and to make sense of their span they need fictive concords with origins and ends, such as give meaning to lives and to poems."

⁴¹Steven Fraade has written of the importance of temporality, and especially retrospection and prospection in the *narrative structure* of Sifre Deuteronomy, a "nonnarrative" text. His discussion of plot and polyphony, the tension between narrative and linearity, was influential in my thinking about narrative in *sugyot*. See Steven Fraade, *From Tradition To Commentary: Torah and Its Interpretation in the Midrash Sifre to Deuteronomy* (Albany: SUNY Press, 1991): 124-127 and n. 10. See also the question at the end of the chapter: "Might the same approach be applied not only to other texts of legal and nonlegal scriptural commentary (or midrash), but also to the pedagogic discourse of the mainly nonexegetical legal digest of the Mishnah, and in turn to its own dialogical commentaries of the two Talmuds." 164.

⁴²This is very similar to, and is influenced by Riffaterre's understanding of subtext. The major difference is that a *sugya* is much smaller than a novel, and therefore the *su*btext will often break the surface. See our discussion above. Boyarin has shown how Riffattere's understanding of narrative elucidates what Boyarin refers to as "syntagmatic" midrashim. *Intertextuality and the Reading of Midrash*, 29-31.

⁴³When I say that the narrative of a *sugya* is the movement from *x* to *y* to *z*, I am attributing that narrative to the "implied author." By invoking the "implied author" of narratology, I avoid some of the problems of having to divine the psychology of the author/editor. It is in essence a reification of the meaning of this *sugya* in this context. Cf. "...while the flesh and blood author is subject to the vicissitudes of real life, the implied author of a particular work is conceived as a stable entity, ideally consistent with itself within the work." Shlomith Rimmon-Kenan, *Narrative Fiction: Contemporary Poetics* (London and New York: Methuen, 1983): 87. See also Ricoeur's discussion of the implied author in *Time and*

The narrative(s) in which the *sugya* is embedded is the story which a culture tells, within which specific legal moments "make sense." As Robert Cover has written, "every prescription is insistent in its demand to be located in discourse – to be supplied with history and destiny, beginning and end, explanation and purpose."[44]

Law is similar to narrative in that it organizes actions thereby giving them meaning as a whole. Actions are given meaning by falling within one another set of laws, or, more accurately, legal meanings. In a contemporary setting, the structurally identical act of eating matzoh means radically different things depending on who is eating it and when – that is, within what context of legal signification does the act fall. If any person eats matzoh during the evening of a day which is not religiously marked, the act is Halakhically/legally insignificant. If that act is done on the first night of Passover, and if the person is Jewish, the act acquires a Halakhic/legal significance – and as a result, a positive valence within this context. If the person is Jewish and the eating occurs on the night of Yom Kippur, the act acquires a different Halakhic/legal significance, and a negative moral valence amongst those who feel bound by the Halakhah. It might also be an act of protest against the system or authority of Halakhah, again, though, this is only intelligible within the signifying context of the Halakhah.[45] This latter holds true also for all acts of civil disobedience.

A legal action, that is, an act which falls within the frame of a system of law, only "means" or "signifies" within that system. The meaning is not inherent in the act, but in the community which tells specific stories about the act. The same legal act, then, can "mean" differently in different communities.[46] In order then to understand a "legal"

Narrative, Vol. 3, trans. Kathleen McLaughlin and David Pellauer (Chicago: The University of Chicago Press, 1988): 160-166.

[44] Robert Cover, "Nomos and Narrative" in *Narrative, Violence, and the Law: The Essays of Robert Cover*, Edited by Martha Minow, Michael Ryan, and Austin Sarat, (The University of Michigan Press, Ann Arbor, 1992): 96. My thinking about law and narrative is totally indebted to Cover's work, even when I disagree with him on particulars.

[45] "... the capacity of law to imbue action with significance is not limited to resistance or disobedience. Law is a resource in signification that enables us to submit, rejoice, struggle, pervert, mock, disgrace, humiliate, or dignify." "Nomos and Narrative," 100.

[46] "All Americans share a national text in the first or thirteenth or fourteenth amendment, but we do not share an authoritative narrative regarding its significance. And even were we to share some single authoritative account of the framing of the text – even if we had a national history declared by law to be authoritative – we could not share the same account relating each of us as an individual to that history. Some of us would claim Frederick Douglass as a father, some Abraham Lincoln, and some Jefferson Davis. Choosing ancestry is a serious

discussion, one needs to understand the larger and smaller narratives that inform the actions being discussed or debated. By larger narratives I refer to narratives of origins, which also account for the authority of the specific system of law. By smaller narratives I mean those that are told about the mundane, and inform the quotidian (from birth to taxes).

Cover has argued further that the spectrum around which law organizes actions is, as with narrative, time. The endpoint for law is an ideal future and law is the bridge to that future. However, the materials for that bridge emerge from the cultural discussion.

> I have argued not only that the nature of law is a bridge to the future, but also that each community builds its bridges with the materials of sacred narrative that take as their subject much more than what is commonly conceived as the "legal."[47]

A prerequisite to understanding the "legal" discussion, is understanding the community's "nomos" – "narratives, experiences, and visions to which the norm articulated is the right response." Therefore, in analyzing any specific *sugya*, I attempt to understand the larger and smaller narratives in which the *sugya* is embedded. This entails answering the question: "What kind of story would need to be told by those who would feel implicated in the *sugya*, in order for the assumptions, norms and demands of the *sugya* to make sense?"[48]

Sugya

All this leads to the importance of starting any understanding of Talmud with the *sugya*. This, of course is not a new supposition. Most Talmud scholars speak of interpreting the *sugya*. However, the theoretical concerns that we raised in the earlier part of this chapter bring into sharp relief the problem of defining the parameters of a *sugya*. Since

---

business with major implications. Thus, the narrative strand integrating who we are and what we stand for with the patterns of precept would differ even were we to possess a canonical narrative text.

The conclusion emanating from this state of affairs is simple and very disturbing: there is a radical dichotomy between the social organization of law as power and the organization of law as meaning." "*Nomos* and Narrative," 112.

[47] Robert Cover "The Folktales of Justice: Tales of Jurisdiction," in *Narrative, Violence, and the Law: The Essays of Robert Cover*, Edited by Martha Minow, Michael Ryan, and Austin Sarat (Ann Arbor: The University of Michigan Press, 1992): 177.

[48] "To state, as I have done, that the problem is one of too much law is to acknowledge the nomic integrity of each of the communities that have generated principles and precepts. It is to posit that *each* 'community of interpretation' that has achieved 'law' has its own *nomos* – narratives, experiences, and visions to which the norm articulated is the right response." "*Nomos* and Narrative," 141.

context is of such paramount importance to reading, one is faced with the problem of stabilizing that context to at least some degree. For this reason I will be using the following working definition of *sugya*:

> A sugya is the primary context of all its parts-attributed and unattributed statements, aggadot, maasim, prooftexts, et al. Its parameters are established both structurally or intratextually, and thematically.

By this definition, though some *sugyot* might be edited from earlier materials, it is unhelpful to speak of the parts of a *sugya* separated from the whole. Though a part of a *sugya* might appear in two different *sugyot*, this doesn't mean that it has a meaning independent of either. Rather, as shown in the previous chapter with regards to the Akiva story in b Ket. and b Ned., a part of a *sugya* could have two different meanings. Therefore I speak of a unit (aggadah, attributed statement, etc.) in a specific *sugya* – that is the "primary context." That unit could have another primary context. In that other primary context it would likely mean something else.

When I speak of a *sugya* it is of the whole that I speak. The parameters of that whole are only seen on the second reading. It is only after I read through and discern the structural, intratextual and thematic elements that I can argue that I have a *sugya*. Though this definition lays itself open to charges of circularity,[49] there is no better option. As I said above, there is no *objective sugya*, there is only *this sugya in this context*. At the same time this definition of a *sugya* is public.[50] The reasons for claiming that the parameters of a *sugya* are *a* and *b*, rather than *y* and *z*, are neither random, nor totally subjective. They are open and accessible to interrogation. It is with these qualifications that I would say that *sugya x says/means y*.[51]

---

[49]Though no more circular than any other attempts at defining *sugya*. For example, the following is Avraham Weiss' definition, mentioned above in Chapter II:
> We give the name *sugya* to any Talmudic give and take, long or short, which is concerned with any subject, as long as it comprises a complete unit in itself. (*The Talmud in its Development*, 3.)

Weiss is not alone in assuming that both "a subject" and "a complete unit" are self-explanatory. He provides no way of determining when a unit or a subject ends.

[50]I am using "public" here as opposed to the Wittgenstinean "private language."

[51]See above note 43.

Praxis

As a first step in a sugyaetic analysis I arrange the statements or lines of the *sugya* graphically.[52] Borrowing freely from Shamma Friedman's criteria, without accepting his historicist assumptions, I work in from the margin. That is, "Tannaitic" material is at the margin, "Amoraic" material is one tab in, and "Stammaitic" material two tabs in.[53] This is done so as to be able to easily pick out recurrent phrases, structures, etc. It should also be stressed that this is the first step in the interpretation, and not a value-neutral act. As Friedman says:

> Any division of the *sugya* is an interpretation, and, not infrequently, there is room for more than one interpretation.[54]

There are then three critical frameworks, or modes of analysis that I employ in reading the sugya. A rhetorical literary analysis will ask the question, following Stanley Fish, "What do parts of the *sugya* do?"

> What makes problematical sense as a statement makes perfect sense as a strategy, as an action made upon a reader rather than as a container from which a reader extracts a message.[55]

This question will be asked especially at sites of conflicted interpretation, that is at those points in the *sugya* when "ambiguities" or "ungrammaticalities" in the text are rendered more acute, rather than ameliorated by the interpretive tradition.[56] The answer, to the question of the rhetorical function of moments in the *sugya*, will be in the ways that

---

[52] The text of all the *sugyot* in the next two chapters is based on the Vilna edition. Changes from the Vilna text are noted in the apparatus and in the body of the work. For the variants I relied on M. S. Feldblum, דקדוקי הסופרים השלם, double checking with the MSS (when possible) whenever a variant was found which significantly affected the meaning of the text.

[53] See the discussion of Friedman's method above, Chapter II part 3. See, too, Friedman's own discussion of his method, and a concise history of the use of graphic devices to differentiate the layers of a *sugya* in "A Critical Study of *Yevamot* X with a Methodological Introduction," 313-319.

[54] "A Critical Study of *Yevamot* X with a Methodological Introduction," 316.

[55] *Is There a Text in This Class?: The Authority of Interpretive Communities* (Cambridge, MA: Harvard University Press, 1980): 23.

[56] "If for example, there is a continuing debate over whether Marlowe should or should not have lied at the end of *Heart of Darkness*, I will interpret the debate as evidence of the difficulty readers experience when the novel asks them to render judgment....In short, critical controversies become disguised reports of what readers uniformly do...." Ibid., 178. The evidence of the continuing interpretive debate in Talmud can usually be found in Rashi and Tosafot, the traditional sidebars to the Talmud from the first printed edition (and even in some of the earlier MSS).

one or another rhetorical move informs the way in which one subsequently reads the *sugya*.[57]

A structural literary analysis will examine the relationships between parts of the *sugya*, in an attempt to move beyond the rhetoric of the linear argument. This type of analysis is akin to what Barthes refers to as "reading the text as if it had already been read."

> ...rereading is here suggested at the outset, ...rereading draws the text out of its internal chronology ("this happens *before* or *after* that")... it contests the claim which would have us believe that the first reading is a primary, naïve, phenomenal reading which we will only, afterwards have to "explicate," to intellectualize...[58]

Noting the structural similarities of the parts[59] of the *sugya* allows one to recognize connections between narrative strands that are not those of the explicit question, answer, prooftext progression.

As a reading practice, I will first analyze the *sugya* line by line. This close reading of the linear argument will point to the places where a simple and seemingly straightforward reading falters. These ungrammaticalities are what will let me move away from reading according to the explicit rhetorical demands of the text (i.e. question, answer, prooftext, etc.). On a second reading I will argue that there is a structure to the *sugya* independent of its linear flow.

Once the parameters of the *sugya*, and a local reading have been completed, an intertextual literary analysis will examine the way in which this sugya is informed by other texts, or cultural constructs, or presupposes those constructions. It is at this point that I can answer the question posed above: "What kind of story would need to be told by those who would feel implicated in the *sugya*, in order for the assumptions, norms and demands of the *sugya* to make sense?"

In the final two chapters of this dissertation I will offer a sugyaetic analysis of two *sugyot* from b Gittin. Both *sugyot* deal with Halakhic issues. The issues they deal with are very different though they intersect

---

[57]This is of course very different from classical rhetorical analysis whose goal is to identify rhetorical forms. See e.g. Henry A. Fischel, "The Uses of Sorites (*Climax, Gradatio*) in the Tannaitic Period," *HUCA*, 44 (1973): 119: "It is the purpose of this article to suggest that the tannaitic and New Testament instances reflect the fashionableness, variety, structure, and function which the sorite possessed in Greco-Roman rhetoric and rhetorical literature of this period and are, with some exceptions, dependent upon the Greco-Roman models."

[58]Roland Barthes, *S/Z: An Essay*, trans. Richard Miller (New York: Hill and Wang, 1974): 15-16.

[59]The "parts" that I refer to are types of comment (e.g. לא שנו, איכא דאמרי, etc.), stories (*ma'asim* brought ostensibly for "legal" purposes, and "sage stories" or other Aggadot), Midrashim, etc.

in what I think are interesting ways. The purpose of the readings will be both as test cases for this methodology, and to contribute to a broader discussion of the construction of gender in Rabbinic literature. I also hope to start a discussion about the impact of the midrashic story of the divorce of God and Israel on the Halakhic discussions of divorce.

6

Framing Women/Constructing Exile: b Gittin 34b-35b

The *sugya* that I present in this chapter (b Gittin 34b-35a) deals with a widow who attempts to collect her *ketubah* payment from the estate of the orphans of her husband. Not reading the sugya according to the demands of its own rhetoric, but rather employing a *sugyaetic* analysis, I discern two competing narrative strands. One strand consists of *lo shanu* ("this rule applies only...") statements, the apodictic statements of Rav and Shmuel. The other strand consists of *ma'asim*.[1] The *stam* (the anonymous layer of the sugya) is the site of the tensions between these differing interpretations.

The two strands exhibit conflicting ideas about the fragility of authority. In the *ma'asim*, the rabbis are reticent to move outside the limitations of an authoritative tradition; women endanger the institutions of law, and men are the law's conservative guardians. Within the *lo shanu* statements, the rabbis are freer to interpret the law in an innovative manner. This whole discussion is embedded in the cultural narrative of exile.

I will read the *sugya* closely, attending to its ungrammaticalities, recurrent phrases, forms, and tropes. Exploiting these, I will place the *sugya* in a larger intertextual web – which informs some of the *sugya's* tensions. For heuristic purposes which will become clear as the reading progresses, I start this reading at the second unit of the *sugya*, and then return to the first unit which serves, in some ways, as a frame or title.

---

[1] A *ma'aseh* is a story or a precedent, but it is also defined by a specific form, i.e. short verbal phrases mostly connected by conjunctions. The three *ma'asim* in our *sugya* are lines 17-24; 40-44; 46-54.

The Sugya

Bavli Gittin 34b-35b[2]

Mishnah

3. A widow may not collect [her *Ketubah*] from the property of orphans save on taking an oath.
4. They refrained from imposing an oath on her.
5. Rabban Shimon ben Gamaliel made a regulation that she should vow to the orphans any [vow] they wish to impose on her, and [then] recover her Ketubah.

Gemara

8. Why is this rule [about an oath] laid down with reference to a widow, seeing that it applies to everybody?
9. Since it is an established rule that "one who seeks to recover payment from the property of orphans cannot recover save on taking an oath."
10. There is a special reason for the mention of a widow.
11. For it might occur to you to say, "Because of her favor (משום חינא) our rabbis were lenient towards her,"
12. We are told [therefore that this is not so].

14. **They refrained from imposing an oath on her.**
15. What was the reason [of this refusal]? Shall we say it is because of that which is attributed to R. Kahana?
16. For R. Kahana said, and others say that R. Yehudah said in the name of Rab:
17. A *ma'aseh* of a certain man in a year of drought,
18. who deposited a *dinar* of gold with a widow.
19. She put it in a jar of flour,
20. and she baked it in a loaf, and gave it to a poor person.
21. In time, the owner of the *dinar* came and said to her, "Give me my *dinar*."
22. She said to him: "May the poison of death have benefit from one of the sons of this woman if I have derived any benefit for myself from your *dinar*.
23. They said: Not many days passed before one of her sons died.
24. When the Sages heard of the incident they remarked: If such is the fate of one who swears truly, so much the more so for one who swears falsely.
25. What was the reason [that she was punished]? Because she had derived advantage from the place of the *dinar*.
26. And what does it mean "one who swears truly"? – As one who swears truly.

---

[2]The Hebrew and Aramaic text is found in Appendix IV. The line numbering is the same in both original and translation. The translation is based on the Soncino translation, which I have changed when I saw a need in order to suit the literary needs of the *sugya*.

27	If that is the reason [why the Rabbis refrained from imposing an oath], why is this rule laid down with reference to a widow; it should apply to a divorced woman also. Why has
28	R. Zera said in the name of Samuel: This rule applies only to a widow, but to a divorced woman an oath is administered.
29	There is a special reason in the case of a widow, because she finds a justification for herself on account of the trouble she has taken on behalf of the orphans.
30	
31	R. Yehudah said in the name of R. Yirmiah b. Abba:
32	Rab and Samuel both stated: this rule applied only [to an oath imposed] in the *Beth Din*, but outside the *Beth Din* an oath may be imposed on a widow.
33	Is this so? Is it not a fact that Rab would not enforce payment of a *ketubah* [by orphans] to a widow?
34	This is a difficulty. This is the version given in Sura. This is the version given in Nehardea:
35	Said R. Yehudah in the name of Samuel: This rule applied only [to an oath imposed] in the *Beth din*, but outside the *Beth din* an oath may be imposed on a widow.
36	And Rab said: Even outside the *Beth din* an oath may not be imposed on her.
37	Rab is following his own reasoning, for Rab would not enforce payment of a *ketubah* to a widow.
38	Why did he not make her take a vow and so let her recover? In the time of Rab, vows were treated lightly.
39	
40	A certain woman came before R. Huna [to enforce payment of her *ketubah*].
41	He said to her: "What can I do for you for Rab would not enforce payment of a *ketubah* to a widow?"
42	She said to him: Is not the only reason the fear that perhaps I have already received part of my *ketubah*?
43	By the Lord of Hosts [I swear that] I have not received anything from my *ketubah*.
44	R. Huna said: Rab admits [that we enforce payment] for one who jumps forward [and takes the oath of her own accord].
45	
46	A certain woman came before Rabbah son of R. Huna [to enforce payment of her *ketubah*].
47	He said to her: "What can I do for you for Rab would not enforce payment of a *ketubah* to a widow,
48	and my father would also not enforce payment of a *ketubah* to a widow?"
49	She said to him: At least grant me maintenance.
50	He said: You are not entitled to maintenance either,
51	since R. Yehudah has said in the name of Samuel: If a woman claims her *ketubah* in the *Beth din*, she has no [claim to] maintenance.
52	She said to him: Turn his seat over! He gives me [the worst of] both authorities.
53	They turned his seat over and put it straight again,

54	but even so he did not escape an illness.
55	
56	Yehudah said to R. Yirmiah Bira'ah:
57	Impose a vow on her in the *Beth din*, and administer an oath to her outside the *Beth din*, and see that the report reaches my ears,
58	since I desire to make this a precedent.
59	
60	[The text above stated:]
61	R. Zera said in the name of Samuel: This rule applies only to a widow, but to a divorced woman an oath is administered.
62	Cannot then a divorced woman recover her *ketubah* on [merely] making a vow? Was not [a communication] sent from there:
63	"So-and-so the daughter of So-and so received a *Get* from the hand of Aha b. Hedia who is also known as Ayah Mari,
64	and took vow binding herself to abstain from all produce whatsoever if she should be found to have received of her *ketubah* anything besides
65	a blanket, a book of the Psalms, a copy of Job and a much worn copy of Proverbs,
66	and we valued them at five *maneh*. When she presents herself to you, empower her to collect the rest."
67	R. Ashi said: The *Get* in that case was a *Get* of a levirate marriage.

Reading The Sugya

The Mishnah's declaration "they refrained from imposing an oath on her" (4), can actually be interpreted in two ways. Either passively as "they were restrained from administering... [by some unidentified outside force]," or actively as "they stopped (or no longer) administered...." The initial question of the sugya (15) assumes the latter.[3] It is this assumption which frames the subsequent *ma'asim* as an answer to a question.

The question is: what brought the Rabbis to stop administering the oath to widows? The answer is: swearing women are dangerous. What is the connection between the *ma'aseh* and the Mishnaic proclamation? A glance at the Palestinian Talmud's discussion of our Mishnah seems to supply an etiology of the idea. P Git. begins its *sugya* with the following midrash:

> At first the women would swear falsely and bury their sons, as it says: to no purpose did I smite your sons (Jer. 2:30).[4]

---

[3] A reading of the Mishnah in the context of M. Gittin 4 might just as easily support the passive reading. The first Mishnahs are all dealing with responses to "historical" events in the form a) ruling; b) occurrence which no longer allowed for ruling to occur; c) *takanah*

[4] בראשונה היו נשבעות לשקר וקוברות את בניהם שנאמר (ירמיה ב) לשוא הכיתי את בניכם.

Framing Women/Constructing Exile

The midrashic rereading of "to no purpose " (לשוא[5]) as "because of oaths of no purpose (שבועות שוא)" is the kernel[6] of the three *ma'asim* in b. Gittin 35a. All the characters that will participate in all the *ma'asim* are already present in this one line: a) the women; b) the false oaths; c) the male victims. These parts become full blown characters in the *ma'aseh*. That this idea of women killing by oath is a prominent force in our sugya, is evidenced by its relationship not only to the first *ma'aseh* but also to the third (46-54). This might be graphically demonstrated as follows:

Women would swear	–> A widow (18)	–> A certain woman came...(46)
and bury	–>May the poison of death ...(22)	–>turn his seat over (52)
their sons	–>one of her sons (23)	–>Rabba son of R. Huna (46/54)[7]

While this might explain the "origin" of the idea (or possibly the trope) of dangerous swearing women, the unattributed (or stammaitic) discussion following the first *ma'aseh* (25-29) points out clearly that its connection with our Mishnah is tenuous at best. Sages' statement in line 24 clears the widow of any charge of wrongdoing. This charge however is brought back and strengthened in lines 25-29.[8] The impact of line 29

The full verse reads as follows (NJPS): To no purpose did I smite your children, they would not accept correction. Your sword has devoured your prophets like a raving lion.

[5]This is a very interesting rereading of the whole verse which continues: אכלה חרבכם נביאיכם כאריה משחית מוסר לא לקחו. The midrash shifts the blame from the people as a whole to women who are liars; and from the death as a punishment enacted by God, to the act of the women (note the *action* taken by each woman accompanying the oath). This is an interesting take on " midrashim of comfort" (מדרשי נחמה).

[6]In Frank Kermode's understanding of "structural" thinking there is a "fabula" which underlies a narrative. In this fabula, all the characters of the narrative are present as "functions". In this way Kermode compares the relation between the betrayal story in Mark and in the other synoptics. The relationship here is not one of dependence or influence in the traditional sense. Cf. Frank Kermode, *The Genesis Of Secrecy: On the Interpretation of Narrative* (Harvard University Press, Cambridge, MA, 1 97g) 78ff esp. 83. Daniel Boyarin has already brought Kermode into the discussion of the relationship of *mashal* and biblical text in Midrash. "...in the midrash text which includes the Written Torah story, the mashal, and the narrative filling which the midrash provides, the mashal itself (the schematic story) is the (necessarily synchronic) *fabula* underlying the narrative elaboration of the biblical text together with its midrashic expansion." *Intertextuality and the Reading of Midrash* (Bloomington: Indiana University Press, 1990): 85.

[7]

<–נשבעות	<– אלמנה (18)	ההיא דאתאי (46)
<–וקוברות	<– יונה סם המות (22)	הפכוה לכורסיה (52)
<–את בניהם	<– אחד מבניה (23)	רבה בר רב הונא (46/54)

[8]Line 27 actually reprises line 8, as if starting over again.

("...because she finds a justification for herself...") is to a large extent generated by the idea of "One who *might* be said to have sworn truly," (26) that is, the widow has a problem with truth.

Sugyaetics

I claimed in the last chapter that the linear progression of a *sugya* is not its defining characteristic. The textuality of the *sugya*, its existence in a literary world and the literary connections that tie it to that world (i.e. its web), pull the reader in many different directions. I want to pursue this a bit, in two different directions. First, by way of a structural literary analysis or an analysis of the internal relationships of the "parts" of the *sugya*. Second, by way of an intertextual literary analysis or an analysis of the relationship between the sugya and other texts, (i.e. the intertexts of the *sugya*).

There are two identifiable types of statements that are seemingly the raw materials of this *sugya*. One is the *ma'aseh,* and the other is the *lo shanu* (this rule applies only...).[9] There are three of each type, though two of the *lo shanu* comments are ostensibly "variants" of the same comment. The relationship between two of the *ma'asim* has already been mentioned above in passing. It would be worth pointing out the extent of the structural and linguistic similarities between all three *ma'asim*. First the first and the third:

I a) A *ma'aseh* of a certain man in a year of drought, who deposited a *dinar* of gold with a widow.
   b) She put it in a jar of flour, and she baked it in a loaf, and gave it to a poor person.
   c) In course of time the owner of the *dinar* returned and said to her, "Give me my *dinar*."
   d) She said to him: "May the poison of death have benefit from one of the sons of this woman if I have derived any benefit for myself from your *dinar*."
   e) They said: Not many days passed before one of her sons died.

III a) A certain woman came before Rabba son of R. Huna [to enforce payment of her *ketubah*].

---

[9]Cf. Shamma Friedman, "A Critical Study of *yevamot* X with a Methodological Introduction," in H.Z. Dimitrovski ed. *Texts and Studies: Analecta Judaica*, vol. 1 (New York: Jewish Theological Seminary of America, 1978): 331-339. In his comments on the second and third *sugyot*, Friedman uses the identification of the לא שנו statements there, to further the understanding of the redaction of the *sugya*. His method is to distinguish between the "original" and later layers of *sugyot* by form critical methods. See my discussion of Friedman's method in Chapter II Part 3, above.

Framing Women/Constructing Exile

b) He said to her: "What can I do for you for Rab would not enforce payment of a *ketubah* to a widow, and my father would also not enforce payment of a *ketubah* to a widow?"
c) She said to him: <u>Give me maintenance</u>.
He said: You are not entitled to maintenance either,
since R. Yehudah has said in the name of Samuel: If a woman claims her *ketubah* in the Beth din, she has no [claim to] maintenance.
d) She said to him: <u>Turn his seat over!</u> He gives me [the worst of] both authorities.
e) They turned his seat over and put it straight again, <u>but even so he did not escape an illness</u>.[10]

The structural similarities between I and III are:

b) legitimate grounds for compensation (i.e. *the story*)
c) demand for compensation
d) introduction of danger[11] as a result of contradictory "legitimate" claims
e) dangerous outcome[12]

In addition both involve a man and a woman – (a) – but despite the changing of some parts of their roles, it is the woman who inflicts harm[13] through her words.

10

I (a) מעשה באדם אחד בשני בצורת, שהפקיד דינר זהב אצל <u>אלמנה</u>
(b) והניחתו בכד של קמח, ואפאתו בפת, ונתנתו לעני
(c) לימים, בא בעל הדינר ואמר לה, <u>תני לי דינרי</u>.
(d) אמרה ליה, <u>יצה סם המות</u> באחד מבניה של אותה אשה אם נהניתי מדינרך כלום.
(e) אמרו, לא היו ימים מועטין <u>עד שמת אחד מבניה</u>.

III (a) <u>ההיא דאתאי</u> לקמיה דרבה בר רב הונא.
(b) אמר לה, מאי אעביד ליך? דרב לא מגבי כתובה לארמלתא, ואבא מרי לא מגבי כתובה לארמלתא.
(c) אמרה ליה, <u>הב לי מזוני</u>.
אמר לה, מזוני נמי לית ליך.
דאמר רב יהודה אמר שמואל, התובעת כתובתה בב"ד אין לה מזונות.
(d) אמרה ליה, <u>הפכוה לכורסיה</u>! כבי תרי עבדא לי.
(e) הפכוה לכורסיה, ותרצוה. <u>ואפילו הכי לא איפרק מחולשא</u>.

[11]On the overturning of the chair as sign of conflict and perceived assault on the Rabbinic authority in a similar context, see PT Yebamoth 15:4 (15a). The anonymous voice records that in response to a radical ruling of Rav (in an Agunah situation) "the staff was burnt, and the chair was burnt." ערקתא יקד וספסלה יקד. See, too, b Ketubot 62b where the inadvertent turning over of Yehuda son of R. Ḥiyya's bed by his father-in-law, causes Yehuda's death.
[12]Cf. the reading of Rabbi Menahem Hame'iri, who cites this last line as a proof that Rabbah b. R. Hunah's opinion was not accepted since he was punished. This reading is generated by Mei'ri's obvious empathy with the woman's claim of unfairness. *Bet Habehfrah 'almasechet Giffin* (Jerusalem: 1977) 149-150.
[13]That the connection between the two ma'asim had been perceived at an early date is indirectly testified to by the printed editions of the first *ma'aseh*. Line 21 (or c) in the printed editions reads: הב לי דינרי in Aramaic. Most of the MSS have

The relationship between the second and third (46-54) *ma'asim* is also obvious. Both have the same introduction (40 & 46), and the same opening line of dialogue. The only differences are those that are due to the fact that they are portrayed as occurring one generation after another.[14] In both *ma'asim* this opening is followed by a confrontation. In the second *ma'aseh* the woman gets what she demands, and there is no apparent danger to the men. The context of the other two *ma'asim*[15] imply, however, that there is a danger to this one too. The woman's response in the second *ma'aseh* (1. 43) recalls the woman's response in the first *ma'aseh* (1. 22). The implication of danger is further supported by the use of the phrase חי ה' צבאות[16] by the woman.[17] The danger is that of the

---

the Hebrew version (see the apparatus). However, it seems to me that the Aramaic represents a reading of the *sugya* which understood a connection between the two *ma'asim*.

[14] This fact in itself is significant and will be dealt with later.

[15] And the lexical connections. In addition to those just mentioned there is of course line 43: חי ה' צבאות אם נהניתי מכתובתי כלום, and line 22: יהנה סם המות באחד מבניה של אותה אשה אם נהניתי מדינרך כלום:

[16] There are only two occurrences of חי ה' צבאות (line 36) in our Hebrew Bible: I Kings 18:15 and II Kings 3:14. The two occurrences are connected thematically in several ways. The first is spoken by Elijah, and the second by Elijah's pupil Elisha. Elisha's relation to Elijah is noted in the story itself (II Kings 3:11) by one of the servants of the King of Israel, as a recommendation of Elisha. Second, both are part of confrontation narratives between the prophets and the king(s) of their times. Third, both narratives have to do with drought, and the power of the prophet to alleviate that drought. The only occurrences of this phrase in Rabbinic literature (Numbers Rabbah 21:6, Deut. Rabbah 10:3, Tanhuma (Buber) Pinhas 5, Pesikta Rabbati 5 [ed. Ish Shalom 1 5b]), as far as I was able to ascertain, are quotations of one of these two verses.
Interestingly, in Pes. Rabbati and Deut. Rabbah the phrase is quoted from I Kings 17:1. In the Masoretic text the verse there reads:
ויאמר אליהו התשבי מתשבי גלעד אל אחאב
חי ה' אלהי ישראל אשר עמדתי לפניו אם יהיה השנים האלה טל ומטר כי אם לפי דברי:
The midrashim quote the underlined phrase as: חי ה' צבאות. (It seems that the LXX had something like: חי ה' צבאות אלהי ישראל.) The significance of this is that it puts this "oath" phrase at the heart of the confrontation and directly connected to the drought.
On הפכוה לכורסיה see Hagai 2:24.

[17] This is an interesting example of what those in Critical Legal Studies refer to as the central paradox: the necessity to have public proof of the private. The woman intuits that it is just this impossible proof that is being demanded (proof that she never profited [נהניתי as in line 16] from her *ketubah*) and she therefore forcefully crosses the line from private to public. Cf. Clare Dalton, "An Essay in the Deconstruction of Contract Doctrine," in Sanford Levinson and Steven Mailouxed. *Interpreting Law and Literature :A Hermeneutic Reader* (Evanston, IL: Northwestern University Press, 1988) esp. 292-293, and the critique by Joan Williams in "Critical Legal Studies: The Death of Transcendence and the Rise of the New Langdells," *New York University Law* Review vol. 62 (June 1987) 429-496.

Framing Women/Constructing Exile

woman who demands, who swears, who confronts the institution of law, and who is adamantly certain of her own integrity. This is the danger of a woman's voice.

This particular framing of the *ma'asim* needs to be contrasted with other frames that have been strongly urged. The Tosafists *ad locum* juxtapose the first *ma'aseh* with statements from b Shavuot 26a and b Nedarim 25b which pardon a person who inadvertently swears falsely (either because the person is forced or mistaken). This would seem to cover our case too. For the Tosafists this is a problem which could not be reconciled by a source theory, since they saw the whole Talmud as one interconnected work. They claim to overcome this difficulty by harmonizing the various sources. Their specific answer is unimportant to us except insofar as it obviously sees each piece of the sugya as existing autonomously and therefore in need of reconciliation with the rest of Talmud.

The Tosafists' question, however, is interesting, and does seem to support our framing of the *ma'aseh*, even though their answer doesn't. They quote the following *ma'aseh* from b. Shavuot 26a:

> Someone said[18]: *a person*[19] (אדם) *utters an oath*[20] this excludes one who is coerced.
>
> How is this? It is like [the case of] Rav Kahana and Rav Asi. When they left Rav, one said "I swear that Rav said such…" And the other said "I swear that Rav said such…" When they went before Rav he agreed with one of them. The other said to him (Rav) "And I have sworn falsely." He (Rav) said "Your heart coerced you."[21]

The Tosafists point out that the circumstances here are closely analogous to the ones in our *ma'aseh* (Gittin 35a). The result however is radically different. There is no imputation of guilt at all, and there is no discussion

---

[18] אמר מר is a technical term which means something along the lines of: "This law was quoted earlier in the discussion." Actually a few lines above. Cf. A. Weiss' discussion of the redactional meaning of אמר מר and גופא in *Redaction History of the Babylonian Talmud; Gufa and Amar Mar* (Warsaw: 1929 [1988]), and *Studies in the Literature of the Amoraim* (Heb.) (New York: Horeb, 1962): 127 ff.

[19] Reading the Lev. verse when a person is a person, i.e in full control of his faculties. (Rashi)

[20] Lev. 5:4.

[21]

אמת מר האדם בשבועה פרט לאנוס.
היכי דמי? כדרב כהנא ורב אסי. כי הוו קיימי מקמי דרב,
מר אמר, שבועתא דהכי אמר רב. ומר אמר, שבועתא דהכי אמר רב.
כי אתו לקמיה דרב, אמר כחד מינייהו.
אמר ליה אידך, ואנא בשיקרא אישתבעי?
אמר ליה, לבך אנסך.

of cosmic punishment wrought by their swearing. In their attempt to harmonize these two sources, the Tosafists claim that a higher level of vigilance would be called for in the *ma'aseh* of the woman since it is a case of a pledge, and she should have known that she would be liable to take an oath. Aside from the fact that there is no Talmudic basis for this assertion, it is contradicted by a *sugya* in b BK 106a.

That *sugya* in b BK concerns the power of an oath to override the testimony of witnesses. If one person claims that another has money belonging to the former, and the second person swears that he doesn't have the money – even if witnesses then testify that the second did have the money, the second person is exempt from repaying the money. The discussion is then widened:

1 "[...the owner of the house shall depose before] God," Rab said, [This applies] even in the case of a deposit. [i.e. that an oath is required, and following upon the oath – no payment is made.]
[...]
3 R. Naḥman sat and related this teaching.
4 R. Aḥa b. Manyumi asked R. Naḥman:
5 "Where is my deposit?" He said: "It was lost."
6 "I take you on your oath." And he said: "Amen."
7 And the witnesses testify that he consumed it, he pays the principle.
8 And if he confessed on his own, he pays the principle, and a fifth, and [brings a] guilt offering. (M Baba Kama 9:7)
9 He said, With what case are we dealing here? For example, when he swore outside of *Beth din*.
10 He said, If so say the end [of the Mishnah].
11 "Where is my deposit?" He said: "It was stolen."
12 "I take you on your oath." And he said: "Amen."
13 And the witnesses testify that he consumed it, he pays double.
14 And if he confessed on his own, he pays the principle, and a fifth, and [brings a] guilt offering. (M Baba Kama 9:8)
15 And if you would think that it is [when he swore] outside of *Beth din* – is there [the payment of] double outside of *Beth din*?[22]

---

[22]The translation is mine, the text is according to MS Hamburg 165.

בבא קמא קו ע"א כת"י המבורג

"והאלהים," (שמות כב:ז) אמר רב, אפילו בפקדון.
דכי כתיב קרא, בפקדון כתיב.
יתיב רב נחמן וקאמר להא שמעתא.
איתיביה רב אחא בר מניומי לרב נחמן,
"היכן פקדוני." א"ל, "אבד."
"משביעכני." ואמר, "אמן."
והעדים מעידים אותו שאכלו, משלם את הקרן.
ואם הודה מעצמו, משלם קרן, חומש, ואשם.
א"ל, הכא במאי עסקינן? כגון שנשבע חוץ לב"ד.
א"ל, אי הכי אימא סיפא.
"היכן פקדתי?" ואמר לו, נגנב."
"משביעכני." ואמר, "אמן."

Framing Women/Constructing Exile   163

The give and take here is challenging Rab's initial statement. The *sugya* continues, and becomes somewhat more involved, though the conclusion of this debate has no bearing on our concerns. What is of interest for the present discussion, however, is what is not in this *sugya*. Lines 5-6 and 11-12 are equivalent to lines 21-22 in our *sugya*. In fact, the case in b BK is far more serious since, it seems, the person there is lying on purpose. Yet, in BK there is no consequence to the false oath which is at all similar to the death of the widow's son.

Saul Lieberman[23] and David Weiss Halivni[24] see the *ma'aseh* in Gittin as an example of the principle articulated in p Shavuot 6:5 (37a), Leviticus Rabbah 6:3 (ed. Margaliot p.135), and Pesikta Rabati (ed. Ish Shalom) 132b: "Whether innocent or guilty do not resort to an oath."[25] They then claim that the Bavli didn't accede to this principle and therefore had to resort to a misreading of the *ma'aseh* (lines 25-26) in order to claim that she actually did swear falsely.

All three of the aforementioned sources append the saying (as a saying) to similar versions of a *ma'aseh* which is structurally related to ours. The other *ma'aseh* involves a woman who has visited a woman friend of hers, and while there she dropped the three dinars that she had wrapped in her belt. They fall into loaves of bread that are to be baked. When she discovers her loss (upon returning home) she returns to the friend and asks for the dinars. The friend then says: "I have no knowledge of them, if I know anything about them may she [that is: herself] bury her son." Her son then dies. (In the Lev. R. and Pesikta version this recurs three times, and in the Pesikta version her original return to the friend's house is at the urging of her husband.)

Notable similarities between Gittin and the others are the following: a woman, baking bread, unwittingly swears falsely and kills her son(s).[26] The most important, seemingly obvious similarity is that all the cases involve *women*. This is, of course, the kernel of the story that is found in the midrash in p Gittin. Recognizing this fact, one sees that we are not

---

והעדים מעידים אותו שגנב, משלם תשלומי כפל.
ואם הודה מעצמו, משלם קרן וחומש ואשם.
ואי סלקא דעתך חוץ לב"ד, חוץ לב"ד מי איכא כפל?

[23]*TK Zeraim* pt. *II* on Tos. Bikkurim (p. 835-6); and cf. *Greek in Jewish Palestine*, p. 124 and n. 74 where Lieberman shows that the saying has a Greek equivalent from the same time (Righteous or unrighteous, flea an oath; Maximus Planudes).
[24]*Sources and Traditions: A Source Critical Commentary on Seder Nashim*, 536-538.
[25]בין זכיי בין חייב לשבועה לא תיעול. In Leviticus Rabbah: למומי לא תיעול.
[26]Some of the differences are equally notable: in Gittin there is a legal transaction which starts the narrative (הפקיד), and (as noted by Halivni) the woman in Gittin swears that she never *benefited* from the money, which is ambiguously true, while in the other *ma'aseh* she swears that she knows nothing of the money, which is more obviously true.

faced with a general principal equally applied to men and women, but, rather, a series of narratives generated by a specific narrative (i.e. the midrash in p Gittin) about women's behavior in relation to oaths (they lie; its dangerous).[27] Not acknowledging this, neither Halivni[28] nor Lieberman frame this ma'aseh with the other *ma'asim* in the *sugya* in Gittin.

The structural or intratextual analysis that I have undertaken here, highlighted the similarities among the three *ma'asim* in our *sugya* in Gittin, and brought into focus the importance of the midrash in p Gittin as the kernel of these *ma'asim*. By the same token, one can see that the differences between the first *ma'aseh* in b Gittin, and the ones cited by Lieberman and Halivni are as crucial as their similarities. Attending to the way in which the midrash informs the *ma'asim*, and the context that the *ma'asim* themselves create, I read the *ma'asim* as representations of the danger women pose to the institutions of law.

This construction of women as dangerous by virtue of their having a voice and making demands on the institutions of law, reinforces another theme of the *ma'asim*: the rabbis' reticence to move outside the limits of authority. The theme is illustrated in line 35, "What can I do for you, for Rab would not...?" and lines 40-41: "What can I do for you, for Rab would not...? and my father would also not...?" Each narrative not only describes but also enacts the rabbis' reticence.[29] In contrast, the *lo shanu* statements of Rav and Shmuel – in the manner of *lo shanu* statements generally – minimize the original lemma's prohibition. By interpreting the Mishnah directly, without invoking a line of tradition as justification, these statements not only describe but also enact the rabbis' willingness to interpret innovatively.

What however, determines this construction of women as dangerous? To answer this we must look to the beginning of the *sugya*

---

[27]Note too that the midrash in p Gittin, is cited in b Ket. 72a (and attributed to R. Nahman) as an explanation of the statement in M Ket. 7:6 that a *woman* who doesn't fulfill her vows (ולא מקיימת נודרת) is one who can be divorced without receiving her *ketubah*.

[28]For a more complete discussion of Halivni's position see Appendix I.

[29]This reticence to move outside the limits of authority is enacted in the first *ma'aseh* in lines 23-24. The other side of a reticence to move outside authority, is a reluctance to take responsibility. This is performed by the movement in "narrative level" in the first *ma'aseh*. The original omniscient narrator who is above the story (17-22), is abruptly replaced by a narrator who is "in the story," and therefore no longer omniscient (23: "They said"). This lower level narration is then interpreted by the Sages (24), who might even be seen as the implied narratees of the implied author of this *ma'aseh*. A second level interpretation then starts at line 25, so that by the time the woman is named as punished, it is at a third remove. This seems to be a literary equivalent to מאי איעביד ליך (47, 41).

(page 154 above). This first part (lines 4-8) is *stammaitic*. Scholarship has long since decided that these "introductory" *sugyot*, often at the beginning of Tractates and chapters, but also at the beginning of specific Mishnah sections, are unique.[30] Whether or not they are late additions they do seem to play the role of "title," that is, they provide a certain framing of the subsequent *sugya* or *sugyot*.

Framing Women/Constructing Exile
Mishnah
3   A widow may not collect [her Ketubah] from the property of orphans save on taking an oath.
4   They refrained from imposing an oath on her.
5   Rabban Shimon ben Gamaliel made a regulation that she should vow to the orphans any [vow] they wish to impose on her, and [then] recover her Ketubah.

Gemara
8   Why is this rule [about an oath] laid down with reference to a widow, seeing that it applies to everybody?
9   Since it is an established rule that "one who seeks to recover payment from the property of orphans cannot recover save on taking an oath."
10 There is a special reason for the mention of a widow.
11 For it might occur to you to say, "Because of her favor (משום חינא) our rabbis were lenient towards her,"
12 We are told [therefore that this is not so].

What does this part of the sugya do? Justification for the question of line 8 is given in line 11. משום חינא (*mishum ḥinah*) is proposed as a possible reason for Rabbinic leniency in the case of a widow. The mishnah's specific wording is construed as precluding this possible misapplication of a ruling. What, however, is משום חינא (*mishum ḥinah*)? The words mean "because of her grace or favor."[31] The ambiguity of the English translation points out the strangeness of the phrase in the original. There are two contradictory explanations given by the traditional commentators. Rashi comments on משום חינא (*mishum ḥinah*) in our *sugya*[32]:

---

[30]See e.g. Avraham Weiss, *The Literary Activities of the Saboraim (Heb.)* (Jerusalem: Magnes Press, 1953): 8-11, and 16.
[31]Acc. to Jastrow. He gets himself embroiled in the whole problematic that interests us here by presenting what is essentially Tosafot's opinion as the 'authoritative' meaning of the phrase, and then adds Rashi's opinion in brackets at the end as "oth. opin." (Cf. *Hebrew Aramaic Dictionary* חן & חנא).
[32]And consistently throughout the Bavli. Rashi is rather forceful in his position, see e.g. his comment on b. Ketubot 97b commenting on the statement "a divorcee also needs ḥen": "for [mishum ḥinah] is a rabbinic ordinance [takkanat ḥachamim] and not [done] for the love of the husband, therefore what difference would it

> So that the men will find favor in the eyes of the women, so that the women will marry them. [33]

משום חינא (*mishum ḥinah*) is a precautionary measure taken to insure that women are not dissuaded from marrying by the possibility that they will be defrauded of their *ketubah* payment wrongfully.

There is no comment in the Tosafot on our *sugya*. However, on 49b the following is attributed to R. Haim:[34]

> He explained *mishum ḥinah* that all would want to marry her...[35]

משום חינא (*mishum ḥinah*) is "protective legislation" intended to persuade potential future husbands to marry a forlorn widow by giving her some money even under questionable circumstances.

It is, of course, impossible to decide between these two interpretations, and this is just the point. The fact that משום חינא (*mishum ḥinah*) is such an obvious site of conflicting interpretations points to its "ungrammaticality" and that what it *does* is different than what it *means*. In the next line (13) the claim is seemingly dismissed out of hand.

However, I would claim that the סד"א... קמ"ל figure[36] is a way of introducing a concept under erasure[37] (to borrow a term from Derrida). What I mean by this is that introducing משום חינא (*mishum ḥinah*) creates a textual web which generates the narrative of the rest of the *sugya*. What exactly the web is (i.e. what intertexts inform the meaning of our *sugya*) will be made clear further on. This is what the first five lines do: they set up the connection "*widow* ↔ חן (*hen*)" without arguing for it. The connection is granted as obvious. What is not granted is merely the appropriateness of its applicability in this situation to justify a legal

---

make to me if she was loved or hated [by her husband]." (and cf. Tosafot there, too, s.v. אלמנה) See the more extensive discussion in Appendix II to this chapter.

But cf. Rashi on this comment (b. Sotah 47a):

אמר רבי יוחנן, שלשה חינות הן חן מקום על יושביו חן אשה על בעלה חן מקח על מקחו.
חן האשה – תמיד על בעלה ואפי' היא מכוערת נושאת חן בעיניו:

(The Talmudic comment also appears in PT Yoma 4:1 41b. in a slightly different context.)

[33] שיהא חן האנשים בעיני הנשים לינשא להם.

[34] Probably Hayyim ben Hananel Ha-Kohen: French Tosafist; second half of the twelfth century.

[35] דפירש משום חינא שיהא הכל קופצין עליה לישאנה... (lit. jump on her to marry her)

[36] "For it might occur to you to say... We are told [therefore that this is not so]."

[37] I would make this claim not only here but as a consistent literary mechanism of the Bavli. See Appendix III for a continuation of this discussion.

Framing Women/Constructing Exile

leniency. Even though it is not accepted as *legal* reasoning, it still has rhetorical power.³⁸

The term חן is a significant one in a discussion of the good woman in the Book of Ben Sirah.³⁹ There is a list (Chap. 26 ed. Kahane p. 54), similar to the one found in Proverbs 31 (though not alphabetical), of the attributes of the "good woman" and the "bad woman".⁴⁰ I want to quote four verses from that chapter:

13. A wife's charm (חן) delights her husband, and her skill puts fat on his bones.
14. A silent wife is a gift of the Lord, and there is nothing so precious as a disciplined soul.

---

³⁸It is like writing "he is not sick" rather than writing "he is well". The effect of the former is to introduce sickness into the discussion, as if the person had written he is ~~sick~~

³⁹On the larger question of the Rabbinic relationship to Sirach or Ben Sirah, see Benjamin G. Wright III, "Some Methodological Considerations On The Rabbis Knowledge Of The Proverbs Of Ben Sira", IOUDAIOS files, 1992, electronic media: "Rather than being inimical to using these proverbs, many rabbis clearly believe them to be as persuasive and effective as both scripture and the sayings of other rabbinic sages." Also: " The Jewish sages had a special relationship with the Wisdom of Sirach. Although not included in the Jewish Bible and ultimately thrust entirely to the periphery, the book remained extremely popular with the Tannaitic and Amoraic authorities in the face of prohibitions against its use." Wright is interested in what I have called the more "traditional" question of influence, but his findings are equally valid for understanding the cultural frame.

⁴⁰Parts of this list are quoted in b Yebamoth 53b (and b Sanhedrin 100b), in the context of a long *sugya* about the "good woman" and the "bad woman" and attributed to Ben Sirah:

כתוב בספר בן סירא: אשה טובה מתנה טובה לבעלה.
וכתיב: טובה בחיק ירא אלהים תנתן אשה רעה צרעת לבעלה.
[...]
אשה יפה אשרי בעלה מספר ימיו כפלים.
העלם עיניך מאשת חן פן תלכד במצודתה.
אל תט אצל בעלה למסוך עמו יין ושכר,
כי בתואר אשה יפה רבים הושחתו ועצומים כל הרוניה.

It is noteworthy that the *sugya in* Yebamoth unfolds within a framework in which a woman is either "wonderful" or "evil". This is, of course, an often noted attribute of discourse *about* women in patriarchal culture. Here the whore – madonna binary opposites are replaced by the midrashic binaries, based on two verses Eccl. 7:26: Now I find woman more bitter than death...; and Proverbs 18:22: He who finds a wife has found happiness (טוב).... It is the "contradiction" between these verses which generates the good-bad dichotomies. The possibility that is left out of course, is that a woman is, like a man, a person who is neither necessarily good nor necessarily evil. A full analysis of the *sugya* in Yevamoth would be beyond the scope of this chapter, though it is significant to note that the *sugya* starts with a statement attributed to R. Elazar which reads Gen. 5:2 (Male and female he created them. .. [i.e. אדם]) to mean: Any man (אדם) who doesn't have a woman is not a man (אדם).

15. A modest wife adds charm to charm (חן על חן), and no balance can weigh the value of a chaste soul. [...]
27. A loud voiced and garrulous wife is regarded as a war trumpet for putting the enemy to flight.[41]

The salient point is that a woman of חן is silent (מחרישה), unassuming (=modest) (בושה), and passive (="chaste")(מושלה בנפשה). On the other hand, the woman who has a voice is considered as a war trumpet for putting the enemy to flight.[42] This is the construction of woman that is determining the reading in our *sugya*. This is what was introduced under erasure in line 11-12.

These are also the very characteristics that are seen in our *sugya* as problematic. The women are neither silent (line 22), nor unassuming (49-52) nor passive (43). Within the cultural and textual web formed by both the midrash and Ben Sirah list[43] it is easy to understand the danger and the fear.[44]

Sugyaetics / Narrative

Let us take a moment to analyze the literary power of the first *ma'aseh*. In setting up the narrative, the reader is introduced to three very sympathetic (if not tragic) characters, in trying times. First, a man who deposits a dinar with a widow in/because of the years of drought. The widow herself is pictured as caring in both accepting the dinar and giving the bread she baked to a poor person. The poor person then leaves the scene. Tragedy is foretold by the fact (which the reader knows) that the dinar is now with the poor person (who seemingly, might be able to make good use of it). The *ma'aseh* itself "claims" to be about the depositor. The significant action however, is done by the widow, while the tragedy strikes her son (who has not been in the narrative up to this point), and we know that the son is stricken by way of the anonymous

---

[41]RSV.

יג. חן אשה ישמח בעלה ועצמותיו ידשן שכלה
יד. מתנת ה' אשה מחרישה ואין מחיר למיסרת נפש.
טו. חן על חן אשה בושה ואין משקל שוה למושלת בנפש.
[...]
כז. אשה גדולת קול ובעלת לשון כשופר מלחמה מחריד תחשב.

See the variants in *The Book of Ben Sira: Text, Concordance and an Analysis of the Vocabulary* (Jerusalem: The Academy of the Hebrew Language and the Shrine of the Book, 1973): 25.

[42]Cf. M Ket. 7:6 wherein the woman of (loud) voice (קולנית) is listed as one who might be summarily divorced without receiving her Ketubah payment.

[43]And reflected in the *sugya* in Yebamoth.

[44]As opposed to e.g. b BK 106a where analogous *legal* situations don't lead to analogous *cultural* ramifications.

Framing Women/Constructing Exile

"they said" (23) rather than the omniscient narrator who tells the rest of the tale.

The confrontation is doubly poignant since it involves, not only a total lack of communication (the widow's statement in line 22 doesn't really answer the demand in line 21), but it also confounds all the supposedly well-founded expectations of what should happen to a person who feeds the hungry in years of drought.[45] Rather than being rewarded, she is tragically punished, and it is the very act of nurturing – feeding[46] – which brings about the tragic death.

It is at this point of tragedy that the narration switches from an omniscient narrator to the fallible, anonymous, "they". This is immediately interpreted further by the sages as being the result of her oath. The context for the failed expectations and the interpretive function of the fallible narrator (i.e. "they"), might very well be the struggle with the fact that proper action does not cause proper reward. The phrase: שנת בצרת [year of drought] (13) appears only once in the Hebrew Bible[47], Jeremiah 17:8[48]:

> He shall be like a tree planted by waters, sending forth its roots by a stream:
> It does not sense the coming of heat, its leaves are ever fresh;
> It has no care in a year of drought, (ובשנת בצרת) it does not cease to yield fruit.

This is part of a promise of divine salvation in times of trouble. The contrast with the *ma'aseh* is obvious. Not only does the woman have faith in God[49], but she is actively doing good in the year of drought, by giving bread to the poor. She does not however receive divine protection for her goodness. Her nurturing, rather, brings death.

There is intertextual evidence that the context of the *ma'aseh* is exile. The year of drought in Jeremiah is a metaphor for times of trouble – and exile is *the* trouble[50] for the Rabbis. The seemingly desperate attempts to interpret this anomalous series of actions (lines 24-27), can all be seen within an attempt to retell the basic story of the community, the narrative

---

[45] E.g. Isaiah 58; 8-14.
[46] Cf. Isaiah 58:8; Proverbs 31:15, 20.
[47] For equally "loaded" uses of the phrase שני בצורת in *ma'asim* see: b Ber. 18b; b Yeb. 15b; (b Ket. 10b); b B.B. 8a, 11a; b Hulin 94a.
[48] NJPS

והיה כעץ שתול על מים ועל יובל ישלח שרשיו ולא ירא כי יבא חם והיה עלהו רענן ובשנת בצרת לא ידאג ולא ימיש מעשות פרי

[49] Cf. Jeremiah 17:7.
[50] Cf. also Jer. 17:3,4 which explicitly lists exile as the trouble.

of origins[51], within which there is a coherent line of authority, and a consistent sense of cause and effect in the world. From this vantage point, the oppositional nature of the *ma'asim* and the overtones of danger, take on new significance.

If the authority of the institutions of law is to be upheld, its stability and anchoring in tradition must be a given.[52] That which opposes that stability (or threatens to expose it as a construct) is dangerous. Within this binary opposition, men are cast in the role of the conservative guardians of tradition, while women are the opposition.[53] Both are locked into their roles (cf. line 47-48). There is a palpable danger that the system will be overthrown.[54] "The system" is the last vestige of the pre-exilic covenantal relationship.

It is not surprising that a halakhic discussion of the collection of ketubah money is embedded in the cultural narrative of exile. Marriage and divorce has been the traditional site of metaphorical conflict between God and Israel. Isaiah (50:1) and Jeremiah (3:8) both use the Deuteronomic divorce laws (24:1-4) in their discussion of the covenantal relationship.[55] Similarly, the Rabbis use the divorce scene, and the dispute over support (i.e. the ketubah payment) as a, if not the, significant site for the discussion of the covenantal relationship.[56] Engagement, marriage, separation and divorce is at the heart of Rabbinic

---

[51] On Narratives of origins see Kermode, *The Sense of an Ending*, and more recently, and in relation to the Rabbis, see Daniel Boyarin, "Diaspora: Generation and the Ground of Jewish Identity," *Critical Inquiry/ 19:4* (Summer 1993), 693-725 (esp. 718-723).

[52] The unease with the wielding of legislative power, and especially legislative reform is succinctly articulated in the last *sugya* on this mishnah (37a), in a statement attributed to R. Yohanan: ‏וכי מפני שאנו מדמין נעשה מעשה?‏ ("And just because we imagine that it is so should we legislate accordingly?") Rashi comments: ‏מדמין: נראה בעינינו וכמדומין אנו כן ולא שמענו מרבותינו‏ ("It seems to us, and we imagine it so, but we did not hear it from our teachers.").

[53] David Biale argues this point on a more universal scale within Rabbinic literature. *Eros and the Jews: From Biblical Israel to Contemporary America* (Basic Books, 1992) p. 48.

[54] Lines 52-54, take on this significance, within this frame. (Cf. Hagai 2:24: "‏והפכתי כסא ממלכתו‏." Targum on Deut. 17:18.) ‏מלך‏ is the term used to describe the term of the exilarch in the Letter of R. Sherirah Gaon.

Also see above n. 16 [on ‏חי ה' צבאות‏].

[55] Michael Fishbane, *Biblical Interpretation in Ancient Israel* (Clarendon Press, Oxford, 1985) 307-312.

[56] In addition to the following midrash cf: Sifri Deut. (Ha'azinu) #306 (ed. Finkelstein p. 330; b San. 105a; Exodus Rabbah 31:10; Tanhuma Mishpatim 11; Numbers Rabbah 1:5; Tanhuma Vayeshev 4; Tanhuma (and Tan. Buber) Numbers 5; Midrash Psalms (Shoher Tov) 139:1 (ed. Buber p. 527). This very partial list is only meant to show that divorce as a site of the existential tensions of the exile, is a motif common to most layers of Rabbinic discourse.

Framing Women/Constructing Exile 171

mythology. A clear example of this, with direct bearing on our *sugya* is the following midrash from Eichah Rabba:[57]

> Another interpretation of "She ... is become like a widow" (Lam. 1:1).
> [...]
> The Rabbis said:
> It is like a king who became angry at his consort. He wrote her a bill of divorce and gave it to her, but then he returned, and grabbed it from her.[58]
> Whenever she wished to marry someone else, the king said to her: Where is the bill of divorce with which I divorced you?
> And whenever she claimed support from him, he said to her: I have already divorced you.
> Similarly, whenever Israel wishes to worship idolatry, the Holy One of Blessing says to them: "Where is the bill of divorce to your mother whom I have dismissed?" (Isa. 50:1)
> And whenever they ask Him to perform a miracle for them, He tells them: I have already cast you off, as it is written, "I cast her off and handed her a bill of divorce" (Jer. 3:8).[59]

The midrash, stressing the indefiniteness of the "as a widow" and not a widow, precisely articulates the existential fears of the exilic situation. Is the covenant broken and irreparable or is there still hope? What is the obligation to the law when there is no obvious recompense?

On this background, it is not at all surprising that the legal discussions which parallel, and in our *sugya*, partake of the language and

---

[57] For an analysis of this text, and a critical apparatus for the text, see David Stern, *Parables in Midrash: Narrative and Exegesis in Rabbinic Literature* (Harvard University Press, Cambridge, MA, 1991) esp. 99-101. The text I am using is the one labeled Ashkenaz in *Parables*, 257. It is in Buber's edition of Eichah Rabbah 46, with some differences. The translation is basically Stern's.

[58] For an explicit parallel, to this seemingly absurdist scene, in a *halakhic sugya* cf. b Gittin 19b:

מיתיבי הרי זה ניטך ותמלתו חרקתו לים או לאור או לכל דבר האבד
וחזר ואמר שטר פסים הוא שטר אמנה הוא מגורשת ולא כל הימנו לאוסרה
ואי אמרת צריכי למיקרייה בתר דקריוה מי מצי אמר לה הכי
לא צריכא דבתר דקריוה עייליה לבי ידיה ואפקיה מהו דתימא חלופי חלפיה קא משמע לן

[59]

ד"א היתה כאלמנה
[...]
ורבנן אמרי:
למלך שכעס על מטרונה וכתב לה גיטה ונתן לה וחזר וחטפו ממנה.
וכל זמן שהיא מבקשת לינשא לאחר הוא אומר לה: היכן גיטיך נירשתיך?
וכל זמן שהיתה תובעת צרכיה הוא אומר לה: כבר גרשתיך.
כך כל זמן שישראל מבקשים לעבוד עבודה זרה אומר להם הקב"ה:
אי זה ספר כריתות אמכם אשר שלחתיה (ישעיה נ:א).
וכל זמן שמבקשים שיעשה עמהם נס, אומר להם:
כבר שלחתיה דכתיב שלחתיה ואתן את ספר כריתותיה (ירמיהו ג:ח).

images[60] of the midrashic discussions are fraught with danger and violent emotion.

This construction of Rabbinic society (the *maasim*) meets the other narrative strand (the לא שנו statements) in the statement attributed to R. Yehudah. (57) His ruling seems to subvert the notion of a need for a static legal structure to insure the line of authority. He, on the contrary, seems to want to assert authority by legislating. He declares, essentially that the students of Rav are wrong. That one must do whatever is required in order to assure that the woman gets her ketubah.[61]

The *sugya*, however, does not end here. Within the narrative context[62] R. Yehudah's demand that he hear that his decree[63] is carried out, is itself fulfilled by the rereading of the לא שנו statement from above[64](28) in light of the narrative in lines 63-66. The message that is sent "from there" (62) seems to accord with R. Yehudah's ruling. She swore and should collect the rest of the ketubah payment. The last line of the sugya subverts this move. The statement attributed to R. Ashi, denies the force of the Palestinian ruling and narrows it to one specific case. Once again though, a significant moment in the *sugya* is a site of conflicting interpretations. Rashi and Tosafot are at odds about how to reread the *ma'aseh* according to R. Ashi's statement.

The force of R. Ashi's remark however, is to bring the *sugya* back to the point before R. Yehudah. This, of course, is the moment of tension which infuses the *ketubah* payment as a site of legal/theological

---

[60]Especially the third *ma'aseh*.

[61]His statement does not, however, challenge the representation of woman as passive. R. Yehudah is commanding that these things be done to her. Line 58, especially the phrase דאעביד בה מעשה is interesting in this regard. It is rarely used in the sense that it seems to be used here. The usual use of דאעביד בה מעשה is in relation to a sacrifice OR as a term meaning that a man has had intercourse with a woman (e.g. b Yeb. 60a-b). This just reinforces the sense here of things being done to her. The phrase also connects the statement back to the first מעשה and perhaps recognizes that that מעשה was really a מעשה באשה.

[62]Cf. Barthes' discussion of the proairetic code (that is the code which Barthes uses to analyze actions and their consequences, including questions and their digressions and answers) in Roland Barthes, S/Z: *An Essay*, trans. Richard Miller (New York: Hill and Wang, 1974) esp. 19.

[63]Saul Lieberman, "ספר מעשים, ספר פסקים" has shown that the word מעשה in many contexts has the meaning of פסק, that is – legal decision.

[64]נמא here is serving an obvious literary function which is not dependent on the outcome of the debate over whether it actually signifies an earlier or later statement than the sugya to which it is "attached". Cf. the article by Avraham Weiss cited above in n. 19.

Framing Women/Constructing Exile   173

discourse. The *sugya* ends, essentially, without a bottom line, and we never hear the voice that will confirm R. Yehudah's ruling.[65]

Narrative/Afterlife Of The Sugya

We have ended up after all, with a somewhat linear narrative following on a nonlinear reading of the *sugya*. We have seen how the *sugya* is a narrative and partakes of the larger cultural narratives.

In addition the *sugya* generates narratives. This is seen in the early and medieval commentaries on the Talmud. The relationships prescribed in the *sugya* later become part of the cultural baggage of the Halakhic tradition. The afterlife of משום חינא is a good example of this.[66]

The central moment of this *sugya* – the crisis of authority – is an issue which repeats itself throughout the *sugyot* in this chapter. On close reading, most of the *sugyot* are about the authority of the institutions of law.[67] It is in creating that authority through interpretation, that the relationships between men and women, and between men, women and the institutions of law are created.

---

[65]It is interesting to note that Alfasi (10th century Babylonian author of the work *Halakhot*, which is the first significant attempt to create a legal code of the Talmud) quotes only the לא שנו line of our *sugya*. This may not seem remarkable, since the common opinion is that Alfasi is only interested in the Halakhic bottom line. What is remarkable is that, in order to achieve a bottom line Alfasi also rearranges the לא שנו statements. In the *Halachot*, Samuel's statement as quoted by R. Zeira (line 28 & 61) appears *only* after R. Yehuda's statement. Neither R. Ashi's statement nor the *ma'aseh* before it are quoted. That Alfasi had to rearrange the *sugya* in this fashion in order to have a linear reading which arrived at a "bottom line" halakhic ruling, indirectly supports our understanding of the *sugya* as it stands as not having a bottom line. For a partisan review of the Halakhic tradition of commentary up to his time, see Menahem HaMei'ri (n.18 above).

[66]See e.g. Responsa of R. Shlomo b. Adret Part 5:90; Responsa of Mahram of Rottenburg part 4:362; Responsa of R. Moshe Isserles g:13. See, also my discussion in Appendix II.

[67]The *sugyot* about מה כה בית דין יפה – מה כה בית דין יפה (33a-35b); the authority of Rabbinic signets (36a); אין בית דין יכול לבטל דברי בית דין חברו – (36b) and on.

Appendix I. David Weiss Halivni On b Gittin 35a

Halivni frames the *sugya* in terms of the debate over whether or not one who swears truthfully is punished. He claims that the Bavli, as opposed to the Yerushalmi (and other Palestinian sources – e.g. Lev. Rabbah, Pes. Rabbati), cannot abide the claim that one who swears truthfully is punished anyway. Or to put it in another light, in the Palestinian sources all swearing is viewed disparagingly and those who indulge in this type of activity are punished. This, according to Halivni, is the reason that the Bavli was forced to "misinterpret" the *ma'aseh* and claim that the woman actually did swear falsely in some way. As Halivni says: "According to this one must explain the *ma'aseh* in its simple sense (כפשוטו), that the widow swore truthfully and even so she was punished, for even one who swears truthfully is punished."[68]

With this explanation Halivni is attempting to explain the ungrammaticality of the claim that she was punished for swearing falsely because she had profited by saving the flour which would have had to fill the space of the dinar. Halivni accomplishes this by framing this sugya with others in which the point is the debate over whether or not one who swears truthfully is punished.[69] We argued above that there were significant differences between the *maasim* in Lev. Rabbah, p Shavuot, Pesikta Rabbati and the *ma'aseh* in our *sugya*. Halivni however, also sees a connection with a statement and *ma'aseh* in Tanhuma (Buber) in which two thousand cities are wiped out for swearing falsely, at the end of which is the same statement as is found in our *sugya*:

ומה הנשבע באמת כך-הנשבע בשקר על אחת כמה וכמה.

I will argue that the *ma'aseh* quoted in this Tanhuma (and its parallels) is different enough from our *maasim* as to problematize Halivni's framing.

The pericopae in full is as follows:

1   Our sages said, he is not even allowed to swear about the truth. In what situation?
    Our sages taught, an Israelite should not be promiscuous with vows or laughter, nor in misleading his fellow [concerning] an oath saying it is not an oath.
    A ma'aseh, at Har Hamelech (Hill of the King) there were two thousand cities, and all of them were destroyed on [account of] a true oath.

---

[68]*Sources and Traditions: A Source Critical Commentary on Seder Nashim*, 537, my translation.
[69]p Shavuot 5:6 37a; parallels in Lev. Rabbah 6:3, Pesikta Rabbati 113b. noted by Halivni on p. 537.

Framing Women/Constructing Exile

> If such is the fate of one who swears truly, so much the more so for one who swears falsely.
> 5   In what manner did they do it? A person would say to his fellow:
> "On oath that I am going to such and such place and I will eat and drink."
> And they would go and do [what they had sworn] and fulfill their oaths.
> For such it is said: If a person incurs guilt etc. (Lev. 5:1)[70]

The differences between this *ma'aseh* and ours are glaring. First, in the original telling, it is not clear who is swearing, or what is being sworn. Second in the interpretation (following the question, line 5, "In what manner did they do it?") there is no confrontation, there is no legal action, there is no story about a specific incident involving a specific person, rather a generalized incident involving thousands.[71] The question then that must be answered is what is the more appropriate frame.

It seems to me that the *mishum ḥinah* discussion determines the reading of this *sugya* towards the frame that I have proffered. Halivni's reading does not take cognizance of the specificity of our *ma'aseh* (and the ones in Lev. Rab., Pes. Rabbati) – i.e. that it is about women. Further, the kernel of the *ma'aseh* which is in p Gittin, supports this framing. The fear here is not of swearing but of women swearing. This difference also comes to light in Halivni's further comments on the sugya.

> "And here, this difference between the Bavli and the Yerushalmi also affects the explanation of the mishnah; according to the Bavli נמנעו מלהשביעה, for perhaps she would swear falsely and *be punished*. And for the Yerushalmi נמנעו מלהשביעה for one is punished even for swearing truthfully."

However the point – in both the Bavli and the Yerushalmi – is that *she* swears and in doing so *she harms*, not that she is punished. This is the crux of the difference between my reading and Halivni's. As I see the significance of the Midrash in the Yerushalmi on Jer. 2:30, dangerous

---

[70]Tanhuma (Buber) Leviticus 16

אמרו רבותינו אפילו על האמת אינו יכול לישבע. למה?
שנו רבותינו, לא יהא אדם מישראל פרוץ בנדרים ולא בשחוק,
ולא להטעות את חבירו בשבועה לומר שאינה שבועה.
מעשה בהר המלך שהיו שם שני אלפים עיירות,
וכולם נחרבו על שבועת אמת.
ומה הנשבע באמת כך-הנשבע בשקר על אחת כמה וכמה.
כיצד היו עושין? אדם אומר לחבירו:
"שבועה שאני הולך למקום פלוני ואוכל ואשתה,"
והולכין ועושין ומקיימין שבועתן. לכך נאמר נפש כי תחטא וגו'.

[71]It is interesting to note (though not necessarily relevant) that the destruction of cities on *Har Hamelech* is recorded in b Gittin 57b. There, however, the number is 6000, and there is no mention of swearing truthfully or falsely.

swearers are always gendered female. Furthermore, neither Talmud is worried that she be punished, but that she harm.

The heart of the issue separating the two readings is whether the Bavli's frame is that of the principle that one is punished for swearing falsely; or whether it is the problem that seems to be structurally at the heart of all the *maasim* in our *sugya*, and is the "title" of our sugya: *women swearing*. In this light the Bavli's question: why was she punished does not proceed from an assumption that there are innocent swearers, but rather that there are no innocent women swearers. This is why the stam in the Bavli must misread in Bloom's sense, rather than misinterpret the *ma'aseh*. For the Bavli the woman, by definition as a woman – that is, dangerous when swearing, cannot be innocent.

Appendix II. Gendering (and) Halakhah

There is an intersection in a number of *sugyot* between the concept of *ḥen* and two other concepts which serve to construct a certain idea of "woman" in relation to marriage and the courts. The other "principles" are:

1. More than a man wants to marry, a woman wants to be married.[72]
2. A person does not desire that his wife should abase herself in court.[73]

The second principle is obviously related to the court system. The abasement in the second phrase, based on the phrase's occurrences,[74] is the appearance in court itself. It might be translated as "...abase herself [by appearing] in court." The first principle, while not explicitly about the courts, is used to justify a lesser form of *ketubah* payment to the wife. It is used as *legal* reasoning, and is employed to explain why a woman collects her *ketubah* money from the lowest grade crops.

Another important characteristic of these "principles," is that they are neither argued for, nor given scriptural support.[75] They are assumed to be true, and then they, in turn are used as part of the "logic" of the legal reasoning. In this way they are building blocks in the construction of gender – that is, the ascription of characteristics to men and women, thereby differentiating roles and activities by gender.[76]

Each of these principles intersects with *mishum ḥinah* in the context of a *sugya*. I will analyze one of these *sugyot*, and then discuss some of the others briefly. The *sugya* is from the fifth chapter of b Gittin (49b-50a).

The *sugya* b Gittin 49b-50a, is generated by a reading of the following lines from the first Mishnah in the fifth chapter of M Gittin:

---

[72].יותר ממה שהאיש רוצה לישא אשה רוצה לינשא e.g. TKet. 12:3 (ed. Zukermandel 234), b Gittin 50a.
[73].אין אדם רוצה שתתבזה אשתו בבית דין e.g. b Ket. 87b.
[74]Cf. b Ket. 87b, b Gittin 46a.
[75]I mean "scriptural" here in the largest sense – neither Biblical nor Mishnaic, etc.
[76]This process is also referred to as "gendering." "Gendering describes the processes and mechanisms that create culturally persuasive notion about what make males men and females women; 'gendering' refers to the cultural assignment of appropriate activities, behaviors, and legal categories to each." Miriam Beth Peskowitz, "The Work of Her Hands': Gendering Everyday Life in Roman-Period Judaism in Palestine (70-250 CE), Using Textile Production as a Case," (Ph.D. diss., Duke University, 1993): 17. Cf. my discussion above in Chapter Five.

> [In cases of] damages we assess the choice land [of the defendant], [In the cases of the claim of] a creditor [we assess] the average land, and [in the case of] a woman's ketubah [payment] – the worst [land].
>
> R. Meir says, even [in the case of] a woman's ketubah [payment we assess] the average land.[77]

The *sugya* is generated by the fact that the Mishnah grouped the three seemingly different cases together. Two different questions are raised. First, if the grouping is as a result of the three cases being equivalent in that they are all legitimate civil actions, and all the plaintiffs have standing, why are the assessments different?[78] Second, who is being assessed in these cases? Our *sugya* is focused on the third clause of the Mishnah's first line:

2   [In the case of] a woman's ketubah [payment] – the worst [land].
3   Said Mar Zutra the son of R. Naḥman, they only said it [in the case of collecting] from orphans, but [in a case of collecting] from [the husband] himself [we assess] the average land.

The statement attributed to Mar Zutra (fourth generation Babylonian Amora) in line 3: "...they only said it [in the case of collecting] from orphans," is the reading which creates the space for the rest of the *sugya*, and supplies the language within which the rest of the *sugya* is written: the poles of "from orphans" vs. "from himself." This way of reading the Mishnah is not the only possible or necessary way. It would, at first glance, seem that the Mishnah was referring to the obvious defendant in the case of *ketubah* – that is, the husband – just as it seemed to be doing in the case of damages and debt. The connection with orphans is only supplied by the next Mishnah (5:2). There we find the principle that is quoted here in line 5: "Payment is collected from orphans only out of the worst [land]." Reading the connection of "the worst [land]" back into our

---

[77] The full text and translation of b Gittin 49b-50a appears at the end of this appendix. The translation is mine, though I consulted the Soncino (Daiches) translation extensively. The abbreviations in the apparatus are the same as for b Gittin 34b-35b.

המזיקין שמין להם בעדית, ובעל חוב בבינונית, וכתובת אשה בזבורית.
רבי מאיר אומר, אף כתובת אשה בבינונית:

[78] In the previous *sugya*, reasons are given for "damages" and "debt." The former from the choice land, so that people should be wary of damaging others' property. The latter from average land so that, on the one hand creditors will be assured of realistic repayment – and therefore they will not stop lending money – while on the other hand, it will stop speculators from lending money for the sole purpose of trying to collect someone's choice property in default.

Framing Women/Constructing Exile

Mishnah, Mar Zutra raises the status of payment for the *ketubah* to the level of a creditor, and reframes the whole discussion.[79]

This "ungrammatical" reading enables the framing section of the *sugya*, and is itself part of the ostensible frame of the whole *sugya*. The body of the *sugya* consists of three structurally similar "Come and here" units (11-16; 18-23; 42-45), leading to the "refutation" of Mar Zutra in line 45. This line of attributed statement/units is interwoven with a stammaitic frame which follows immediately upon Mar Zutra's statement, and a stammaitic "digression" (24-40) whose problems have fueled centuries of discussions in the commentaries.[80]

4   [If only] "from orphans," – why is this rule laid down with reference to a woman's ketubah [payment]? [It applies in] every case. For we learned:
5   "Payment is collected from orphans only from the worst [land]."
6   Rather, [this is] not [the proper understanding]. [It refers to collecting] from him.
7   [Actually] it still [refers to the case of collecting] from orphans. And it is necessary [to specify] a woman's *ketubah*.
8   For it might occur to you to say, "Because of her favor the rabbis were lenient towards her,"
9   We are told [therefore that this is not so].

It is immediately apparent that this section is almost identical in structure to the first part of the *sugya* that was at the heart of this chapter, b Gittin 34b-35a.

8a   Why is this rule [about an oath] laid down with reference to a widow, seeing that it applies to everybody?
9a   Since it is an established rule that "one who seeks to recover payment from the property of orphans cannot recover save on taking an oath."
10a There is a special reason for the mention of a widow.
11a For it might occur to you to say, "Because of her favor (משום חינא) our rabbis were lenient towards her,"
12a We are told [therefore that this is not so].

---

[79]The reification of attributed statements is not to be taken beyond the level of the implied author, as always. See the discussion in chapter five above, and especially n. 33.

[80]The whole concept of a קבלן דכתובה (29ff.) is problematic. Cf. Menaḥem HaMe'iri:

וקבלנות של כתבה קשה לפרש לפרש שקבלנות של בעל חוב הוא שיש שם מעות ואומר לו תן לו ואני נותן או תן לו ואני קבלן, אבל של כתבה שאין שם מעות שהרי על כתבת מנה מאתים אנו עסוקים היאך הוא נעשה קבלן...(213).

Though he gives an answer, its clear that this whole section is ungrammatical.

Lines 4 and 8a (the subscript, as above, refers to b Gittin 34b-35a) question the specificity of the (different) Mishnaic laws. Lines 5 and 9a are prooftexts for a wider reading of the laws. Lines 7 and 10a reaffirm the necessity of the narrow reading. Lines 8-9 and 11a-12a is the reason that one might have misunderstood the wider law, thereby necessitating the narrower law, and this reason's dismissal. These last two lines in the two *sugyot* are identical, and function in similar ways as being written "under erasure." I will claim that it is this introduction of the cultural baggage of the woman of *ḥen* which informs the rest of the *sugya*.

The first "Come and hear" unit, attributed to Rava (fourth generation Babylonian Amora), reads R. Meir's statement in the Mishnah as a sourcetext (12). The possibility is raised that R. Meir is referring to collecting payment from orphans (13). This possibility is dismissed as a result of the principle articulated in the second Mishnah and cited also in the opening section of the *sugya* ([5] 14): "Payment is collected from orphans only from the worst [land]." Thus, R. Meir's statement must be referring to collecting from the husband, and R. Meir's statement is a reaction to the fact that the Mishnah lets the husband pay from the worst land (15). This possibility is also dismissed, and the section finishes:

16   No, it still [refers to the case of collecting] from orphans. And a woman's *ketubah* payment differs because of *ḥinah*.

That is, R. Meir's statement does actually refer to collecting from orphans, and the reason that a woman's *ketubah* payment differs from the general rule governing collecting from orphans is *ḥinah*. This last, of course, means that collecting from the better type of grain would convince her to marry – or convince others to marry her. That which was cited under erasure, is re-cited.

The second "Come and hear" unit (18-23) is attributed to Abayye (fourth generation Babylonian Amora). The moves are almost identical to the previous unit, but the results are opposite. The beginning of Mishnah 5:1 is quoted as a sourcetext (19 [≈ 12]). The possibility is raised that this is referring to collecting payment from orphans (20 [= 13]). This possibility is challenged by an implicit reference to the general rule about collecting from orphans of Mishnah 2 (≈ 14). Thus the Mishnah's statement must be referring to collecting from the husband (21 [=15]). This conclusion, however, is immediately questioned in the next line (22), and redefined in the final line of the unit (23 [≈ 16]). The Mishnah, then, is not referring to collecting the payment from the orphans. Then again, neither is it referring to collecting the money from the husband. The person who is actually dunned in the Mishnah, is the father who became a guarantor for the *ketubah* payment (among others) of his son.

Framing Women/Constructing Exile

The third "Come and hear" unit is attributed to Rabina (fifth or seventh generation Babylonian Amora) (42). The sourcetext in this unit, is also the unit's bottom line:

43   [It is] of the essence of the ordinance [that a woman's *ketubah* payment is from the worst land]: "More than a man wants to marry, a woman wants to be married."

The *sugya* has come full circle. Mar Zutra and then Rava read the Mishnah as referring to orphans. Abayye through Aḥa b. Yaakov (third generation Babylonian) reads it as referring to the father as guarantor. Rabina reads the "worst land" provision as an essential part of the understanding of the *Ketubah* payment (44), and returns the Mishnah to its "naive reading."

The digression after the second "Come and hear" unit reinforces the sense that, if it is read linearly, the *sugya* goes nowhere and accomplishes nothing. Indeed, Alfasi in his *Halakhot* doesn't mention this *sugya* at all. There is no give and take between the positions,[81] and the "digression" (24-40) serves mainly to introduce the civil law notions of guarantor and קבלן, and, then, to show why they are unusable (32,39).

What we are left with, is the cultural baggage of *mishum ḥinah* and the principle that more than a man wants to marry, a woman wants to be married. Together, this generates a representation of woman who is eager to participate as a silent and unassuming part of the system. The woman does not demand anything, since her reward is in her marriage, and she need no more. The cultural stakes are great. If women choose not to play, as it were,[82] the game is over. They are represented therefore, as

---

[81]This is reinforced by the use of the introductory formula: "Said X, Come and hear," rather than the much more common "Come and hear" without attribution. (A search of the Davka Judaic Classics CD-ROM 2.0 shows that there are 173 of the "Said X, Come and hear" type, as opposed to 1262 of the unattributed type. The relation is similar – 50 out of 361 – if the search is confined to the Order *Nashim.*) As has been pointed out the dispute form is "Said R. X..., And R . Y said...." The presentation here is not of this form, which reinforces the sense that what is happening is not a dispute but "something else." See the discussion of this form in Shamma Friedman, "A Critical Study of *Yevamot X* with a Methodological Introduction," 349 and n. 30. See too, my discussion above Chapter II, Part 3.

[82]Rashi consistently states the cultural stakes very clearly, as in the following quote attributed to Rashi "First Edition" in the שיטה מקובצת to b Ket. 97b: "*Mishum ḥina*, so that the men will find favor in the eyes of the women, so that they will say 'we will marry men, for if a husband dies or divorces [us] we needn't abase ourselves in going to court.'" R. Bezalel Ashkenazi, *Sefer Shittah Mekubetzet Vehu Hidushey Ketubot* (Tel Aviv: Avraham Ziony, 1965): 1262. Another interesting element of this comment is the fact that the reasoning of "a person does not desire that his wife should abase herself in court," is subsumed in the

having a stake in participating, even while being a threat if they participate in the institutional or judicial part of the game.[83] The *sugya* does not "accomplish" anything halakhically, yet, culturally it has "accomplished" much.

The idea of women being a threat if they participate in the institutional or judicial part of the game, is reinforced by the second principle that we cited at the outset: "A person does not desire that his wife should abase herself in court." In all the contexts in which this principle appears, the one thing about it which is left unquestioned is its basic premise. That premise is that women who appear in court are abasing themselves. There is a seeming contradiction between the role of a woman, and the appearance in court. Yet, this assumption itself is not questioned.

The assumption that women who appear in court shame themselves is a part of the construction of men, women and the institutions of law which we saw before with *ḥen*. The construction of shame and honor is a forceful way of representing this difference in the roles of men and women.[84] This discourse of the "nature" of men and women[85] also informs the medieval commentaries on the Talmud. A brief comment of Rashi will illustrate this point. There is a short comment in b Ket. (84a) on the following lines of M Ket. 9:2:

> One who died, and left a wife, a creditor, and heirs, and he also had a deposit or a loan in the possession of others.
> R. Tarfon said, this shall be given to the weakest amongst them.[86]

R. Tarfon's statement makes it easier for one who, for whatever reason, won't be able to win the harder fight of collecting immediately from land, to collect something eventually. The Talmudic comment is generated by the rare phrase: to the weakest. Two opinions are cited:

---

understanding of *mishum ḥina*. In the *sugya* in b Ket, these are two independent reasons. On the identity and existence of the "First Edition" (מהדורא קמא) of Rashi see Jonah Fraenkel, *Rashi's Methodology in his Exegesis of the Babylonian Talmud* (Heb) (The Magnes Press, Jerusalem, 1980): 7-15. Whether the author of this particular comment is Rashi or one of his students, the description of the cultural stakes stands.

[83] As in the *ma'asim* in the *sugya* 34b-35b.
[84] And cf. in Chapter VII the use and abuse of Psalms 45:14 in b Gittin 1 2a-1 3a, and in the subsequent commentary and halakhic tradition.
[85] Cf. esp. the series of ...דרכה של איש (It is the way for a man to...) statements, b Kid. 2b, and especially their *legal* ramifications.
[86]

מי שמת והניח אשה ובעל חוב ויורשין, והיה לו פקדון או מלוה ביד אחרים.
רבי טרפון אומר ינתנו לכושל שבהן.

Framing Women/Constructing Exile 183

> R. Yosi in the name of R. Ḥanina says, to the one who is weakest in proof.
>
> R. Yoḥanan says, to the *ketubah* payment of the wife, because of her grace (*mishum ḥinah*).[87]

Rashi comments on the phrase "to the *ketubah* payment of the wife," as follows:

> She is called the weakest, since it is not her way to go after the property of the dead person, and find out where he had any land.[88]

Rashi's interpretation, based on what is "natural" ("it is not her way...") is generated by the same cultural construct that sees a woman as submissive, silent, and not involved in the judicial institutions.

---

[87] The Soncino translation here (S. Daiches) has "...in order to maintain pleasantness [between her and her husband]." In the notes though (84a n. 12), three alternatives are supplied. This is a wonderful enactment of a site of conflicting interpretation.

[88] לכתובת אשה – היא קרויה כושל שאין דרכה לחזור אחר נכסי המת ולבקש היכן יש לו קרקע: Rashi is still consistent in his interpretation of *mishum ḥina* as the men finding favor in her eyes:

משום חינא – שימצאו האנשים חן בעיני הנשים ויהיו נשאות להן שלא תדאגנה להפסיד כתובתן:

גיטין דף מט ע"ב-נ ע"א

כתובת אשה בזיבורית:
אמר מר זוטרא בריה דרב נחמן, לא אמרן, אלא מיתמי. אבל מיניה דידיה בבינונית.
'מיתמי' מאי איריא כתובת אשה? אפילו כל מילי נמי. דהא תנן,
5 "אין נפרעים מנכסי יתומים אלא מן הזיבורית."
אלא לאו, מיניה.
לעולם מיתמי, וכתובת אשה איצטריכא ליה.
סלקא דעתך אמינא משום חינא אקילו בה רבנן,[89]
קא משמע לן.
10

אמר רבא, תא שמע,
רבי מאיר אומר כתובת אשה בבינונית.
ממאן? אילימא מיתמי, לית ליה לרבי מאיר הא דתנן,
"אין נפרעים מנכסי יתומים אלא מן הזיבורית?"
15 אלא לאו, מיניה. – מכלל דרבנן סברי בזיבורית.[90]
לא, לעולם מיתמי. ושאני כתובת אשה משום חינא.

אמר אביי, תא שמע,
הניזקין שמין להן בעידית, ובעל חוב בבינונית, וכתובת אשה בזיבורית.
20 ממאן? אילימא מיתמי, מאי איריא כתובת אשה? אפילו כל הני נמי.
אלא לאו, מיניה.
אמר רב אחא בר יעקב, הכא במאי עסקינן?
כגון שנעשה ערב למקי בנו, לבעל חוב בנו, ולכתובת כלתו.
והאי כי דיניה, והאי כי דיניה.
25 ניזקין ובעל חוב דמחיים גבו אידו נמי כי מגבי כמחיים מגבי.
כתובת אשה דלאחר מיתה נביא, ולאחר מיתה ממאן גביא – מיתמי.
אידו נמי כי מגבי, כלאחר מיתה מגבי.

ותיפוק ליה, דערב דכתובה לא משתעבד. בקבלן.
30 הניחא למאן דאמר קבלן, אף על גב דלית ליה נכסי ללוה משתעבד, שפיר.
אלא למאן דאמר אי אית ליה משתעבד, אי לית ליה לא משתעבד. מאי איכא למימר?
איבעית אימא בדהוו ליה ואישתדוף, ואיבעית אימא כל לגבי בריה שעבודי משעבד
נפשיה. איתמר,
ערב דכתובה דברי הכל לא משתעבד,
35 קבלן דבעל חוב דברי הכל משתעבד,
ערב דבעל חוב וקבלן דכתובה פליגי.
איכא למאן דאמר אף על גב דלית ליה נכסי ללוה משתעבד,
ואיכא למאן דאמר אי אית ליה משתעבד אי לית ליה לא משתעבד.
והלכתא בכולהו אף על גב דלית ליה-משתעבד, בר מערב דכתובה,
דאף על גב דאית ליה-לא משתעבד.

נ ע"א

---

[89] בה רבנן] מן_1, אקילו בה א, בה רבנן נבה ו, רבנן נבה דפוס
[90] מכלל דרבנן סברי בזיבורית] ליתא מ

40   מאי טעמא? מצוה הוא דעבד, ולא מידי חסרה.

אמר רבינא, תא שמע,
מעיקרא דתקנתין יותר ממה שהאיש רוצה לישא אשה רוצה לינשא.
ואי סלקא דעתך מיתמי, האי משום דיתמי הוא.
45   תיובתא דמר זוטרא תיובתא.[91]

---

[91] דמר זוטרא תיובתא] ליתא מ

Bavli Gittin 49b-50a

2   [In the case of] a woman's *ketubah* [payment] – the worst [land].
3   Said Mar Zutra the son of R. Naḥman, they only said it [in the case of collecting] from orphans, but [in a case of collecting] from [the husband] himself [we assess] the average land.
4   [If only] "from orphans," – why is this rule laid down with reference to a woman's ketubah [payment]? [It applies in] every case. For we learned:
5   "Payment is collected from orphans only from the worst [land]."
6   Rather, [this is] not [the proper understanding]. [It refers to collecting] from him.
7   [Actually] it still [refers to the case of collecting] from orphans. And it is necessary [to specify] a woman's *ketubah*.
8   For it might occur to you to say, "Because of her favor the rabbis were lenient towards her,"
9   We are told [therefore that this is not so].
10
11 Said Rava: Come and hear,
12 R. Meir says, even [in the case of] a woman's ketubah [payment we assess] the average land.
13 From whom? If I were to say from the orphans, does R. Meir not accept that which we have learned:
14 "Payment is collected from orphans only from the worst [land]?"
15 Rather, [this is] not [the proper understanding]. [It refers to collecting] from him – as inferred from the fact that the rabbis hold [that even a *ketubah* collected from the husband is collected from] the worst [land].
16 No, it still [refers to the case of collecting] from orphans. And a woman's *ketubah* payment differs because of her favor.
17
18 Said Abayye: Come and hear,
19 [In cases of] damages we assess the choice land [of the defendant], [In the cases of the claim of] a creditor [we assess] the average land, and [in the case of] a woman's *ketubah* [payment] – the worst [land].
20 From whom? If I were to say, from the orphans – why is this rule laid down with reference to a woman's ketubah [payment]? [It refers] even to all these others, too.
21 Rather, [this is] not [the proper understanding]. [It refers to collecting] from him.
22 Said R. Aḥa b. Yaakov, with what [type of situation] are we dealing here?
23 [We are dealing with a situation where,] for example, he was made a guarantor for the damages [due from] his son, towards the creditors of his son, and for the *ketubah* of his daughter-in-law.
24 Each item then follows its own rule.
25 Damage awardees and creditors who collect payment in the lifetime [of the person responsible] – [so,] when he [the father/guarantor] is forced to pay, he is forced to pay as though in the lifetime [of the person responsible].

26	A woman's *ketubah* which is [usually] collected after the death [of the person responsible]; and after the death, from whom is it collected? From the orphans.
27	[So,] when he [the father/guarantor] is forced to pay, he is forced to pay as though after the death [of the person responsible].
28	
29	But cannot this rule be derived from the fact that a guarantor for a *ketubah* is not responsible? [We speak] of a *kabbelan* [go-between, who is held responsible.]
30	This sits well for the one who says that a *kabbelan* is responsible even though the borrower has no property.
31	But, for one who says that if the borrower has [property] he is responsible, if the borrower has no [property] he is not responsible, what is to be said?
32	If you like I can say [that we suppose it to be a case in which] he had [property] which was subsequently destroyed, or if you like I can say that in respect of his son a man would in all cases regard himself as responsible.
33	It has been stated:
34	[With regard to] a guarantor of a *ketubah*, all say that he does not become responsible,
35	[With regard to] a *kabbelan* towards a creditor, all say that he does become responsible,
36	[With regard to] a guarantor towards a creditor, and a *kabbelan* of a *ketubah*, they differ.
37	Some are of the opinion that even though the debtor had no property they become responsible,
38	and some are of the opinion that if he had property they become responsible, but if he had no property they do not become responsible.
39	The law in all these cases is that even if [the debtor] had no property – [the guarantor] becomes responsible, save in the case of a guarantor of a *ketubah*, for even if [the husband] had property he does not become responsible.
40	What is the reason? He performed a *mitzvah*, and he does not cause the woman any loss.
41	
42	Said Rabina: Come and hear,
43	[It is] of the essence of the ordinance [that a woman's *ketubah* payment is from the worst land]: "More than a man wants to marry, a woman wants to be married."
44	And if it would occur to you [that the Mishnah refers to collecting] from orphans, then the reason would be that they are orphans.
45	The refutation of Mar Zutra [is] a refutation.

Appendix III: סלקא דעתך אמינא...קמ"ל and Writing Under Erasure

An obvious and close to hand example of the "סלקא דעתך אמינא...קמ"ל" figure as introducing concepts under erasure, is the first *sugya* of the fourth chapter of b Gittin.[92] The *sugya* is an unattributed *sugya* which strongly reads each phrase of the Mishnah in order to open it up for concerns that are the Bavli's and not the Mishnah's. (This reading is strongly reminiscent of the style of reading of Bible verses found in Midrash Halakhah.) Each of these concerns is introduced "under erasure" by the phrase "You would have said... We are told [therefore that this is not so]" (מהו דתימא...קמ"ל), except for the first which is introduced by "and we do not say..." (ולא אמרינן). I read this first limb as a variation of the מהו דתימא...קמ"ל figure, which functions in the same way, or does the same thing.[93] The Mishnah begins as follows:

> If one sends a writ of divorce (get) to his wife, and he overtook the messenger
> or sent another messenger after him, and said to him, "The writ of divorce that I gave to you is nullified,"
> then it is nullified.[94]

The *sugya* begins:

> [The Mishnah] does not say 'overtook *him*' (הגיעו), but simply overtook (הגיע),
> that is to say, even accidentally;
> and we do not say in that case that he merely desires to trouble his wife.[95]

Introducing the concept of "troubling" (לצעורא) into this part of the Mishnah is hard to understand. The Talmud is suggesting that when a man has sent a divorce to his wife, and then he finds (or comes upon) the

---

[92] Cf. Menahem Kahane, "*Gilui Da'at Ve'ones Begittin*," *Tarbiz* 62, 2, Jan-Mar 1993: 225-263, who from very different premises, and for different reasons comes to similar conclusions about the *sugyot* generated by the first Mishnah:

נמצינו למדים, כי יש מכנה משותף לסוגיות הנפרדות של הגמרא בפתיחה ובסיום של הדיון במשנה הראשונה של פרק השולח. שתי הסוגיות הללו הן סוגיות סתמיות ומאוחרות, כנראה סבוראיות, המנהלות פולמוס סמוי עם עמדתו של רבא ונוקטות בדעת אביי הסובר, לפי האינטרפרטאציה המופשטת שלהן, שגילוי דעת לאו מילתא הוא. (233)

[93] See the beginning of Appendix II for another example of the סד"א...קמ"ל figure.

[94]
השולח גט לאשתו והגיע בשליח,
או ששלח אחריו שליח, ואמר לו: גט שנתתי לך בטל הוא;
הרי זה בטל.

[95]
הגיעו לא קתני אלא "הגיע"-
ואפילו ממילא.
ולא אמרינן לצעורה הוא דקא מיכוין.

Framing Women/Constructing Exile

messenger, and cancels the divorce – we actually believe that he canceled the divorce, and the divorce is nullified. We don't impute to the husband an unattested desire to not nullify the divorce, but merely to harass his wife. In other words we don't explain the actions of the husband against the husbands proffered explanation of them (or their "face value").

Aside from the fact that ascribing the motive of לצעורא, in this case, is counterintuitive it is not clear what the hypothesis of לצעורא actually is. The term itself is a site of conflicting interpretation. Rashi in his commentary on the *sugya* says:

> And we don't say: [that] he didn't intend to nullify it but, rather, to just trouble her for a month or two. *For if he wanted to nullify it he would have run after him [the messenger] to nullify it.*

On the other hand the Tosafot comment:

> And we don't say: ...I would have thought that *since he didn't bring witnesses to it [the nullification] he doesn't want to nullify it.*

It is, of course, impossible to decide between these two interpretations, and this is just the point. The fact that לצעורא (in order to trouble) is such an obvious site of conflicting interpretations points to its "ungrammaticality" and that what it *does* is different than what it *means*. In the very line that it is introduced, the claim is seemingly dismissed out of hand. However, what it does is introduce a narrative of conflicting wishes between husband and messenger, husband and wife, and husband and court; ultimately a narrative arc which calls into question the ability of a *get* (writ of divorce) to reach its intended address. This is the narrative kernel of all the *maasim* in the *sugya* of b Gittin 33a-34b – that is, the final *sugya* on this Mishnah.

Appendix IV: The Text

נישין דף לד ע"ב-לה ע"ב[96]

משנה

אין אלמנה נפרעת מנכסי יתומים אלא בשבועה,
נמנעו מלהשביעה.

5   התקין רבן שמעון בן גמליאל[97] שתהא נודרת ליתומים כל מה שירצו וגובה כתובתה.

גמרא

מאי איריא אלמנה, אפילו כולי עלמא נמי?
דהא קיימא לן, 'הבא ליפרע מנכסי יתומין לא יפרע אלא בשבועה.'
10   אלמנה אצטריכא ליה.
סלקא דעתך אמינא | משום חינא אקילו רבנן גבה,[98]
קא משמע לן

נמנעו מלהשביעה:

15   מאי טעמא? אילימא משום דרב כהנא.
דאמר רב כהנא ואמרי לה אמר רב יהודה אמר רב,[99]
מעשה באדם אחד בשני בצורת,
שהפקיד דינר זהב אצל אלמנה,
והניחתו בכד של קמח,
20   ואפאתו בפת, ונתנתו לעני,
לימים, בא בעל הדינר ואמר לה, תני לי[100] דינרי,
אמרה ליה, יהנה סם המות באחד מבניה של אותה אשה אם נהניתי מדינרך כלום.
אמרו, לא היו ימים מועטין עד שמת אחד מבניה.

---

[96] I use the Vilna text as a starting point, significant changes from the Vilna text are noted in the appartatus and explained in the chapter. The major resource for the apparatus is Meyer S. Feldblum, דקדוק סופרים: מסכת נישין (New York: Yeshiva University Press, 1966). The following are the most common abbreviations: מ – Munich 95; א – Arras 969; א₁ – Oxford 368, MS Opp. 248; ו – Vatican 140; ו₁ – Vatican 130; ו₂ – Vatican 127. For a description of the manuscripts see Feldblum, 9-13. Cf. the list "Manuscripts of the Babylonian Talmud" by Michael Krupp in Abraham Goldberg, "The Babylonian Talmud," in Shmuel Safrai ed. *The Literature of the Sages, First Part: Oral Torah, Halakha, Mishna, Tosefta, Talmud, External Tractates* (Philadelphia: Van Gorcum, Assen/Maastricht, Fortress Press, 1987): 351-360. Krupp identifes the Arras MS as number 889. Vatican 130 was published in a facsimile edition in אוסף כתבי יד של הטיק (Jerusalem: Makor, 1974).

[97] רבן שמעון בן גמליאל] קפל, רבן גמליאל הזקן דפוס

[98] אקילו רבנן גבה] אקילו בה רבנן וא

[99] דאמר רב כהנא ואמרי לה אמר רב יהודה] ליתא ה₁, דאמר רב כהנא אמר רב ו₁, דאמר רב כהנא ואמרי לה אמר רב ח

[100] תני לי] ואה₁, תן ה ז, הבי לי ו₁ דפוס

וכששמעו חכמים בדבר אמרו, מה מי שנשבע באמת כך, הנשבע לשקר[101]
על אחת כמה וכמה.

25 מאי טעמא איענשה? דאישתרשי לה מקום דינר.
ומאי 'מי שנשבע באמת?' כמי שנשבע באמת.
אי משום הא, מאי איריא אלמנה? אפילו גרושה נמי. אלמה
אמר רבי זירא אמר שמואל, לא שנו אלא אלמנה אבל גרושה משביעין אותה.
30 אלמנה שאני, דבההיא הנאה דקא טרחה קמי דיתמי אתיא לאורויי היתרא.

אמר רב יהודה אמר רבי ירמיה בר אבא,
רב ושמואל דאמרי תרוויהו לא שנו אלא בב"ד אבל חוץ לבית דין משביעין אותה.
איני? והא רב לא מגבי כתובה לארמלתא?
קשיא. בסורא מתנו הכי, בנהרדעא[102] מתנו הכי.
35 אמר רב יהודה אמר שמואל, לא שנו אלא בבית דין אבל חוץ לב"ד משביעין אותה.
ורב אמר אפילו חוץ לב"ד [103]אין משביעין אותה.
רב לטעמיה, דרב לא מגבי כתובה לארמלתא.
וליאדרה וליגבייה! בשני דרב קילי נדרי.

40 ההיא דאתאי לקמיה דרב הונא,
אמר לה, מה אעביד ליך? דרב לא מגבי כתובה לארמלתא.
אמרה ליה, מידי הוא טעמא, אלא דלמא נקיטנא מידי מכתובתי.
חי ה' צבאות אם נהניתי מכתובתי כלום.
אמר רב הונא, מודה רב בקופצת.

45 ההיא דאתאי לקמיה דרבה בר רב הונא.
אמר לה, מאי אעביד ליך? דרב לא מגבי כתובה לארמלתא,
ואבא מרי לא מגבי כתובה לארמלתא.[104]
אמרה ליה, הב לי מזוני.
50 אמר לה, מזוני נמי לית ליך.
דאמר רב יהודה אמר שמואל, התובעת כתובתה בב"ד אין לה מזונות.
אמרה ליה, הפכוה[105] לכורסיה! כבי תרי עבדא לי.
הפכה לכורסיה, ותרצה.[106]
ואפילו הכי לא איפוק מחולשא.

55 אמר ליה רב יהודה לרב ירמיה ביראה,
אדרה בב"ד, ואשבעה חוץ לב"ד, ולייתי קלא וליפול באודני,
דבעינא כי היכי דאעביד בה מעשה.

---

[101]לשקר] מה[1]או, בשקר ה, על שקר דפוס
[102]בנהרדעא] בפומבדיתא ו
[103]אין] מו[1], נמי אין דפוס
[104]ואבא מרי לא מגבי כתובה לארמלתא] ליתא א (תראה שבגלל הדומת)
[105]הפכוה] מ, ליהפכוה וו[1]א, אפכוה דפוס
[106]לכורסיה ותרצה] ותרצה לכורסיה ו

נופא,

אמר רבי זירא אמר שמואל, לא שנו אלא אלמנה אבל גרושה משביעין אותה. ונרושה דאדרה לא? והא שלחו מתם,

"איך פלוניתא בת פלוני קבילת גיטא מן ידא דאחא בר הידיא דמתקרי איה מרי, ונדרת, ואסרת כל[107] פירות שבעולם עלה, דלא קבילת מכתובתה אלא: גלופקרא אחד, וספר תהלים אחד, וספר איוב, וממשלות בלואים. | ושמנום בחמשה מנה. לכשתבא לידכם הגבוה את השאר."

אמר רב אשי, ההוא גט יבמין הוה.

---

[107]כל] סוף₁, ליתא דפוס

7

Women and Slaves: A Reading of Gittin 12a-13a

Introduction

The *sugya* that I analyze in this chapter (b Gittin 12a-13a), deals broadly with the obligations of a man to support his wife and/or slave, and whether or not the man can unilaterally end that obligation.

The method of this chapter will be similar to the previous chapter. First I will analyze the *sugya* part by part. This close reading of the linear argument will point to the places where this reading falters. These ungrammaticalities are what, in the final reading will let us move away from reading according to the rhetorical demands of the text (its linearity, its mimetic level). On a second reading I will argue that there is a structure to the *sugya* independent of its linear flow. This structure will enable us to situate the *sugya* within the tensions of a larger cultural discourse. Finally, I will return to read the *sugya* in light of its ungrammaticalities, the concerns of its images, in short the narrative of its subtext.[1]

One focal point of my reading of this *sugya* will be the way in which it conflates the constructions of women and slaves. One of the indices of this conflation is the use of terminology that is marked female – by way of its (statistically) "common" usage – to discuss sexually (though perhaps not culturally and definitely not legally) male slaves. This is one of only three *sugyot* in the Bavli which apply the term מעשה ידים (lit. handiwork; "whatever one earns") to slaves. The other two *sugyot* are b Gittin 37b-38a,[2] and the parallel of that *sugya* in b Yebamot 46a. The term

---

[1]See my discussion of subtexts and ungrammaticalities in Chapter V, above.
[2]The use of the term in that *sugya* is also unique inasmuch as it is dealing with the question of whether a non-Jew ("idolator") can buy another non-Jew for a slave.

is regularly applied to women. The only Tannaitic source that applies the term to slaves is one that is also quoted in our sugya – Tosefta Makkot 2:8[3] (lines 20ff.) This is the only *sugya* in which the phrase *ma'aleh...mezonot* (provides... with food) is used in reference to a male[4] – a slave (lines 58, 76). It is often used in the Bavli in reference to women (fiancee[5]/ wife[6]).

The Sugya

Bavli Gittin 11b-13a[7]
Mishnah

3   One who says: 'Give this writ of divorce [*get*] to my wife', and 'this bill of emancipation to my slave',
4   If he wishes to renege on both, he may – these are the words of R. Meir.
5   And Sages say, in [the case of] women's divorce [he may renege], but not in [the case of] emancipations of slaves.
6   For a benefit may be conferred on a person in their absence, but a disability may be imposed on him only in his presence.
7   For if he wishes not to feed his slave – he is permitted; but [if he wishes] not to feed his wife – he is not permitted.
8   He said to them: does he not invalidate his slave from eating *Terumah* just as he invalidates his wife [from eating *Terumah*]?
9   They said to him: Because he is his property [קנינו].
10 Gemara
11 For if he wishes not to feed, etc.
12   We understand from here that a master can say to his slave: 'Work for me and I will not feed you'.

The possibility is raised that a non Jew might not be able to buy another non-Jew's *body* but only his "handiwork."
[3]Ed. Zukermandel p. 440.

עבד שגלה לעיר מקלט אין רבו חייב במזונותיו
ולא עוד אלא שמעשה ידיו לרבו,
האשה שגלתה לעיר מקלט בעלה חייב במזונותיה
ואם אמר צאו לה מעשה ידיה במזונותיה הרשות בידו:

[4]Though in b B.M. 92b male slaves are included among a list of *dependent* persons for whom the husband/father/master is *ma'aleh mezonot*. In that *sugya*, as in ours, the question of whether or not a master might tell his slave "work for me but I won't pay you," is raised. This might suggest that (legal) gendering is along power lines, as has been suggested with regard to the construction of sexuality in the ancient world by Bernadette J. Brooten *Love Between Women: Early Christian Responses to Female Homoeroticism* (Chicago: University of Chicago Press, 1996), and John Winkler, The *Constraints of Desire: The Anthropology of Sex and Gender in Ancient Greece* (New York, London: Routledge, 1990), esp. chap 1.
[5]E.g. b Ketubbot 2a
[6]E.g. b Ketubbot 58b
[7]The original text of the *sugya*, with an apparatus, is in the Appendix at the end of this chapter. The translation is mine, although I used the Soncino translation as a starting point. The abbreviations in the apparatus are the same as in the apparatus to b Gittin 34b-35b. See Chapter VI, Appendix IV, n. 96.

Women and Slaves: A Reading of Gittin 12a-13a

13   With what [case] are we dealing here? – That he [the master] said to him [the slave] 'Let your earnings suffice to feed yourself.'

14   Similarly [in the case of] a wife That he said to her 'Let your earnings suffice to feed yourself.'

15   Why [is this] not [allowed in the case of a] wife? When the wife does not earn enough.

16   [Let us say that] the slave also doesn't earn enough.

17   "A slave that is not worth the food of his stomach – what would his master and mistress want him for?"

18

19   Come and hear:

20 "If a slave was exiled to [one of] the cities of refuge[8] his master is under no obligation to support him,

21 and moreover whatever he earns belongs to his master." (T. Mak. 2:8)

22   We understand from here that a master can say to his slave: 'Work for me and I will not feed you'.

23   With what [case] are we dealing here? – That he [the master] said to him [the slave] 'Let your earnings suffice to feed yourself.'

24   In that case why does it say that what he earns belongs to the master? That is [referring to] the extra [earnings beyond that which is sufficient for food]. Extra [earnings] is obvious.

25   What is it that you would have said, "Since [the master] does not give him when he does not have, he should also not take from him when he does have!"

26   We are told [therefore that this is not so].

27   And what is different [about the case of] "to the cities of refuge?" It might occur to you to say, [since] the Torah[9] said "and live"[10] – it is incumbent [upon the master] to provide extra support (*living*).

28   We are told [therefore that this is not so].

29   But since the end [of the passage quoted] teaches:

30 "But if a woman was exiled to a city of refuge, her husband is under obligation to support her."

31   This is obviously because he did not say to her ['Let your earnings suffice to feed yourself.'] For if he told her, why should he be obligated?

32   And since it is the case here that he didn't tell her, that is also the case in the first part of the passage.

33   No, in all cases he told her/him, but [the case of] the woman is when she can't earn enough [to support herself].

34   But since the end [of the passage quoted] teaches:

35 If he says to her 'Use your earnings for your support,' he is within his rights.

36   This is obviously because in the earlier case he did not tell her.

37   This is what it said: If she can earn *sufficiently* and he says to her 'Use your earnings for your support,' he is within his rights.

38   What is the point of stating [the case where] she can earn sufficiently?

---

[8] see Deut. 4:41-43.
[9] lit. "the Merciful One"
[10] Deut. 4:42

39	You would have said, "the honor of the king's daughter lies in privacy," (Psalms 45:14).
40	We are told [therefore that this is not so].
41	
42	Let us say [that it is the same] as [a difference of opinion between] Tannaim.
43	Rabban Shimon ben Gamaliel says: A slave can say to his master in a year of drought,
44	'Either maintain me or let me go free'.
45	And Sages say: It is up to the master.
46	Is it not that they are divided in this – that the one holds that a master can say [to his slave: 'Work for me and I will not feed you.'] and the other holds that he cannot say?
47	Do you really think so? [In that case why does it say] 'Either maintain me or let me go free'?
48	It should say 'Either maintain me or let me keep my earnings in place of my maintenance'.
49	And further, why should the rule apply especially in years of drought?
50	Rather, with what [case] are we dealing here? – That he [the master] said to him [the slave] 'Let your earnings suffice to feed yourself,' and in a year of drought he didn't earn enough.
51	Rabban Shimon ben Gamaliel holds: 'Either maintain me or let me go free,
52	So that people will see me and have pity on me.'
53	And the rabbis hold, one who pities a free man will also pity a slave.
54	
55	Come and hear that Rab said:
56	One who dedicates [to the Sanctuary] the hands of his slave, that slave borrows, eats, works and repays [the loan].
57	We understand from here that a master can say to his slave: 'Work for me and I will not feed you'.
58	With what [case] are we dealing here? – [A case] in which [the master] supplies him with food.
59	If so why does he borrow money to eat? For extra [food beyond **12b** what his master would give him].
60	The Sanctuary should say to him, 'Just as you could do without extras until now,
61	so you can do without extras now.'
62	The Sanctuary itself prefers this, since it is for the improvement of its slave.
63	He "works and repays [the loan]" – how is this possible since each penny he earns is sanctified as he earns it? [He earns and pays] in amounts smaller than a *perutah*.
64	This view is borne out [by this other dictum], for Rab says:
65	If one dedicates to the Sanctuary the hands of his slave, [the slave] works and eats.
66	For if he doesn't work, who would work for him?
67	If you say that the first statement [refers to a case] in which [the master] provides [the slave's food], and [the master] cannot [say to

Women and Slaves: A Reading of Gittin 12a-13a

the slave work for me though I won't feed you]; while the second statement [refers to a case] in which [the master] doesn't provide [the slave's food] – all is well.

68 But if you say that the first statement [refers to a case] in which [the master] does not provide [the slave's food], and [the master] can [say to the slave work for me though I won't feed you];

69 [what is the sense of saying] 'for if he doesn't work, who would work for him?' – Whoever so wants, will work for him.

70 We, rather, understand from here that he cannot [say to the slave work for me though I won't feed you], this we understand.

71

72 Come and hear that R. Yohanan says:

73 One who cuts off the hand of another's slave, pays the slave's loss of time, and medical expenses to his master, and the slave lives on charity.

74 We understand from here that a master can say to his slave: 'Work for me and I will not feed you'.

75 With what [case] are we dealing here? – [A case] in which [the master] supplies him with food.

76 If so, why [does it say] he lives on charity. For extra [food].

77 If this is so, it should not say "lives on" (ניזון) but "is supported by" (מתפרנס).

78 We, rather, understand from here that he can [say to the slave work for me though I won't feed you], this we understand.

79

80 The Master said: "he pays [the slave's] loss of time, and medical expenses to his master,"

81 Loss of time is obvious. Medical expenses needed [to be mentioned].

82 Surely the medical costs are the slave's, for he needs them for his cure?

83 This too must be stated in view of a case where it was calculated that he requires five days [treatment] and by the application of a painful remedy he was cured in three.

84 You would have said, [the extra money because of] the pain is his, we understand from here [that it is not].

85

86 We learned: R. Eliezer said: We said to Meir, Is it not a benefit for a slave to get out from under his master to freedom?

87 He said to us: It is a disability for him, since if he was the slave of a priest he can no longer eat of the *Terumah*.

88 We said to him: If the priest chooses not to feed him or give support him, is he not permitted to do so?

89 He said to us: If the slave of a priest runs away, or if the wife of a priest flouts her husband, they can still eat of the *Terumah*,

90 but this one cannot.

91 For a woman, however, certainly it is a disadvantage [to be divorced] since she becomes disqualified to eat the *Terumah* [if she was married to a priest] and forfeits her maintenance [in any case]?

92 What did they say to him, and what did he reply to them?

198   *Rereading Talmud*

93   This is what he said to them: You have refuted me in the manner of maintenance, but what answer can you give in the matter of the *Terumah*?
94   For if you should say that, if the master likes, he can throw the writ of emancipation to the slave and so disqualify him – [I answer that] the slave can [prevent this by] leaving him and running away. |
95   If the slave of a priest runs away, or if the wife of a priest   **13a**
          flouts her husband,
96   they can still eat of the *Terumah*, but this one cannot.
97   For a woman, however, certainly it is a disadvantage [to be divorced] since she becomes disqualified to eat the *Terumah* [if she was married to a priest] and forfeits her maintenance [in any case]?
98   He answered them well.
99   Raba said: That is [the point of] the answer of the Rabbis [recorded] in the Mishnah, 'because he is his property,'
100   for if [the master] wants he can take four *zuz* from any [non-priestly] Israelite, and disqualify him wherever he is.
101   As to R. Meir, leaving aside the slave of a priest – what might he say about the slave of an Israelite?
102   R. Shmuel bar R. Isaac said, because it disqualifies him from a Canaanite slave woman.
103   On the contrary, it permits him to a free woman.
104   A slave prefers a common woman; she may be treated with disregard, she is always at his call, she is open to all his sexual advances.

The Sugya At First Sight

The *sugya*[11] is generated by Mishnah Gittin 1:6:[12]

3   One who says: 'Give this writ of divorce [*get*] to my wife', and 'this bill of emancipation to my slave',
4   If he wishes to renege on both, he may – these are the words of R. Meir.
5   And Sages say, in [the case of] women's divorce [he may renege], but not in [the case of] emancipations of slaves.
6   For a benefit may be conferred on a person in their absence, but a disability may be imposed on him only in his presence.
7   For if he wishes not to feed his slave – he is permitted; but [if he wishes] not to feed his wife – he is not permitted.
8   He[13] said to them: does he not invalidate his slave from eating *Terumah* just as he invalidates his wife [from eating *Terumah*]?

---

[11] It is the second *sugya* on this Mishnah.
[12] Actually, the first part of M Gittin 1:6 since in the division of the Mishnayot in the Mishnah MSS (as opposed to the division in the Talmud), there is no 1:7. 1:6 continues to the end of the chapter – it adds two lines more than we have here.
[13] R. Meir. The Munich MS and Vatican 120 both have "R. Meir said to them." I think that this is a reading which is influenced by the *sugya* which quotes the Tos. in which this statement is attributed to R. Meir by name (line 87ff).

Women and Slaves: A Reading of Gittin 12a-13a

9   They said to him: Because he is his property[14] [קנינו]

The *sugya* is commenting on the line "For if he wishes not to feed his slave...." The recurring question of the *sugya* is whether or not a master may tell his slave: "Work for me and I will not feed you."

I will now introduce the first part of the *sugya* in order to ground a purely formal description of the parts of the *sugya* as a whole.

11 **For if he wishes not to feed, etc.**
12 We understand from here that a master can say to his slave: 'Work for me and I will not feed you'.
13 With what [case] are we dealing here? – That he [the master] said to him [the slave] 'Let your earnings suffice to feed yourself.'
14 Similarly [in the case of] a wife That he said to her 'Let your earnings suffice to feed yourself.'
15 Why [is this] not [allowed in the case of a] wife? When the wife does not earn enough.
16 [Let us say that] the slave also doesn't earn enough.
17 "A slave that is not worth the food of his stomach – what would his master and mistress want him for?"

This first part of the *sugya* introduces one of the two types[15] of "formal units" found in the *sugya*. There are four units of this type. The type can be mapped as follows:

---

[14]The implication of this answer is that is that it is *only* because the slave is property that he (the slave) is invalidated, and therefore there is a great difference between the slave and the wife (contra "R. Meir"). MS Vat 130 ($_1$1) has the interestingly problematic reading: "Because he invalidates his wife as his acquisition" (see the notes to the Hebrew text). This reading would seem to be granting the point of "R. Meir," while claiming that it did not matter – since the reason for invalidation of the wife *here in the case of Terumah* is exactly that she is (for this purpose) "as his acquisition." This variant/reading is especially interesting in that it is problematizing the differentiation slave/wife in a way that I will argue that the *sugya* is also doing. The fact that this reading is not in any of the three important manuscripts of the Mishnah (ק,פ,ל), might suggest that this scribe (or whatever text the scribe was working from) was influenced by a unique reading of the *sugya* here. It cannot, however, be dismissed out of hand that we are merely dealing with a scribal error, since the previous line is somewhat similar to this line. That possibility is, of course, far less interesting. It should be noted that the readings of Vat. 130 are consistently unique or surprising in this *sugya*, and that the expert opinion is that the MS is accurate and important for its variant readings. Rabbi Moshe Hirshler, ed., מסכת כתובות עם שינויי נוסחאות מכתבי היד של התלמוד ועם השואות להבאות מגמרא בח"ל, נאותים וראשונים (Jerusalem: Machon Hatalmud Hayisraeli Hashalem, 1972): 67.

[15]This is a very minimal, descriptive claim at this point. These are parts of the larger *sugya* that are structurally similar. The reason for this taxonomy is to establish on "purely formal grounds" the points at which the *sugya* might resonate intratextually, and not to make any claim for the existence of these units beyond this *sugya* (or my description of it). This last disclaimer is to some extent contra Jacob Neusner's unstated claim that his description of Talmud, that is his

i.   Introductory source text
ii.   "We understand from here that a master can say to his slave: 'Work for me and I will not feed you'."
iii-?.   "With what [case] are we dealing here?" and discussion leading to…
LAST LINE. The "point," conclusion.

In the first unit, which we cited above, part i is quoted from the Mishnah (line 11). It is set off as a unit, and has no introductory formula. The other units of this type have introductory formulas ("Come and hear") to introduce part i (19, 55,73). Part ii is a constant in all the units of this type (12, 20, 57, 75). Part iii is a rereading of part i, in light of the challenge of part ii – the possibility that, a master can say to his slave: 'Work for me and I will not feed you'. The discussion generated by this question always leads to a "point" or "conclusion" – part iv (17, 25, 27, 40, 70, 79).

All of the units except the first have a formulaic ending for the "conclusions," either "we are told…" (קא משמע לן) or "we understand from here…" (שמע מינה). The second unit (ll. 19-40) of this type has three "conclusions." This, however, is in part because it deals with the source text by halves, and therefore doesn't introduce the second half with the "Come and hear" formula, but with "but look at the continuation of the quoted source" (30, 35). The "conclusions" are all, in one way or another, unexpected or obtuse – "ungrammatical." Two are verses quoted midrashically and/or decontextualized, one (the first) seems to be a saying of some sort. And the other two, which are straightforward, contradict each other outright.

The second type of formal unit may be mapped as follows:

i.   Introduction of a Tannaitic source.[16]
ii.   A seemingly independent sub-*sugya* attached to the Tannaitic source, which is a "commentary" on it.

There are two units of this second type (42-53; 87-105).

The trajectory of the linear argument, of the *sugya* as a whole, is odd in itself. It can be mapped as:

---

division of *sugyot* into lines and units of text, is a neutral activity. See above chapter three on Neusner's "analytic translation."
[16] 42: "Let us say it is as the Tannaitic debate…" לימא כתנאי; 87: "It has been taught [in a Tannaitic source]…"תניא, The former source (43-45) is not found in any other extant early Rabbinic text; the latter source is in some ways parallel to our Mishnah and also to Tosefta Gittin 1:5 (ed. Lieberman, 247), however it also differs from them in important ways.

1. Mishnah: the master need not support his slave.
2. Talmud: [thesis] therefore we may assume that the master need not support his slave.[17]
3. Conclusion: We learn from here that the master need not support his slave. QED (79)

Militating against accepting the linear argument at face value are several considerations. First, as is obvious, it is a tautological argument — the conclusion is no more, and no less than the original statement. Though it is true that tautologies, while they might not help anybody, don't hurt anybody either — there is an enormous effort in marking this tautology as a tautology which demands *"darsheni"* (explicate me).

Second, there are actually two separate and opposing conclusions in the *sugya*. In the mapping above we followed the Halakhic tradition, beginning with Alfasi,[18] which accepts the conclusion that appears later in the *sugya* (79) as being the "bottom line".[19] However, the unit immediately prior to this one (55-70) arrives at the opposing conclusion, and also ends off with the Talmudic equivalent of QED:[20] the repetition of the ending phrase "we understand from here" before and after the conclusion. (70)[21]

Third, as noted above, all the "conclusions" along the way are, in various ways "ungrammatical."

---

[17]In truth, the move that is repeated in each of these units is to suppose that when the Mishnah says that a Master might refuse to support a slave, this is not implying a work situation ('Work for me and I will not feed you'). This supposition is wholly unnecessary in order to explain the Mishnah. It is, however, a necessity for the *sugya* to "work."

[18]Isaac Alfasi (5a) [10 cent. Halakhist, wrote the *Halakhot*, a Halakhic "digest" of the Bavli printed at the end of the standard (Vilna) editions.] only quotes the final "come and hear" unit, prefacing it with ומסקנא (and the conclusion is). cf. R. Shlomo ben Aderet (*Rashba*; 1235-1310) and R. Yom Tov ben Abraham (*Ritva*; ca. 1270-ca. 1342)*ad locum* (*Novellae of the Rashba to the Talmud: Gittin*, Mossad Harav Kook, Jerusalem 1986, p. 107; *Novellae of the Rashba to the Talmud: vol. four Gittin*, Mossad Harav Kook, Jerusalem, 1980, p.66

[19]It is doubly surprising that this is the unit chosen as the conclusion, since it is the weakest one on logical grounds. The conclusion arrived at (79) is based on an unproven distinction between two usually synonymous terms ניזון and מתפרנס. cf. Rashi (1040-1105) and Ritva *ad locum*. Both commentaries attempt to support this differentiation as linguistically founded without pointing to any other instance where the differentiation is maintained. Ritva also notes that this conclusion could contradict the conclusion reached by the explanation of the Baraiita of R. Shimon ben Gamaliel (42-53).

[20]שמע מינה...שמע מינה.

[21]Vat. 130 (₁) does not have the second ending phrase שמע מינה in line 60, although all other MSS do.

Reading

Now let us return for a more substantive analysis of the first unit, quoted above (page 199). The basic problem with the unit is that the last line (17) doesn't seem to answer the question posed by the second line (12). What is at stake here, seemingly, is not whether or not it is logical for a person to own a slave, if that slave doesn't earn his keep. The question is whether a master might tell his slave to buy his own food from his earnings – even if the slave will not earn enough to do this.[22] The expected answer would have been either, "yes, a master might tell his slave to buy his own food from his earnings – even if the slave will not earn enough to do this," or "no a master may not tell his slave to buy his own food from his earnings – if the slave will not earn enough to do this." The "answer" we read seems more of a folk saying, or an epigram than an answer to the question. There are scholars who have "attributed" this saying to Ben Sira.[23] Whether or not the *sugya* was quoting Ben Sira (and in fact, there is no saying in Ben Sira that exactly matches our saying here), the discussion of the relationship towards, and the control of slaves there is very helpful in understanding the cultural concerns governing the discussion here – the tension between oppression and mercy.

For now though, we will just note that this statement points us to another statement later on in the *sugya* which also is unadorned with formal ending phrases. This is the last line of the *sugya* :

104   A slave prefers a common[24] woman; she may be treated with disregard, she is always at his call, she is open to all his sexual advances.

This statement seems to be a saying of some kind, also. Its sole claim to authority is as a truism – that is, descriptive rather than prescriptive. Both statements come at the end of more or less technical legal discussions and cap them with a bit of folk wisdom.

---

[22]Cf. Tosafot *s.v. eved nami*. "…it should have been said outright, that he [the master] is not obligated to feed him [the slave], since he said to him: 'Let your earnings suffice to feed yourself.'"

[23]See the list at the end of Benjamin G. Wright III, "Some Methodological Considerations on the Rabbis' Knowledge of the Proverbs of Ben Sira," IOUDAIOS files, 1992, electronic media (send message: <get bwsira article> to listserv@lehigh.edu). Wright cites the saying from b Baba Metziah 65a, but it is essentially the same as here.

[24]This follows the Soncino translation. הפקירא also has the connotations of wanton on the one hand, and unowned on the other. Cf. the usage of הפקר מנהג in describing (by R. Hiyah) the act of forcing a master to free a woman who was half slave and half free (b Gittin 38b).

Women and Slaves: A Reading of Gittin 12a-13a   203

Let us leave this tenuous link hanging for now and move to the second "Come and hear" unit (19-40). The source that is introduced is a *beraitta* that is also found (with slight variations) in Tosefta Makkot 2:8:[25]

1. If a slave was exiled to one of the cities of refuge[26] his master is under no obligation to support him,
2. and moreover whatever he earns belongs to his master.
3. But if a woman was exiled to a city of refuge, her husband is under obligation to support her.
4. If he says to her 'Use your earnings for your support,' he is within his rights.

The *beraitta* is discussed in two parts. The first two lines are explicated in the same manner as the first unit, leading, though, to two "conclusions" (19-28). Then the second half of the *beraitta* is introduced in order to complicate, or renew, the discussion leading to a further "conclusion" (29-40).

This unit is ostensibly a continuation of the question left hanging after line 14, whether a master may force his slave to work for him while not feeding him. The specific scenario introduced is the unlikely situation (especially in sixth century Babylonia or thereabouts) of a slave who has killed a person accidentally, and run to one of the cities of refuge for safety. Since the ruling in that case is that the master need not support him, it seems that our question is answered. A variable however is introduced which confutes this ready assertion (23). In truth the *beraitta* (as now reread by the anonymous tradent represented in our *sugya*) refers to a case in which the master had told the slave "Use your earnings for your support," and the earnings (referred to in line 2 of the *beraitta* above) that go to the master are those that are in excess of the amount needed for support (24). It is then asked that if the intent was only the money in excess of maintenance, wouldn't this be understood even without an explicit teaching? The *sugya* continues:

25   What is it that you would have said, "Since [the master] does not give him when he does not have, he should also not take from him when he does have!"
26   We are told [therefore that this is not so].
27   And what is different [about the case of] "to the cities of refuge?" It might occur to you to say, [since] the Torah[27] said "and live"[28] – it is incumbent [upon the master] to provide extra support (*living*).

---

[25]Ed. Zukermandel p. 440
[26]See Deut. 4:41-43.
[27]Lit. "the Merciful One"
[28]Deut. 4:42

28   We are told [therefore that this is not so].

Two points are being introduced here "under erasure." The first (25) is more or less clear and we will leave it for now.[29] The second is far from clear.[30] First the "prooftext" that is cited makes no mention of slaves at all. The immediate context in Deuteronomy 4 is as follows:[31]

> 41. Then Moses set aside three cities on the east side of the Jordan
> 42. to which a manslayer could escape, one who unwittingly slew a fellow man without having been hostile to him in the past; he could flee to one of these and live;
> 43. Bezer, in the wilderness in the Tableland, belonging to the Reubenites; Ramoth, in Gilead, belonging to the Gadites; and Golan, in Bashan, belonging to the Manassites.

Line 22 is a midrashic rereading of verse 42 "and live" – reading it now as an imperative (*and support*). It also extends it to slaves. However, this Midrashic reading of Deut. 4 brings us no closer to understanding why this rule had to have been taught regarding a city of refuge. If I would have thought that "it is incumbent [upon the master] to provide extra support," how could I have dismissed line 25? And if I would have said: "Since the master does not give him anything when he does not earn, he should not take anything from him when he does earn!" in regard to any situation, and not just a city of refuge, then we are back to the question: "And why does this rule apply especially to cities of refuge?" In other words, these two premises are mutually exclusive. Line 25 supposes that there might be a reason for a special consideration (with or without the city of refuge consideration) since the master cuts off support. Line 27 supposes that there might be special consideration because it is a city of refuge. Line 25 however is within the context of the city of refuge law here, and is dismissed. How, then, does the premise behind the second question even begin? That is, there obviously is no frame within which there should be special consideration – why assume that there is one? One cannot simply posit that there is a claim for special treatment in the case of a city of refuge, immediately after having dismissed the possibility of a claim for special consideration in the case of a city of refuge.

---

[29]We will return to the idea of master-slave relations later.
[30]One measure of this is the way in which the Tosafot *ad locum* attempt to clarify the point.
[31]NJPS.

41   אז יבדיל משה שלש ערים בעבר הירדן מזרחה שמש.
42   לנס שמה רוצח אשר ירצח את רעהו בבלי דעת והוא לא שנא לו מתמל שלשם, ונס אל אחת מן הערים האל וחי.
43   את בצר במדבר בארץ המישר לראובני, ואת ראמת בגלעד לגדי ואת גולן בבשן למנשי.

The point of this is not to challenge those who are skilled in it, to engage in *pilpul* and harmonize the unit, rather to settle for a moment on its strangeness, its ungrammaticality, and its "unreadability."[32] And to raise the question, "what is this section doing?"

The second half of this unit rereads the second half of the *beraitta* quoted above. Line 4 of the *beraitta* is understood as saying:

37   ...If she can earn *sufficiently* and he says to her 'Use your earnings for your support,' he is within his rights.

The *sugya* asks: Why bring in "sufficient"? And continues:

39   You would have said, "the honor of the king's daughter lies in privacy," (Psalms 45:14).
40   We are told [therefore that this is not so].

The fascinating side to these lines is that there is a twofold move that is necessary in order to make sense of them. First, there is a midrashic reading of the verse. In its original context it means:

All glorious is the princess within,... (KJV)[33]
...with all kinds of wealth. The princess is decked... (RSV)[34]
...goods of all sorts. The royal princess,... (NJPS)

Glorious or *wealth* or *goods* (כבודה) is read as *honor* (כבודה) and the final syllable of *inside* (פנימה) is taken as a possessive suffix, changing the meaning to *her privacy*. The result is that a verse which in its original context was part of an exhortation to a "Tyrian lass" to give herself up to her king (12. ...*let the king be aroused by your beauty;...*), is now read as a description of the ideal modest Jewish woman.[35] Then this descriptive

---

[32]This in Jacques Derrida's sense: "The unreadable is not the opposite of the readable, but the ridge that also gives it momentum, movement, sets it in motion." "Living On •Border Lines," in Harold Bloom, Paul de Man, Jacques Derrida, Geoffrey H. Hartman, J. Hillis Miller, *Deconstructionism and Criticism* (The Seabury Press, New York, 1979) p. 116. Unreadability is an indicator that a text is signifying in a different way.
[33]Following the LXX.
[34]In this and the NJPS translation, the first phrase of the verse is understood as the end of the thought of the phrase in the verse that precedes it. The full verse is translated as follows:
(12)13. the people of Tyre will sue your favor with gifts, the richest of the people (13)14. with all kinds of wealth. The princess is decked in her chamber with golden-woven robes; [RSV]
13. O Tyrian lass, the wealthiest people will court your favor with gifts, 14. goods of all sorts. The royal princess, her dress embroidered with golden mountings, 15. is led inside to the king; [NJPS] (the understated disclaimer "Meaning of Heb. uncertain" is given in a note).
[35]I would note that at this point when the (Jewish) daughter of a king is being made modest, the slave is on his way to lasciviousness. See the discussion below

statement is given normative implications.[36] The only way that the hypothesis of line 39 could mean anything, is if we follow Rashi's interpretation and read:

39 You would have said, "the honor of the king's daughter lies in privacy," [*and therefore she would not go out in public to earn money for herself*].

There are two Midrashic traditions connected with this verse which supply something of a larger context. Both traditions, read the verse as a whole:

כל כבודה בת מלך פנימה ממשבצות זהב לבושה.

Both traditions understand that the intertext for the gold embroidered garments – משבצות זהב – is the high priest's robes of Exodus 28:13: ועשית משבצת זהב. The verse is then reread as: "The glory of the daughter of the king is her modesty, thereby she will have the gold embroidered garments as her own." That is, if she is modest she will merit having her offspring serving as high priests.[37] Or in some traditions: "The glory of the daughter of the king is her modesty, her garments [i.e. her modesty] are greater than the priesthood." This latter reading takes the prefix "מ" in the sense of "[greater] than."[38] In either tradition there is a connection between the priesthood and the Temple and the modest woman. Be this as it may, in our *sugya* the verse itself signifies a discourse of "proper"[39] behavior.[40]

---

page 216. Further, as noted above, the discussion of this unit is centered on *ma'aseh yadayim* usually a term only applied to women, here applied to the slave.
[36]This is closely related to the discussion of יותר ממה שהאיש רוצה לישא אשה רוצה לינשא and אין אדם רוצה שתתבזה אשתו בבית דין. See Chapter VI Appendix II.
[37]This reading is associated with the earlier Palestinian tradition of the story of a woman who merited seeing two (or three) of her sons serve in the high priesthood on the same day. When asked by the Rabbis the reason for this high honor, she ascribes it to her modesty (p Yoma 1:1 4b; p Meg. 1:10 13b; p Hor. 3:2 12b; Lev. R. 20:11; Pes. de Rab Kahana 26 (ed. Mandelbaum p.399)). It is interesting to note that when this story appears in the Bavli (Yoma 47a) the Rabbis dismiss the woman's understanding of why she merited the honor, saying "Many have done as you did, and it did not help them." Rashi there in his commentary (s.v. *lo ra'u*) inserts the Midrash as something that he "saw in the Palestinian Talmud...."
[38]This reading is associated with a general panegyric towards modesty, taking God's talking to Moses in the privacy of the Tent of Meeting as a starting point. (Numbers R. 1:3; Ruth R. 4:9; Tanḥuma Vayishlaḥ 6; Tanḥ. Buber 85b).
[39]And cf. with the discussion of משום חינא, Chapter VI above.
[40]This meaning of the verse became so ingrained that Rashi, at times just quotes the verse with no further explanation, *as* an explanation itself of modesty-related behavior, e.g. b Abodah Zara 18a, b. Erubin 100b.

The next unit is of the other "type." A *beraitta* is introduced with the formulaic phrase: "Let us say that it is the same as [a difference of opinion] between Tannaim." (42)

43   Rabban Shimon ben Gamaliel says: A slave can say to his master in a year of drought,
44   'Either maintain me or let me go free'.
45   And Sages say: It is up to the master.

The sub-*sugya* which explicates the *beraitta* attempts to position the debate between R. Shimon ben Gamaliel and Sages as the debate over whether or not a master may tell his slave 'work for me and I won't feed you'. (46) (RShbG-no; Sages-yes). Noting the peculiarity of both the demand to be set free and the situation of the event in a year of drought (47-49) the *beraitta* is reread as only discussing a situation wherein, in a year of drought, the master had told his slave "Use your earnings for your support" (50). The *beraitta* is reconstructed at the end as:

51   Rabban Shimon ben Gamaliel holds: 'Either maintain me or let me go free,
52   So that people will see me and have pity on me.'
53   And the rabbis hold, one who pities a free man will also pity a slave.

This unit ends, as do the first and the last, with something more akin to a descriptive statement than a legal inference. The statement is introduced here with the term *savar* (or its plural), meaning "logically infer," or "imply," but also "speculate" or "believe." And unlike the first and the last units these statements are attributed by the anonymous tradent of our *sugya* to the named Tannaim – as the underlying reasoning behind their statements. The significance of this unit for us, is that it introduces a conceptual shift in the *sugya* by placing the slave on a more fluid arc between freedom and slavery, and placing the slave in a relationship of mercy and charity with the community. The term "freedom" is introduced here for the first time and connects this unit with the last unit (87-105) where the discussion, to an extent, revolves around freedom. Of course, no conclusion is reached *vis a vis* the question of whether or not a master may tell his slave "work for me and I won't feed you". The discussion of mercy/charity is engaged again in the next unit.

The next two units seemingly end up proving opposite conclusions. These units are of the first type, and both open with the "Come and hear" formula. The first of the two (55-70) contrasts two somewhat similar statements attributed to the first generation Babylonian Amora Rav. The first statement is:

56   One who dedicates [to the Sanctuary] the hands of his slave, that slave borrows, eats, works and repays [the loan].

That which is "dedicated" (הקדש) may not be used for profane purposes. Since the slave's hands are dedicated, all his handiwork is dedicated. For this reason, the slave borrows money and then uses it to buy food which he eats. The money which he then earns already belongs to the debtor and is not dedicated. After deflecting the possibility that this might mean that a master might tell his slave to work without being fed, by situating Rab's statement in a case when the master is supplying him with food, (and following up on some of the problematics that emerge from the fact that this is a case of "dedication") (57-63) the second statement is introduced:

64   ...for Rab says:
65   If one dedicates to the Sanctuary the hands of his slave, [the slave] works and eats.
66   For if he doesn't work, who would work for him?

Coming off of the statement that the slave might earn small amounts of money (63), this statement of Rab's is brought as a proof of this contention. While contradicting a strict reading of the earlier Rab statement, in context it is not a contradiction, since the amount earned here is below the minimum.

Line 66 is actually a comment on, and an explanation of Rab's statement quoted in 65.[41] It is necessary insofar as this comment is actually a setup for the conclusion:

67   If you say that the first statement [refers to a case] in which [the master] provides [the slave's food], and [the master] cannot [say to the slave work for me though I won't feed you]; while the second statement [refers to a case] in which [the master] doesn't provide [the slave's food] – all is well.

The important point here being that in the second case too, the master *cannot* say to the slave work for me though I won't feed you. This is the reason that the slave works: "for if he doesn't work, who would work for him?" It being understood that he is using his handiwork for his upkeep.

However, if we understand the first statement as referring to the situation in which the master does not provide food for his slave, and he *can* say to the slave work for me though I won't feed you, we are in a quandary. For in this situation, the explanation "for if he doesn't work, who would work for him," doesn't concern us – the master has no

---

[41]Line 66 is Aramaic while Rab's statement is Hebrew. The introduction to Rab's statement (for Rab says) is also Aramaic – both in line 64 and 55. This just seems to mean that this unit is of a piece.

obligation to feed him. "...Whoever so wants, will work for him." (69) And if this is the case – how can Rab say that the slave works and eats (65)?

70   We, rather, understand from here that he cannot [say to the slave work for me though I won't feed you], this we understand.

This concluding argument is, of course, dependent on reading Rab's second statement as contradicting Rab's first statement[42] (thereby necessitating the frame of *provides/doesn't provide*), and then reading line 66: "for if he doesn't work, who would work for him?" as Rab's own argument (thereby showing that Rab obviously held that one cannot say to his slave work for me though I won't feed you).[43]

---

[42]Instead of reading it less strictly as basically synonymous with the first statement. There is no necessity to read an order into the list of the first statement.

[43]Halivni claims that the reading in l.56 should be המקדיש עבדו (If one dedicates his *slave* to the Sanctuary, not his slave's *hands*), as the Tosafot here suggest. He argues for this on two grounds: 1. Its hard to support the proposition (necessitated by the current reading) that the same words "If one dedicates to the Sanctuary the hands of his slave" mean two different things – once that the master supplies him with food, once that he doesn't. 2. It is hard to claim at the same time that "he borrows and eats" (56) means for that which is in excess of what is necessary, while "works and repays" in that same sentence, means very small increments of less than a prutah.

If, however, we take the reading המקדיש עבדו in the first statement, and assume that both statements deal with the situation in which the master does not provide the slave with food, there is no contradiction with the second statement. The difference between the two is a result of the fact that in the earlier one, the slave himself is "dedicated" (הקדש), and therefore anything the slave makes is likewise dedicated. Therefore, if anyone wants to enjoy the work of the slave it must first be redeemed – and this, claims Halivni, is what לוה (usually "borrows") means here – while the slave himself, being dedicated can eat of dedicated food. In the later statement the slave himself is not dedicated, and therefore cannot eat dedicated food, and since the master cannot say 'work for me and I will not feed you' – the slave may eat as much as his support should be, and the rest is dedicated.

It seems that there are two objections to this argument. First, Halivni is substituting one problematic understanding of a phrase for another. Its just as cumbersome to read לוה as redeemed as it is to read המקדיש ידי עבדו as in two different contexts. Second it is easier to understand why, within the context of this *sugya*, this phrase was used when we realize that the only time it is used is in relation to a wife e.g. Mishnah Ketubot 5:7 (and its Parallel in Tosefta Arakhin 3:7): המקדיש מעשי ידי אשתו הרי זו עושה ואוכלה This follows on the other "crossover" usages between slave and woman that we have seen in this *sugya*.

The next unit – which ends with a conclusion, opposite that of the previous unit[44] – is also a "Come and hear" unit. This phrase introduces a statement attributed to R. Yohanan:

72 Come and hear that R. Yohanan says:
73 One who cuts off the hand of another's slave, pays the slave's loss of time, and medical expenses to his master, and the slave lives on charity.

It seems then that there is no obligation of support on the master, and he may in effect say to the slave work for me though I won't feed you. (74) Again this is deflected (as in the previous unit) by situating R. Yohanan's statement in a case in which the master is supporting the slave. However, this gambit is blocked by a two pronged attack. First the objection is raised that if the master is actually supporting the slave – why might he live on charity. When this is answered by saying that the charity is only for "extras," a lexical challenge is mounted:

77 If this is so, it should not say "lives on" (ניזון) but "is supported by" (מתפרנס).
78 We, rather, understand from here that he can [say to the slave work for me though I won't feed you], this we understand.

We noted above (page 201, note 19) that this lexical differentiation is rather weak, as the two terms are usually seen as synonymous.[45] Be that as it may, we have come to a second "conclusion."

The next unit (80-84) is somewhat of a secondary unit of the last one. The introductory formula אמר מר (lit. "The Master said") actually means "in relation to the source/statement discussed/mentioned above...." This unit is reviewing the second half of the statement attributed to R. Yohanan (73): "...he pays the slave's loss of time, and medical expenses to his master." From this part of the statement we ascertain that even when there is suffering associated with medical treatment, the recompense for that suffering is not the slave's but the master's. That is if he healed quicker at the expense of his own suffering (i.e. stronger medicine) he does not get to keep the money allotted for the unused days of healing – they belong to the master.

---

[44]This is not a serious problem for the traditional commentaries since the first conclusion can be attributed to Rab and the second to R. Yohanan. The stature of these two make it permissible for them to be in conflict.
[45]And see Tos. Ket. 7 (end). Interestingly, Jastrow (*A Dictionary of the Targumim, the Talmud Babli, and Yerushalmi, and the Midrashic Literature*, P. Shalom Publishers, Brooklyn, NY, 1967) in an attempt to take this differentiation seriously translates ניזון as "to be fed, sustained" (p. 387), and התפרנס as "to be provided for, to be supported" (p. 1231). However, the citations he translates for ניזון are translated as "to be supported." What is to be granted is that the verb פרנס is used more often in regards to צדקה.

Women and Slaves: A Reading of Gittin 12a-13a   211

This brings us to the final unit (86-104). This unit is in some ways an explication of and expansion upon lines 6-9 of the Mishnah. However if we compare the Mishnah with, first, the *beraitta* quoted here,[46] and then with the rest of the *sugya* – we will see that there are important differences. First the Mishnah and the *beraitta*:

Mishnah	Beraitta in our *sugya*
5. And Sages say, in [the case of] women's divorce [he may renege], but not in [the case of] emancipations of slaves.	
6. For a benefit may be conferred on a person in their absence, but a disability may be imposed on him only in his presence.	86. R. Eliezer said: We said to Meir, Is it not a benefit for a slave to get out from under his master to freedom?

The most striking difference is the use of the word "freedom." The Mishnah, in discussing whether or not it is a benefit, talks about the disadvantages that the slave (and the woman) might (or might not) suffer. However, for the slave the issue is freedom[47] as it is articulated in line 86. The unit's trajectory however, moves from this firm stance wherein freedom is an obvious desiderata for the slave to the last line of the *sugya* where the idea is broached that a slave would rather be a slave. This trajectory itself is somewhat unbalanced, since on one side R. Eliezer is seemingly lauding the virtues of freedom and the onerous hardships of

---

[46]This *beraitta* is also significantly different than Tosefta Gittin 1:5 (ed. Lieberman p.247). See Lieberman's remarks in *Tosefta Ki-Fshuta* on 247:33-34 (vol. VIII, p.791).
[47]The fact that a woman's leaving her husband might also be an escape to freedom (and therefore a case of "benefiting her in absence") is not raised. The only situation in which the possibility is entertained that a divorce might be a benefit to the woman is in a *sugya* in b Yebamoth 118b. The situation there is one in which the husband grants a divorce to his wife so that she should not have to marry a levir. The possibility that her feelings towards the levir are less than totally rapturous is raised:

בעא מיניה רבא מרב נחמן, המזכה גט לאשתו במקום יבם מהו?
<u>כיון דסניא ליה</u> זכות הוא לה, חכין לאדם שלא בפניו.
<u>או דלמא כיון דזימנין דרחמא ליה</u> חוב הוא לה ואין לאדם שלא בפניו.

The *sugya* concludes, however, with a construction of women in which they would rather be married to anybody at all, than remain single.

תא שמע דאמר ריש לקיש, טב למיתב טן דו מלמיתב ארמלו.
אביי אמר, דשומשמנא גברא כורסיה בי חדתא רמו לה.
רב פפא אמר, דנפצא גברא תיקרי בסיפי בבא ותיתיב.
רב אשי אומר, דקולסא גברא לא בעיא טלפחי לקדרא.
תנא וכולן מזנות ותולוח בבעליהן.

Alfasi, in the *Halakhot*, interpolates the first part of b Yebamoth 118b into our *sugya*.

slavery, while Meir is going on about a small minority of slaves who might be the slaves of Priests. They would not be benefiting from manumission since they would no longer be able to eat *Terumah*. The sub-*sugya* appended to the *beraitta* deepens the odd rift between the positions (92-98).

The turning point of the unit starts at line 100. This statement attributed to Rava explains the last clause of the Mishnah: "Because he is his property.":

100   for if [the master] wants he can take four *zuz* from any [non-priestly] Israelite, and disqualify him wherever he is.

In that case there is no advantage to being the slave of a priest, since that advantage is always hanging by a thread of the master's good will. The next line poses the question to "Meir." :

101   As to R. Meir, leaving aside the slave of a priest – what might he say about the slave of an Israelite?

That is, why would it be a disability for the slave of an Israelite?

102   R. Shmuel bar R. Isaac said, because it disqualifies him from a Canaanite slavewoman.
103   On the contrary, it permits him to a free woman.

And then out of left field - the final word:

104   A slave prefers a common woman; she may be treated with disregard, she is always at his call, she is open to all his sexual advances.

Two things happen with this one statement. First, we are now talking of a slave as an entity unchanging over time. Slavery is not a matter of status but, in the Aristotelian sense, soul. Writers from Aristotle, in the *Ethics*, to Ben Sira grappled with the question of slavery by assuming that there were those who were fit for it.

Second, the slave is identified with the sensual and the sexual. Again, from Aristotle and on, the sensual has always fallen on that side of the ledger marked feminine – along with matter (as opposed to form), body (as opposed to mind), and the particular (as opposed to the universal). In Mishnah Sotah 3:4 R. Joshua, in a statement that comments on why women shouldn't learn Torah, says "A woman desires one measure [of food], and lasciviousness, more than nine measures [of food] and asceticism (פרישות)." Again in this reproduction of the binary opposites mind (study of Torah) and body, privileging body is marked female – in the same way that the slave is marked female by asserting that he privileges the body.

Women and Slaves: A Reading of Gittin 12a-13a 213

As the end of this examination of the trees of the *sugya* is reached I will step back and survey the forest. The unit types that I have identified would not stand up to more than a superficial taxonomy. Based on the ideal type we constructed – only one unit actually fits (73-79). As markers however, they serve their purpose: they highlight the "conclusions" in each of the units. If we abandon the types for the moment, but map the "conclusions" we find an interesting pattern. There are nine "conclusions" and they might be arranged in something of a loose chiastic structure as follows:

A. "A slave that is not worth the food of his stomach – what would his master and mistress want him for?" (17)
    B. You would have said, "Since the master does not give him anything when he does not earn, he should not take anything from him when he does earn!" We are told [therefore that this is not so]. (25-26)
    Ba. It might occur to you to say, [since] the Torah said "and live" – it is incumbent [upon the master] to provide extra support (*living*). We are told [therefore that this is not so].(27-28)
        C. You would have said, "*the honor of the king's daughter lies in privacy*," (Psalms 45:14). We are told [therefore that this is not so] (39-40)
            D. Rabban Shimon ben Gamaliel holds (*savar*): 'Either maintain me or let me go free, So that people will see me and have pity on me.' And the rabbis hold (*savri*), one who pities a free man will also pity a slave.(51-53)
        C_1. We, rather, understand from here that he cannot [say to the slave work for me though I won't feed you], this we understand. (70)
    Ba_1. We, rather, understand from here that he can [say to the slave work for me though I won't feed you], this we understand. (79)
    B_1. You might think that in this case the extra pain is his; We are told [therefore that this is not so]. (85)
A_1. A slave prefers a common woman; she may be treated with disregard, she is always at his call, she is open to all his sexual advances. (105)

First the formal structure. The three points of the triangle – A, D, A_1 – are all descriptive statements about slaves, without introductory formulae. I pointed out above that A and A_1 share stylistic similarities. Ba and C are both verse based. C_1 and Ba_1 are "conclusions" to the "say to the slave work for me though I won't feed you dilemma." B and B_1 are rejected leniencies in the treatment of slaves. The term freedom (חירות) appears in D and A_1 – and while the term doesn't appear elsewhere, the possibility is raised that a slave might be other than a slave at A.

Seen in this way, it seems to me that there are two discourses, which both intersect and remain in tension with each other. One level of discourse is within what I would call the moral economy of slavery – the balance between oppression and mercy that is of the essence of commercial slaveholding. This is akin to the discussion in Ben Sira (33:24(25)-31(33)):[48]

> Fodder and a stick and burdens for an ass; bread and discipline and work for a servant.
> Set your slave to work, and you will find rest; leave his hands idle, and he will seek liberty.
> Yoke and thong will bow the neck, and for a wicked servant there are racks and tortures.
> Put him to work, that he may not be idle, for idleness teaches much evil.
> Set him to work, as is fitting for him, and if he does not obey make his fetters heavy.
> Do not act immoderately toward anybody, and do nothing without discretion.
> If you have a servant, let him be as yourself, because you have bought him with blood.
> If you have a servant treat him as a brother for as your own soul you will need him,
> If you ill-treat him, and he leaves and runs away, which way will you go to seek him?

Both the oppression and cruelty (*Yoke and thong... racks and tortures...* /10, 59, 73), and the mercy (*...treat him as a brother* /20, 45) are part of the economy of slavery.[49]

---

[48]RSV. There are some differences between the Greek Sirach and the Hebrew as found or reconstructed – mainly though, in verse order. The differences, on the whole, do not change the sense of the discussion. One noteworthy difference is verse 25(26): Set your.... The Hebrew version is reconstructed as: "Set your slave to work, *so that he does not seek rest; if he raises his head up, he will rebel against you..*" see *Sefer Ben Sirah HaHashalem*, ed. M.Z. Segal, for the MS variants. His reconstruction is as follows:

מספוא ושוט ומשא לחמור ומרדות מלאכה לע[בד].
הע[בד] עבדך שלא יבקש נחת ואם נשא ראשי יבג[ד בך].
העבד עבדך שלא ימרוד כי הרבה רעה ענ[שה בטלה].
[על ועבו]ן חמר תומכו על עבד רע [מהפכת ויסורים.
הפקידהו בעבודה כראוי לו ואם לא ישמע] הרב[ה אסוריו].
ואל תותר על כל אדם ובלא משפט [אל תעש דבר].
אחד עבדך [י]הי כ[מוך] כי במשף [חסרתנו].
אחד עבדך כאח חשבה[ו] [ואל] תקנא ב[דם נפשך].
כי אם עניתו יצא ואבד באיזה ד[רך תבקשנו].

[49]"The slave system of the ancient world rested on force and cruelty. Yet direct physical violence by master on slaves was frequently criticized. The doctor Galen's father chided men who 'had bruised a tendon while striking their slaves on the teeth.... I have seen a man [Galen added] strike a slave in the eye with a reed pen.'

"Galen knew of a landowner in Crete, 'in other respects an estimable person,' who would fall upon his servants 'with his hands, and even sometimes with his feet, but far more frequently with a whip or any piece of wood that happened to be handy.'" Peter Brown, *The Body and Society: Men, Women and*

At the same time there is a movement from A to D to A_1. This trajectory is engaged in a discourse about, rather than within slavery. At A the slave is an object which it is either worthwhile, or not, to keep. (*what would his master and mistress want him for?*) The slave has no voice. At D the slave has a voice that might demand freedom ("*Either maintain me or let me go free*"). At A_1 the slave has humanity, but it is of lower order. Further, the slave is no longer interested in freedom, but is naturally slavish. (*A slave prefers a common woman...*) There is no resolution to the tension between and within these two discourses – just as there is no bottom line to the *sugya*.

Rereading

The next step is to go back and pick up the loose threads of signification that were left hanging.

Miriam Peskowitz, in her work on *ma`aseh yadeha*, writes the following:

> Texts may have multiple meanings and resonances. The concept of *ma`aseh yadeha* serves another purpose besides answering a particular problem of property ownership within marriage. Ideologically it emphasizes a difference between female wage-earners and male wage-earners. *It is significant that a masculine equivalent to this phrase does not appear in Tannaitic writings.* There is no concept which remands the labor of a free male, whether adult or minor, father or son, to another. Male workers own their wages while female workers do not; males and females are differentiated by the legal ownership of their earnings. The legal rubric of *ma`aseh yadeha* bestows the monetary value of this work to the working woman's legal guardian; simultaneously it signifies a realm of gender difference among workers.[50] (Emphasis added)

There are two significant points in this citation that are relevant to our discussion. First, the legal rubric of *ma`aseh yadeha* is not coincidentally associated with women. It is not a larger category of labor in which women are a subset. Women are the only *free* persons who are affected by this rubric. It is a significant differentiation between male and female labor. Male labor produces income for the male laborer. Female labor

---

Sexual Renunciation in Early Christianity (New York: Columbia University Press, 1988): 12. The citations are from *de cognoscendis animi morbis* 1.4.

Clement, too, in the *Paidagogos* comes down against whistling, or finger snapping for slaves' attention (2.66.1), while at the same time he mentions without comment that runaway slaves get branded as punishment (3.10.4). Thanks to Denise Kimber Buell for these references.

[50]Miriam Beth Peskowitz, "'The Work of Her Hands': Gendering Everyday Life in Roman-Period Judaism in Palestine (70-250 CE), Using Textile Production as a Case" (Ph.D. diss., Duke University, 1993): 114-115.

produces income for another. *Ma'aseh yadayim*, then, is labor that is gendered female.

Second, Peskowitz states that there is no male equivalent to the phrase in Tannaitic writings. This statement is true with the exception that has been noted in our *sugya*. T Makkot 2:8, which is also quoted in our *sugya* (ll. 20ff.) uses the masculine term *ma'aseh yadav*. Further, our *sugya* is one of only three *sugyot* in the Bavli which use the concept *ma'aseh yadayim* to refer to anyone other than a woman. The effect of this usage then, is to mark the labor of slaves as female labor. This is true structurally – a slave laborer produces income for another (מעשה ידיו לרבו, l. 21) just as female labor does. Also, the relationship that this situation engenders is that of a man to one who is not a man, that is one who is gendered female.

This is reinforced in our *sugya* by the use of the concept *ma'aleh mezonot*. This too is a term which is gendered female. Ours is the only *sugya* in which the term is used in reference to a man. The man which the term refers to, however, is a slave who is marked as female by this usage. The economy of *ma'aleh mezonot* and *ma'aseh yadayim* – which is the core around which our *sugya* revolves – is an economy that is moderated by a dominant male figure. The other participants in this economy are other than male.

A second loose thread which I would call attention to now is the fact that women appear in the *sugya* at first and then fade away after the second "unit" (40) and don't reappear until the last unit. The first two units, generated by the template of line 7 (slave vs. woman), discuss both women and slaves. After line 40, women aren't discussed at all until the final unit. The final unit picks up the Mishnaic discussion again, but with significant differences as we noted above. In the last lines of the final unit the discussions of slaves and women (free [104], and not [105]) mesh.

A third loose thread or ungrammaticality is the problematic fit of the two midrashic prooftexts (27 & 39, or Ba & C). As we noted above (page 204), the first midrashic prooftext (27), Deut. 4:42, raises two different questions. First, there is no frame within which the premises needed to support the challenge of line 27, can coexist with the premises needed to support the challenge of line 25. Second, the prooftext itself has nothing to do with slaves. Slaves are not mentioned in the whole section in Deuteronomy 4 from which the prooftext is quoted.

The second midrashic prooftext (39), Psalms 45:14, is equally ungrammatical. It is only understood after it is reread midrashically (something that is only implied in the *sugya*), and then that midrashic rereading is given normative implications. (See above page 205.)

These loose threads, or hermeneutic signposts, point to a narrative subtext. The two midrashic prooftexts introduce – under erasure[51] – the fact of place (both geographic, and "proper"), and the idea of movement. The first prooftext speaks of cities of refuge – subsequently defined as places of exile[52] (line 20) – "to which a manslayer could escape." The movement is *away* to a place that is *there* (שמה), or that is *beyond* (בעבר הירדן). The second prooftext introduces the notion of "proper" place, and the movement is *inside*. At the point at which the slave and the woman "cross paths," they are headed in opposite directions, going to different places.

When they appear together again, however, in the last lines of the *sugya*, the slave is going *inside* to slavery (the opposite of הוציאני לחירות), and the woman is moving *outside* (the "proper") to wantonness (the הפקירא / unowned / unbounded – מופקר: "One who abandons [המפקיר] his slave, the slave goes *out* free.").[53] At the point that the slave and woman meet, the slave is once again gendered female. He prefers slavery (it is his "natural" place) since it provides for his sexual needs (105). As we noted above (page 212), in Mishnah Sotah 3:4 R. Joshua, in a statement that comments on why women shouldn't learn Torah, says "A woman desires one measure [of food], and lasciviousness, more than nine measures [of food] and asceticism (פרישות)." The privileging of the sexual is marked female. In our *sugya* both the implied woman and the slave of the last line, are gendered female.

Reaching Towards the End

This reading of the *sugya* points to the way in which the gendered body is created by the legal discourse. "Maleness" is defined by autonomy, ownership and freedom. Everything else is placed in relation to this marker. Women can also be gendered male in this equation: in relation to slaves. This is evident in the first "conclusion": "A slave that is not worth the food of his stomach – what would his master and mistress want him for?" (17) The master and mistress in this situation own the slave. His labor earns for them. The (biologically) male slave is in the paradoxical position of being gendered female in relation to the

---

[51]Cf. the discussion of the סדא...קמ"ל trope (and related tropes) in Chapter VI and Appendix 3.
[52]Note that in M Makkot 2:1 the Mishnah lists those who are exiled (אלו הן הגולין), and only in 2:4 does the Mishnah ask to where are they exiled (להיכן גולין), at which point cities of refuge are mentioned. This is just by way of stressing that *exiling* is not an incidental point.
[53]B Gittin 39a.

(biologically) female mistress who (along with the master) is gendered male.⁵⁴

At the same time this reading marks movement in the *sugya* – outwards (הוציאני)/inwards (פנימה) – which mirrors or reflects the larger movement of the narrative of Exile. The movement outwards or beyond, is a movement to exile (גלה). The movement inward is intertextually connected with the Temple, and high priests. The third unit is involved in a discourse of compassion and the year of drought. This too, as I argued in the previous chapter, is part of the discourse of Exile.

The discourse of exile is a discourse of instability or disorder. Exile is a lack of control, a return to chaos. As Jonathan Smith has written:

> While the exile is an event which can be located chronologically as after A.D. 70, it is above all a thoroughly mythic event: the return to chaos, the decreation, the separation from the deity analogous to the total catastrophe of the primeval flood.⁵⁵

The discourse of slavery, on the other hand, is a discourse of stability. The fact that a slave *wants* to be a slave, has a slavish *nature*, reinforces the order and stability of the community.⁵⁶ The fact that both

---

⁵⁴Cf. the discussion of women philosopher-rulers in Plato's *Republic* in Elizabeth V. Spellman, *Inessential Woman: Problems of Exclusion in Feminist Thought* (Boston: Beacon Press, 1988): 32-33. Spellman argues that some of "contradictions" in Plato's statements about women can be better understood according to the hypothesis that Plato uses the term "woman" ambiguously. "Plato's thinking of people as made up of body and soul allows for at least three different configurations of 'woman.'"

⁵⁵Jonathan Z. Smith, *Map Is Not Territory: Studies in the History of Religion* (Chicago: University of Chicago Press, 1978): 119.

⁵⁶See, e.g., Aristotle's discussion in Book I of the *Politics*, trans. H. Rackham (Cambridge, MA: Harvard University Press, 1972): "The first coupling together of persons then to which necessity gives rise is that between those who are unable to exist without one another, namely the union of female and male for the continuance of the species... and the union of natural ruler and natural subject for the sake of security... so that master and slave have the same interest. ...Hence every city-state exists by nature, inasmuch as the first partnerships so exist; for the city-state is the end of the other partnerships, and nature is an end..." (7)It is significant for the larger exilic frame that I am arguing for to note where Aristotle's argument is headed: "...From these things therefore it is clear that the city-state is a natural growth, and that man is by nature a political animal, *and a man that is by nature and not merely fortune citiless is either low in the scale of humanity or above it*..." (emphasis added.)(9). On Aristotle's treatment of both women and slavery as coming within a discourse of the stable society see Arlene Saxenhouse, "Aristotle: Defective Males, Hierarchy, and the Limits of Politics," in ed. Mary Lyndon Shanley & Carole Pateman, *Feminist Interpretations and Political Theory* (University Park, PA: Pennsylvania state University Press, 1991):40-41. On the significance of the hearth as symbol of place and home see

women and slaves have a "proper place" might in some way ward off the chaos of foreign topography.[57] To quote Smith once more:

> When the world is perceived to be chaotic, reversed, liminal, filled with anomie. Then man finds himself in a world which he does not recognize; and perhaps even more terrible, man finds himself to have a self he does not recognize. Then he will need to create a new world, to express his sense of a new place.[58]

The larger narrative that the *sugya* partakes of is the narrative of Exile. In the construction of order in relations within society, as in relations between people and the institutions of law, the chaos of Exile, it seems, is tamed.[59]

Jean Pierre Vernant, *Myth and Thought Among the Greeks* (Routledge and Kegan Paul, London, 1983): 130ff.

[57] In this regard it is significant that the *sugyot* generated by the first Mishnah in this chapter of Gittin (especially from 4a-8a) are dealing with geography or (I would claim) mapping. Cf. the *sugya* generated by the dispute between Rav and Shmuel (6a):

בבל רב אמר כארץ ישראל לגיטין.
ושמואל אמר כחוץ לארץ.

[58] *Map Is Not Territory*, 146. And cf.: "Through the magic of words [Judaism] attempted, in the great rabbinic legal enterprise, to construct a mythical cosmos, a portable homeland in which any Jew might dwell." (187 n. 66)

[59] Interestingly enough, the Maharal, Rabbi Judah Loew Ben Bezalel of Prague (1525-1609) also understands exile as a disorder, a move away from the natural place. Cf. *Nezach Yisrael*, Chapter 1:

נצח ישראל פרק א'

ועוד יש לבאר ענין הגלות תחלה, כי הגלות בעצמו הוא ראיה והוכחה ברורה על הגאולה ורזה, כי אין ספק כי הגלות הוא שנוי ויציאה מן הסדר, שהש"י סדר כל אומה במקומה הראוי לה וסדר את ישראל במקום הראוי להם שהוא ארץ ישראל, והגלות מן מקומם הוא שנוי ויציאה לגמרי וכל הדברים כאשר הם יוצאים ממקום הטבעי והם מחוץ למקומם, אין להם עמידה במקום הבלתי טבעי להם רק הם חוזרים למקום הטבעי, כי אם היו נשארים במקום הבלתי טבעי להם, היה הבלתי טבעי נעשה טבעי, ודבר זה אי אפשר שיהיה הבלתי טבעי נעשה טבעי.

"There is a need to explain the concept of Exile first, for the Exile itself is a proof and a clear argument for the Redemption, and this because there is no doubt that the Exile is a change, and a going out of the order. For God set every people in the place fitting for them, and set Israel in the place fit for them which is the Land of Israel, and the Exile from their place is a complete change and going-out. And regarding all things, when they go out of the natural place and they are outside their place, they have no existence in that place which is unnatural for them. They, rather, return to the natural place, for if they were to remain in their unnatural place, the unnatural place would become natural, and this thing is impossible – that the unnatural would become natural."

For an overview of the Maharal's understanding of exile see "Judah Loew Ben Bezalel," in *Encyclopedia Judaica* (Jerusalem: The Macmillan Company, 1971): 10:378.

Of specific interest for the *sugya* of b Gittin 12a-13a, is the following comment in *Nezach Yisrael* Chapter 9:

Appendix: The Text

בבלי גטין י"א ע"ב-י"ג ע"א

משנה

האומר תן גט זה לאשתי ושטר שחרור זה לעבדי,
אם רצה לחזור[60] בשניהן יחזור, דברי רבי מאיר.
וחכמים אומרים, בגיטי נשים אבל לא בשחרורי עבדים. 5
לפי שזכין לאדם[61] שלא בפניו ואין חבין לו אלא בפניו,
שאם ירצה שלא לזון את עבדו רשאי ושלא לזון את אשתו אינו רשאי.
אמר להם,[63] והרי הוא פוסל את עבדו מן התרומה כשם שהוא פוסל את אשתו?[62]
אמרו לו מפני שהוא קניין.[64]

גמרא 10

שאם ירצה שלא לזון כו':
שמעת מינה יכול הרב לומר לעבד עשה עמי ואיני זנך.
הכא במאי עסקינן דאמר ליה צא מעשה ידיך במזונותיך.[65]
דכוותה גבי אשה, דאמר לה צאי מעשה ידיך במזונותיך.
אשה אמאי לא? אשה בדלא ספקה. 15
עבד נמי בדלא ספיק,
עבדא דנהום כרסיה לא שויא-למריה ולמרתיה למאי מיתבעי?

תא שמע,

"עבד שגלה לערי מקלט אין רבו חייב לזונו. 20
ולא עוד אלא שמעשה ידיו לרבו."[66]
שמע מינה, יכול הרב לומר לעבד 'עשה עמי ואיני זנך.'
הכא במאי עסקינן? דאמר לו 'צא מעשה ידיך במזונותיך.'[67]
אי הכי מעשה ידיו אמאי לרבו?[68] להעדפה. העדפה פשיטא.
מהו דתימא, כיון דכי ליה לית ליה, לא יהיב ליה, כי אית ליה נמי לא לישקול מיניה. 25
קא משמע לן.

ועיקר הגלות הוא לנשים כי הנשים הן יושבות ביותר במקומן ובבתיהן כי כל כבודה בת מלך פנימה.

"And the principle part of exile is for the women, for the women are the ones who sit mostly in their places and their houses for all the honor of the daughter of the king is inside."

The implication of Psalms 45:14 in a discourse of place and Exile is very stark in this statement.

[60] לחזור] להחזיר קם,פס .
[61] לאדם] לו לאדם מ,מבש
[62] כשם...אשתו] ליתא מ, כשם שפוסל אשתו מן התרומה 1,2 כשם...אשתו מן התרומה מ,ר
[63] אמר להם] אמר להם ר' מאיר מ,1
[64] שהוא קניינו] שהוא פוסל את אשתו כקניינו 1
[65] במזונותיך] מ,1,2,, למזונותיך דפוס
[66] תוספתא מכות ב:ח (צוק עמ. 440)
[67] במזונותיך] למזונותיך דפוס
[68] מעשה ידיו אמאי לרבו] מאי מעשה ידיו לרבו מ, אמאי מעשה ידיו לרבו 1,2,

ומאי שנא לערי מקלט? סלקא דעתך אמינא, א' רחמנ'[70] "וחי"[69]-עביד ליה חיותא טפי.
קא משמע לן.
והא מדקתני סיפא,

"אבל אשה שגלתה לערי מקלט בעלה חייב במזונותיה,"
מכלל דלא אמר לה. דאי אמר לה בעלה אמאי חייב?
ומדסיפא דלא אמר לה, רישא נמי דלא אמר ליה.
לעולם דאמר ליה. ואשה בדלא ספקה.[71]
והא מדקתני סיפא,

"ואם אמר לה צאי מעשה ידיך, במזונותיך רשאי."
מכלל דרישא דלא אמר לה.
הכי קאמר, ואם מספקת, ואמר לה צאי מעשה ידיך במזונותיך, רשאי.
מספקת מאי למימרא?
מהו דתימא, "כל כבודה בת מלך פנימה," (תהילים מח:יד)
קא משמע לן.

לימא כתנאי,
רבן שמעון בן גמליאל אומר, יכול העבד לומר לרבו בשני בצרו',[72]
'או פרנסני או הוציאני לחירות.'
וחכמים אומרים, הרשות ביד רבו.
מאי לאו, בהא קמיפלגי-דמר סבר יכול לומר ומר סבר,[74] אינו יכול לומר.[73]
ותיסברא, האי 'או פרנסני או הוציאני לחירות'-
'או פרנסני או תן לי מעשה ידי במזונותי'[75] מיבעי ליה.
ועוד מאי שנא בשני בצרו'?[76]
אלא הכא במאי עסקינן? דאמר לו 'צא מעשה ידיך למזונותיך' ובשני בצרו'[77] לא ספק.
רבן שמעון בן גמליאל סבר 'או פרנסני או הוציאני לחירות,'
כי היכי דחזו לי אינשי ומרחמין עלי.
ורבנן סברי, מאן דמרחם אבני חרי אעבד נמי רחומי מרחם.

תא שמע, דאמר רב,
המקדיש ידי עבדו, אותו העבד לוה ואוכל ועושה ופורע.
שמע מינה יכול הרב לומר לעבד 'עשה עמי ואיני זנך.'
הכא במאי עסקינן? במעלה לו מזונות.
אי הכי אמאי[78] לוה ואוכל? להעדפה.

---

[69] דברים ד:מב
[70] א' רחמנ'] פ, ליתא דפוס
[71] לעולם דאמר ליה. ואשה בדלא ספקה] לעולם דאמר לה. ובדלא ספק] ו₁
[72] בצרו'] מו₂, בצורת דפוס
[73] לומר] מו₁, ליתא דפוס
[74] לומר] ו₁, ליתא דפוס
[75] במזונותי] מו₁, בפרנסתי דפוס ליתא ו₁
[76] בצרו'] מו₂, בצורת דפוס
[77] בצרו'] מו₂, בצורת דפוס
[78] אמאי] מו₁ו₂, למאי דפוס

60 ולימא ליה הקדש עד האידנ'[79] סגי לך בלא העדפה,
   השתא[80] נמי תיסגי לך בלא העדפה.
   הקדש גופיה ניחא לי', דלשבח[81] עבדיה.
   'עשה ופורע' קמא קמא קדיש ליה, בפחות משוה פרוטה.
   הכי נמי מסתברא, דאמר רב
65 המקדיש ידי עבדו עשה[82] ואכל.
   דאי לא עבדא, מאן פלח ליה?
   אי אמרת בשלמא הך במעלה ואינו יכול והא בשאינו מעלה-שפיר.
   אלא אי אמרת הך בשאינו מעלה ויכול,
   דאי לא עבדא מאן פלח ליה-מאן דבעי ניפלחיה.
70 אלא לאו שמע מינה אינו יכול, שמע מינה.[83]
   תא שמע, דאמר רבי יוחנן,
   הקוטע יד עבדו של חבירו, נתן שבתו ורפואתו לרבי, ואותו העבד ניזון מן הצדקה.
   שמע מינה, יכול הרב לומר לעבד, עשה עמי ואיני זנך.'
   הכא במאי עסקי'? במעלה לו מזונות.
75 אי הכי אמאי ניזון מן הצדקה? להעדפה.
   אי הכי, "ניזון"? "מתפרנס" מיבעי ליה.
   אלא לאו, שמע מינה יכול, שמע מינה.

80 אמר מר, נתן שבתו ורפואתו לרבו.
   שבתו פשיטא. רפואתו איצטריכא ליה.
   רפואתו דידיה היא, דבעי איתסויי ביה.
   לא, צריכא. דאמדוה לחמשא יומי ועבדו ליה סמא חריפא ואתסי בתלתא יומי.
   מהו דתימא, צערא דידיה הוא, קא משמע לן.
85
   תניא: אמר רבי אלעזר, אמרנו לו למאיר והלא זכות הוא לעבד שיוצא מתחת[84] רבו לחירות.
   אמר לנו, חוב הוא לו, שאם היה עבד כהן פוסלו מן התרומה.
   אמרנו לו, והלא מה אם ירצה שלא לזונו ושלא לפרנסו-רשאי.
   אמר לנו, ומה אילו עבד כהן שברח ואשת כהן שמרדה על בעלה, הלא אוכלין בתרומה.
90 וזה אינו אוכל.
   אבל אשה חוב הוא לה, שכן פסלה מן התרומה ומפסידה מן המזונות.
   מאי קאמרו ליה, ומאי קא מהדר להו?
   הכי קאמר להו, השבתוני על המזונות, מה תשיבוני על התרומה?
   וכי תימרו, אי בעי זריק ליה גיטא ופסיל ליה-שביק ליה וריק ואזיל לעלמא. |
95 ומה אילו עבד כהן שברח ואשת כהן שמרדה על בעלה,
   הלא אוכלים בתרומה וזה אינו אוכל-

---

[79] האידנ'] מ1ו2, השתא דפוס
[80] השתא] מ1ו2, והשתא דפוס
[81] דלשבח] מ1ו2, כי הכי דלשבח דפוס
[82] עשה] מ1, אותו העבד עשה דפוס
[83] שמע מינה] ליתא ו1
[84] מתחת רבו] מ1ו2, מתחת ידי רבו דפוס

אבל אשה חוב הוא לה, שכן פוסלת מן התרומה ומפסידה מן המזונות.[85]
שפיר קאמר להו.
אמר רבא, היינו דקא מהדרי ליה במתני' 'מפני שהוא קנינו.'
דאי בעי, שקיל ארבעה זוזי מישראל ופסיל ליה כל היכא דאיתיה.
ולרבי מאיר, תינח עבד כהן-עבד ישראל מאי איכא למימר?
אמר רבי שמואל בר רב יצחק, מפני שמפסידו משפחה כנענית.
אדרבה, הרי הוא מתירו בבת חורין?
עבדא בהפקירא ניחא ליה-זילא ליה, שכיחא ליה, פריצה ליה.

---

[85] אבל אשה חוב הוא לה, שכן פוסלת מן התרומה ומפסידה מן המזונות] ו1, אבל אשה חוב הוא לה, שכן פסלה מן התרומה מ, ליתא דפוס

Bibliography

Editions

ששה סדרי משנה. Commentary by Hanoch Albeck. Tel Aviv: Dvir, 1988.

The Tosefta: According to Codex Vienna, With Variants From Codices Erfurt, Genizah MSS. and Edition Princeps (Venice 1521) Together With a Brief Commentary. Edited by Saul Lieberman. *The Order of Nashim.* New York: Jewish Theological Seminary of America, 1973.

Tosephta: Based on the Erfurt and Vienna Codices, With Parallels and Variants. Edited by M. S. Zuckermandel. Jeruslame: Wahrmann Books, 1970.

Babylonian Talmud Codex Hamburg (165). facsimile edition. Jerusalem: 1969.

Babylonian Talmud Codex Munich (95). facsimile edition. Jerusalem: Kedem, 1970.

Manuscripts of the Babylonian Talmud from the Collection of the Vatican Library. facsimile edition. Jerusalem: Makor, 1972.

Tractate 'Abodah Zarah of the Babylonian Talmud: MS Jewish Theological Seminary of America. Edited by Shraga Abramson. New York: Jewish Theological Seminary of America, 1957.

Feldblum, Meir Simchah. דקדוקי סופרים: מסכת גיטין. New York: Yeshiva University Press, 1966.

The Babylonian Talmud. Edited by I. Epstein. Various translators. London: Soncino, 1935-1952.

מדרש איכה. Edited by Solomon Buber. Vilna: Romm, 1899. Reprint, n.d.

Midrash Bereshit Rabba: Critical Edition with Notes and Commentary. Edited by J. Theodor and Ch. Albeck. Jerusalem: Wahrmann Books, 1965.

Commentaries

Adret, Shlomo b. Avraham, חידושי הרשב"א. Edited by Yisrael Sklar. Jerusalem: Mossad Harav Kook, 1986.

Alashvili, Yom Tov b. Avraham, חידושי הריטב"א. Edited by Eliyahu Lichtenstein. Jerusalem: Mossad Harav Kook, 1979.

Ashkenazi, Bezalel, ספר שיטה מקובצת. Tel Aviv: Avraham Ziony, 1965).

Hameiri, Menaḥem, בית הבחירה על מסכת גיטין. Edited by Kalman Shlesinger. Jerusalem: Mossad Harav Kook, 1964.

Sefer ha-Mordekhai to Tractate Gittin. Edited by Mayer E. Rabinowitz. In *Texts and Studies: Analecta Judaica*, vol. 2., part 2 edited by H. Z. Dimitrovski. New York: Jewish Theological Seminary of America, 1990.

General

Albeck, Chanoch. מבוא לתלמודים, Dvir, Tel Aviv, 1969).

Aminoah, Noah. עריכת מסכת קידושין בתלמוד הבבלי, Tel Aviv: Levin-Epstein - Modan, 1977).

Bal, Mieke. *On Story Telling : Essays in Narratology.* Sonoma, California: Polebridge Press, 1991.

Barthes, Roland. *S/Z: An Essay.* Translated by Richard Miller. New York: Hill and Wang, 1974.

Bloom, Harold. *A Map of Misreading.* Oxford: Oxford University Press, 1975.

Boyarin, Daniel. *Carnal Israel: Reading Sex in Talmudic Culture.* Berkeley: University of California Press, 1993.

_____.*Intertextuality and the Reading of Midrash.* Bloomington: Indiana University Press, 1990.

_____. "'Language Inscribed by History on the Bodies of Living Beings,' Midrash and Martyrdom." *Representations*, 1989.

_____. *Sephardi Speculation: A Study in Methods of Talmudic Interpretation* (in Hebrew). Jerusalem: Ben Zvi Institute, 1989.

_____. "Reading Androcentrism Against the Grain: Women, Sex and Torah Study." *Poetics Today* 12 (1991): 29-52.

———. "המדרש ותמעשה-על החקר ההיסטורי של ספרות חז"ל." in *Saul Lieberman Memorial Volume*, ed. Shamma Friedman, 105-117. New York and Jerusalem: Jewish Theological Seminary of America, 1993.

Brooks, Roger. "Shamma Friedman on b. Yebamot 88a – b," *Semeia* 27 (1983): 63 – 75.

Brooten, Bernadette J. *Love Between Women: Early Christian Responses to Female Homoeroticism*. Chicago: University of Chicago Press, 1996.

Brown, Peter. *The Body and Society: Men, Women and Sexual Renunciation in Early Christianity*. New York: Columbia University Press, 1988.

Chatman, Seymour. *Story and Discourse*. Ithaca, New York: Cornell University Press, 1978.

Cover, Robert. "The Folktales of Justice: Tales of Jurisdiction." In *Narrative, Violence, and the Law: The Essays of Robert Cover*, edited by Martha Minow, Michael Ryan, and Austin Sarat, 173-201. Ann Arbor: The University of Michigan Press, 1992.

———. "Nomos and Narrative" in *Narrative, Violence, and the Law: The Essays of Robert Cover*, edited by Martha Minow, Michael Ryan, and Austin Sarat, 95-172. Ann Arbor: The University of Michigan Press, 1992.

———. "Violence and the Word." In *Narrative, Violence, and the Law: The Essays of Robert Cover*, edited by Martha Minow, Michael Ryan, and Austin Sarat, 203-238. Ann Arbor: The University of Michigan Press, 1992.

Culler, Jonathan. *Structuralist Poetics: Structuralism, Linguistics, and the Study of Literature*. Ithaca, New York: Cornell University Press, 1975.

Dalton, Clare. "An Essay in the Deconstruction of Contract Doctrine." In *Interpreting Law and Literature: A Hermeneutic Reader*, edited by Sanford Levinson and Steven Mailloux, 285-318. Evanston, IL: Northwestern University Press, 1988.

Derrida, Jacques. "Living On · Border Lines." In *Deconstructionism and Criticism*, Harold Bloom, Paul de Man, Jacques Derrida, Geoffrey H. Hartman, J. Hillis Miller. New York: The Seabury Press, 1979.

———. *Limited Inc*. Evanston, IL: Northwestern University Press, 1990.

Donovan, Josephine. *Feminist Theory: The Intellectual Traditions of American Feminism.* New York: Frederick Ungar, 1985.

Eagleton, Terry. *Ideology: An Introduction.* London: Verso, 1991.

_____. *Literary Theory: An Introduction.* Minneapolis: University of Minnesota Press, 1983.

Elon, Ari. עלמא די *Shdamot* 114, March (1990).

Epstein, J.N. *Introduction to Amoraitic Literature.* Jerusalem: The Magnes Press, Hebrew University, 1962.

Feldblum, Meyer S. *Talmudic Law and Literature: Tractate Gittin.* New York: Yeshiva University Press, 1969.

_____. "Prof. Avraham Weiss – An Appreciation of His Method in Talmudic Research and A Summary of His Conclusions," in Hebrew. In The *Abraham Weiss Jubilee Volume: Studies In His Honor Presented by His Colleagues and Disciples on the Occasion of His Completing Four Decades of Pioneering Scholarship.* New York: Yeshiva University Press, 1964.

Fischel, Henry A. "Story and History: Observations on Greco-Roman Rhetoric and Pharisaism." In *Origins of Judaism* vol. II part 1. edited by Jacob Neusner, New York & London: Garland Publishing Inc., 1990. pp. 245-274. Originally published in *American Oriental Society Middle West Branch, Semi-Centennial Volume, Asian Studies Research Institute Oriental Series*, 1969, pp. 59-68.

_____. "The Uses of Sorites (*Climax, Gradatio*) in the Tannaitic Period." *HUCA* 44, (1973): 119-151.

Fish, Stanley. *Is There a Text in This Class?: The Authority of Interpretive Communities.* Cambridge, MA: Harvard University Press, 1980.

_____. Chapters 1-5,7 in *Doing What Comes Naturally: Change, Rhetoric, and the Practice of Theory in Literary and Legal Studies.* Durham: Duke University Press, 1989. .

_____. "Fish vs. Fiss." In *Interpreting Law and Literature: A Hermeneutic Reader*, edited by Sanford Levinson and Steven Mailloux, 251-268. Evanston, IL: Northwestern University Press, 1988.

Fiss, Owen M. "Objectivity and Interpretation." In *Interpreting Law and Literature: A Hermeneutic Reader*, edited by Sanford Levinson and Steven Mailloux, 229-249. Evanston, IL: Northwestern University Press, 1988.

Fraade, Steven. *From Tradition To Commentary: Torah and Its Interpretation in the Midrash Sifre to Deuteronomy*. Albany: SUNY Press, 1991.

Fraenkel, Jonah "שאלות הרמנויטיות בחקר סיפור האגדה," *Tarbiz* 47,(1978): 139-172.

_____. "Bible Verses Quoted in Tales of the Sages." In *Studies in Aggadah and Folk-Literature*, edited by Joseph Heinemann, Dov Noy. Scripta Hierosolymitana vol. 22, Jerusalem, Magnes Press, 1971.

_____. "Paranomasia in Aggadic Narratives." In *Studies in Hebrew Narrative Art Throughout the Ages*, edited by Joseph Heinemann, Samuel Werses, 27-51, Scripta Hierosolymitana, Vol. 27. Jerusalem, Magnes Press, 1978.

_____. דרכי האגדה והמדרש. Israel: Yad LaTalmud, 1991.

_____. עיונים בעולמו הרוחני של סיפור האגדה. Tel Aviv: Hakibbutz Hameuchad Publishing House Ltd., 1981.

_____. *Rashi's Methodology in His Exegesis of the Babylonian Talmud* (in Hebrew). Jerusalem: The Magnes Press, 1980.

Fried, Charles. "Sonnet LXV and the 'Black Ink' of the Framers' Intention." In *Interpreting Law and Literature: A Hermeneutic Reader*, edited by Sanford Levinson and Steven Mailloux, 45-51. Evanston, IL: Northwestern University Press, 1988.

Friedman, Mordechai Akiva. *The* Ketubba *Traditions of Eretz Israel*. Vol. 1 of *Jewish Marriage in Palestine: A Cairo Geniza Study*. New York: Tel Aviv University and The Jewish Theological Seminary of America, 1980.

_____. *The* Ketubba *Texts*. Vol. 2 of *Jewish Marriage in Palestine: A Cairo Geniza Study*. New York: Tel Aviv University and The Jewish Theological Seminary of America, 1981.

_____. "Tamar, a Symbol of Life: The 'Killer Wife' Superstition in the Bible and Jewish Tradition." *AJS Review* 15, No. 1 (Spring 1990): 23-61.

Friedman, Shamma. "A Critical Study of *Yevamot* X with a Methodological Introduction." In *Texts and Studies: Analecta Judaica*, vol. 1., edited by H. Z. Dimitrovski, 277-441. New York: Jewish Theological Seminary of America, 1978.

_____. "להתהוות שינויי הנירסאות בתלמוד הבבלי." *Sidra* vol. 7(1991) pp. 67-102.

Froula, Christine. "The Daughter's Seduction: Sexual Violence and Literary History." In *Feminist Theory in Practice and Process* edited by Micheline R. Malson, Jean F. O'Barr, Sarah Westphal-Wihl, and Mary Wyer, 139-162. Chicago: University of Chicago Press, 1989.

Frye, Northrop. *Anatomy of Criticism: Four Essays*. Princeton, New Jersey: Princeton University Press, 1957.

Genette, Gérard. *Figures of Literary Discourse*. Translated by Alan Sheridan. New York: Columbia University Press, 1982.

Gilbert, Sandra M., and Susan Gubar. "The Mirror and the Vamp: Reflections on Feminist Criticism." In *The Future of Literary Theory*, edited by Ralph Cohen, 144-166. New York: Rutledge, 1989.

Goldberg, Abraham, "התפתחות הסוגיא בתלמוד הבבלי ומקורותיה," Tarbiz 32, (1962-63): 143-152.

_____. "The Babylonian Talmud." In *The Literature of the Sages, First Part: Oral Torah, Halakha, Mishna, Tosefta, Talmud, External Tractates*, edited by Shmuel Safrai, 323-343. Philadelphia: Van Gorcum, Assen / Maastricht, Fortress Press, 1987.

Goodblatt, David. "The Babylonian Talmud." In *Aufstieg und Niedergang der römischen Welt*, II, Band 19.2, edited by Wolfgang Haase, 257-336. Berlin, New York: Walter de Gruyter, 1979.

Greenblatt, Stephen. "Shakespeare and the Exorcists." In *After Strange Texts: The Role of Theory in the Study of Literature*, edited by Gregory S. Jay and David L. Miller. Alabama: University of Alabama Press, 1985.

Halivni, David Weiss. *Midrash, Mishnah, and Gemara*. Cambridge, MA: Harvard University Press, 1986.

_____. *Sources and Traditions: A Source Critical Commentary on Seder Moed: Tractate Shabbath*. Jerusalem: Jewish Theological Seminary, 1982.

_____. *Sources and Traditions: A Source Critical Commentary on Seder Moed: Tractates Yoma to Ḥagiga,*

_____. *Sources and Traditions: A Source Critical Commentary on Seder Nashim,*

Hauptman, Judith. *The Development of the Talmudic Sugya*. Lanham: University Press of America, 1988.

Hezser, Catherine. *Form, Function, and Historical Significance of the Rabbinic Story in Yerushalmi Neziqin*. Tübingen: Mohr, 1993.

Iser, Wolfgang. *The Act of Reading: A Theory of Aesthetic Response*. Baltimore: Johns Hopkins University Press, 1978.

Jacobs, Louis. *Structure and Form in the Babylonian Talmud*. Cambridge: Cambridge University Press, 1991.

_____. *The Talmudic Argument: A Study in Talmudic Reasoning and Methodology*, Cambridge: Cambridge University Press, 1984.

Jones, Ann Rosalind. "Writing The Body: Toward an Understanding Of l'Écriture féminine." In *The New Feminist Criticism: Essays On Women, Literature and Theory*, edited by Elaine Showalter, 361-377. New York: Pantheon Books, 1985.

Kahane, Menahem. "גילוי דעת ואונס בגיטין," *Tarbiz* 62,.2, Jan-Mar 1993: 225-263.

Kalmin, Richard. "The Modern Study of Ancient Rabbinic Literature: Yonah Fraenkel's *Darkhei ha'aggadah vehamidrash*." *Prooftexts: A Journal of Jewish Literary History*. 14, 2 (1994): 189-204.

_____. *The Redaction of the Babylonian Talmud: Amoraic or Saboraic?* Cincinatti: Hebrew Union College Press, 1989.

Kaplan, Julius, *The Redaction of the Babylonian Talmud*. New York: Bloch Publishing Company, 1933.

Kermode, Frank. *The Genesis Of Secrecy: On the Interpretation of Narrative*. Cambridge, MA: Harvard University Press, 1979.

_____. *The Sense of an Ending: Studies in the Theory of Fiction*. London: Oxford University Press, 1967.

Klein, Hyman. "Gemara and Sebara." *Jewish Quarterly Review* 38 (1947-48): 67-91.

_____. "משמעותו של המונח 'אי אתמר הכי אתמר' בתלמוד הבבלי." *Tarbiz* 31 (1960-61): 23-42.

_____. "*Gemara*" and "*Sebara*" in *Baba Metziah 60b-64a*, Jerusalem: Akademon, 1978.

_____. "Gemara Quotations in Sebara." *Jewish Quarterly Review* 43 (1952-3): 341-363.

_____. "Some Methods of Sebara." *Jewish Quarterly Review* 50 (1959-60): 124-46.

Kolodny, Annette. "Dancing Through the Minefield: Some Observations on the Theory, Practice and Politics of a Feminist Literary Criticism." In *The New Feminist Criticism: Essays On Women, Literature and Theory*, edited by Elaine Showalter, 144-167. New York: Pantheon Books, 1985.

_____. "A Map for Rereading: Gender and the Interpretation of Literary Texts." In *The New Feminist Criticism: Essays On Women, Literature and Theory*, edited by Elaine Showalter, 46-62. New York: Pantheon Books, 1985.

Kraemer, David. "Scripture Commentary in the Babylonian Talmud: Primary or Secondary Phenomenon," *AJS Review* 14, no. 1, Spring (1989): 1-15.

_____. *The Mind of the Talmud: An Intellectual History of the Bavli*, New York: Oxford University Press, 1990.

Lane, Jessica. "The Poetics of Legal Interpretation." In *Interpreting Law and Literature: A Hermeneutic Reader*, edited by Sanford Levinson and Steven Mailloux, 269-284. Evanston, IL: Northwestern University Press, 1988.

Laqueur, Thomas. *Making Sex: Body and Gender From the Greeks to Freud*. Cambridge, Massachusetts: Harvard University Press, 1990.

Levinson, Sanford. "Law as Literature." In *Interpreting Law and Literature: A Hermeneutic Reader*, edited by Sanford Levinson and Steven Mailloux, 155-173. Evanston, IL: Northwestern University Press, 1988.

Lieberman, Saul. *Tosefta Ki-Fshutah*: Part VIII Order Nashim. New York: Jewish Theological Seminary of America, 1973.

Lightstone, Jack N. *The Rhetoric of the Babylonian Talmud, Its Social Meaning and Context*. Waterloo, Ontario: Wilfrid Laurier University Press, 1994.

Maimonides, Moses. *The Guide of the Perplexed*. Translated with an introduction and notes by Shlomo Pines. Chicago: University of Chicago Press, 1963.

Minow, Martha "Introduction: Robert Cover and Law, Judging, and Violence." In *Narrative, Violence, and the Law: The Essays of Robert Cover*, edited by Martha Minow, Michael Ryan, and Austin Sarat, 1-11. Ann Arbor: The University of Michigan Press, 1992.

Moi, Toril. *Sexual/Textual Politics: Feminist Literary Theory*. London: Methuen & Co., 1985.

Neusner, Jacob. *The Bavli's One Voice: Types and Forms of Analytical Discourse and their Fixed Order of Appearance*. Atlanta: Scholars Press, 1991.

_____. *Canon and Connection: Intertextuality in Judaism*. New York: University Press of America, 1987.

_____. "Did the Talmud's Authorship Utilize Prior 'Sources'? A Response to Halivni's *Sources and Traditions*." In *Ancient Judaism, Debates and Disputes*, 135-180. Atlanta: Scholars Press, 1984.

_____. *How to Study the Bavli: The Languages, Literatures, and Lessons of the Talmud of Babylonia*. Atlanta: Scholars Press, 1992.

_____. *Judaism, The Classical Statement: the Evidence of the Bavli*. Chicago: University of Chicago Press, 1986.

_____. *Midrash as Literature: The Primacy of Documentary Discourse*. Lanham, New York, London: University Press of America, 1987.

_____. *The Principal Parts of the Bavli's Discourse: A Preliminary Taxonomy*. Atlanta, Georgia: Scholars Press, 1992.

_____. *The Rules of Composition of the Talmud of Babylonia: The Cogency of the Bavli's Composite*. Atlanta: Scholars Press, 1991.

_____. *The Talmud of Babylonia: An American Translation: XVIII.A: Gittin Chapters 1-3*. Atlanta: Scholars Press, 1992.

_____. *The Talmud of Babylonia: An American Translation: XVIII.B: Gittin Chapters 4-5*. Atlanta: Scholars Press, 1992.

_____. *Translating the Classics of Judaism: In Theory and In Practice*. Atlanta: Scholars Press, 1989.

Newman, Louis. "Shamma Friedman on b. Yebamot 87b – 88a." *Semeia* 27 (1983): 53 – 61.

Nye, Andrea. *Feminist Theory and the Philosophies of Man*. London: Croom Helm, 1988.

Peskowitz, Miriam Beth. "'The Work of Her Hands': Gendering Everyday Life in Roman-Period Judaism in Palestine (70-250 CE), Using Textile Production as a Case." Ph.D. diss., Duke University, 1993.

Pomeroy, Sarah. *Goddesses, Whores, Wives and Slaves*. New York: Schocken Books, 1976.

Richards, I. A. *How to Read a Page*. New York: W.W. Norton & Co. 1942.

_____. *The Philosophy of Rhetoric*. New York: Oxford University Press, 1936.

Ricoeur, Paul. *Time and Narrative*. Vol. 1. Translated by Kathleen McLaughlin and David Pellauer. Chicago: The University of Chicago Press, 1984.

Rifattere, Michael. *Fictional Truth*. Baltimore: Johns Hopkins University Press, 1990.

_____. *The Semiotics of Poetry*. Bloomington: Indiana University Press, 1984.

Rimmon-Kenan, Shlomith. *Narrative Fiction: Contemporary Poetics*. London and New York: Methuen, 1983.

Rosaldo, M. Z. "The Use and Abuse of Anthropology: Reflections on Feminism and Cross-cultural Understanding." *Signs: Journal of Women in Culture and Society*, 5, 3 (1980): 389-417.

Rosenthal, David. "עריכות קדומות המשוקעות בתלמוד הבבלי." In *Mehqerei Talmud* edited by Yaacov Sussman, David Rosenthal, 155-204. Jerusalem: Magnes Press, 1990.

Saussure, Ferdinand de, *Saussure's First Course of Lectures on General Linguistics (1907) : From The Notebooks of Albert Riedlinger*, French text edited by Eisuke Komatsu ; English [ed. and] translation by George Wolf. Tarrytown, N.Y.: Pergamon, 1996.

Saxonhouse, Arlene "Aristotle: Defective Males, Hierarchy, and the Limits of Politics." In *Feminist Interpretations and Political Theory* edited by Mary Lyndon Shanley and Carole Pateman, 32-52. University Park: Pennsylvania State University Press, 1991.

Schor, Naomi. *Reading in Detail: Aesthetics and the Feminine*. New York: Methuen, 1987.

Schüssler Fiorenza, Elizabeth. *In Memory of Her: A Feminist Theological Reconstruction of Christian Origins*. New York: Crossroads, 1983.

_____. *But She Said: Feminist Practices of Biblical Interpretation*. Boston: Beacon Press, 1992.

Showalter, Elaine. "Toward a Feminist Poetics." In *The New Feminist Criticism: Essays On Women, Literature and Theory*, edited by Elaine Showalter, 125-143. New York: Pantheon Books, 1985.

Smith, Jonathan Z. "What a Difference a Difference Makes." In *To See Ourselves as Others See Us: Christians, Jews, "Others" in Late Antiquity*, edited by Jacob Neusner and Ernest S. Frerichs. Chico, California: Scholars Press, 1985.

Smith, Jonathan Z. *Map Is Not Territory: Studies in the History of Religion*. Chicago: University of Chicago Press, 1978.

Spellman, Elizabeth V. *Inessential Woman: Problems of Exclusion in Feminist Thought*. Boston: Beacon Press, 1988.

Stern, David, *Parables in Midrash: Narrative and Exegesis in Rabbinic Literature*. Cambridge, MA: Harvard University Press, 1991.

Sussman, Yaacov. "ושוב לירושלמי נזיקין" *Mehqerei Talmud* edited by Yaacov Sussman, David Rosenthal, 55-133. Jerusalem: Magnes Press, 1990.

Veeser, H. Aram. "The New Historicism." In *The New Historicism Reader*, edited by H. Aram Veeser, 1-32. New York, London: Routledge, 1994.

Wegner, Judith Romney. "Shamma Friedman on b. Yebamot 88b-89a." *Semeia*, 27 (1983): 77 – 91.

Weiner, David. "Shamma Friedman's Methodological Principles," *Semeia*, 27 (1983): 47 – 51.

Weiss, Abraham, התהוות התלמוד בשלמותו. New York: Alexander Kohut Memorial Foundation, 1943.

_____. על היצירה הספרותית של האמוראים. New York: Horeb, 1962.

_____. *The Talmud in its Development, Vol. One* (in Hebrew) New York: Philipp Feldheim, 1954.

_____. *The Literary Activities of the Saboraim* (in Hebrew) Jerusalem: Magnes Press, 1953.

Weller, Shulamith, "קובץ הסיפורים בסוגיית כתובות דף ס״ב ע״ב-ס״ג ע״א." in Meir Ayali, editor, *Tura: Studies in Jewish Thought: Simon Greenberg Jubilee Volume*. Tel Aviv: Hakibbutz Hameuchad Publishing House, 1989: 95-108.

White, Hayden. *Tropics of Discourse: Essays in Cultural Criticism*. Baltimore and London: Johns Hopkins University Press, 1978.

Winkler, John J. *The Constraints of Desire: The Anthropology of Sex and Gender in Ancient Greece.* New York, London: Routledge, 1990.

Wyschogrod, Edith. *Saints and Postmodernism: Revisioning Moral Philosophy.* Chicago and London: University of Chicago Press, 1990.

Yassif, Eli. "מחזור הסיפורים באגדת חז"ל." *Jerusalem Studies in Hebrew Literature* 12 (1990): 103-145.

Index

Aggadah 71, 74-89, 97 & n. 69, 98-120

Albeck 24, 32 n. 78

Alfasi 1, 173 n. 65, 181, 201, 211 n. 47

Barthes, Roland 150

bet din 11-15, 28-32

body, construction of 143, 144, 217

Boyarin, Daniel 1 n. 2, 4, 5, 42, 48 n. 17, 71-72, 89-122, 138, 142, 157 n. 6, 170 n. 51

Cover, Robert 132, 146-147

Derrida, Jacques 205 n. 32

divorce 6, 11-15, 170-198, 211

    document of (get) 11-19

    nullification of (nullification of get) 11-15, 188-189

    as metaphor 151, 170

    in prophets 138-141

    in midrash 140 n. 24

Dylan, Bob 137

exile 140, 153, 165, 169-171, 217-219

Feldblum, Meir Simha 10

feminist theory 4, 90, 144

(see also gender, hermeneutics of suspicion)

Fish, Stanley 27 n. 65, 28 n. 67, 149

Fraenkel, Jonah 1 n. 3, 4, 42, 57 n. 36,

Friedman, Shamma 4, 5, 8, 32f, 34-42, 44, 57 n. 36, 158 n. 9

gender 143-144, 212, 217

    construction of 6, 144, 164-178, 170, 181-182

    gendering 177-183, 194, 216-218

    as power 199 n. 4, 217-218

    (see also body, construction of)

Goldenberg, Robert 28 n. 68, 32 n. 78,

Greenblatt, Stephen 90

halakha 1, 6, 60, 72, 84, 94, 96, 102, 103, 131, 146, 173 & n. 65, 177-183

Halivni, David Weiss 4, 5, 8, 24 n. 53, 25-32, 33 n. 78, 35 n. 89, 36 n. 91, 44, 121, 163, 174-176, 209 n. 43

Heinemann, I. 32 n. 78, 71 n. 1

hermeneutics of suspicion 144

historiography 92, 141-143
intertextuality 31, 45-49, 135-141, 158, 218
Janus element 106
Kaplan, Hyman 55 n. 31
Kermode, Frank 1 n. 1, 157 n. 6
Ketubah 98, 154, 165-178, 170, 172-173, 177
Klein, Hyman 1 n. 4, 5, 32 n. 78, 35-36
law 6, 28, 153, 161, 170-173
legal reasoning 166-167, 177
legal theory 146-7, 170-173, 217, 219
Lieberman, Saul 32 n. 78, 163
Lightstone, Jack N. 4 n. 9, 35 n. 90
literary structure, mapping of 8, 35
literary theory 1-5
    formalism, genre criticism 44-47, 73-76
    hermeneutic index 31, 65, 137
    Marxist 91, 92
    New Criticism 72, 73-89, 90-93
    New Historicism 72, 89-122
    misreading 176
    (see also narrative, feminist theory, subtext)
ma'aseh 72, 153-165, 174-176, 189
Maimonides, Moses 74, 132-133, 135
manuscript variants 4 n. 9, 30, 81, 159 n. 13, 199 n.14

marriage 97-117, 170-171, 177, 181-183, 181 n. 82, 215
midrashic reading 55 n. 31, 205-206, 132-139
narrative 132-133, 144-147, 164, 166, 168-173, 193
    law as 132
    sugya as 145
Neusner, Jacob 4, 5, 29 n. 70, 32 n. 78, 42, 43-69, 122, 199 n. 15
    intertextuality 45-49
    Mishnah exegesis 58-60, 62, 64
    systemic literature 47
    traditional literature 46-47
    translation, theory of 49*ff*
Old Historicism 141-142
Peskowitz, Miriam 215-216
prozbul 12 n. 19, 13, 28-31
rabbinic culture 21
Rashi 1, 18, 30, 165, 181 n. 82, 206 n. 40
rhetoric 59-60, 149, 150 & n. 57, 166-167, 199-201
reading against the grain 117-120, 131
Riffaterre, Michael 135-137, 140
Safrai, Shmuel 141
Saussure, Ferdinand de 135
sexuality 90, 98-103
sabbatical year (*shmitah*) 28-32
slaves/slavery 193-219
    owning slaves 213-215

Index

source criticism 2, 8, 25-28, 34, 57-69, 161
Spellman, Elizabeth V. 218 n. 54
Springsteen, Bruce 136-137
stam/stammaitic statements 8, 12, 18, 23, 35 n. 89, 36, 39, 55, 149, 153, 176, 179
stammaim 26, 32 n. 78, 41
subtext 117, 140-141, 193, 217
sugya 97, 119, 147-148
    definition of 10-11, 148
    historical definition of 16-17, 19
    introductory sugyot 165
    literary development of 11-19, 26
sugyaetics 5, 49, 122, 131-151, 153, 158-165, 168-173, 193-194
    literary analysis 149, 158
    praxis 149-151
Talmud
    closing of the Talmud 2, 7
    dehukim 26-27, 30-32, 41
    as discourse 93
    divided into gemara and sebora 36
    fixing literary form 3, 9-10, 20-21, 24, 121
    as literature 3
    redaction criticism 2-3, 7-14
    redaction history 44
    source criticism 2
    technical terms
        dispute form 39

    as writing under erasure 166-167, 180, 188-189, 204, 217
talmudic culture 7
textual difficulties 15, 19
Tosafot/Tosafists 1, 30 n. 74-75, 161
ungrammaticalities 15, 134, 137, 141, 145, 149, 150, 153, 166, 174, 179, 189, 193, 200, 201, 216
    dehukim as 26-27, 30-32, 95, 105
Wegner, Judith Romney 35 n. 89, 41 n. 103
Weiner, David 34 n. 89
Weiss, Avraham 2-3, 4, 5, 7-25, 32 n. 78, 165 n. 30
    fixing literary form 3, 9-10, 20-21, 24, 121
widow 153-161, 165-166, 168-170
women 37-42, 153-219
writing under erasure 166-167, 180, 188-189, 204, 217

Index of Hebrew
and Aramaic terms

איכא דאמרי 9
איתמר נמי 9, 21, 23-24
אפקעת קידושין .... 29 n. 70,
התהוות ספרותית 24
לא אמרן אלא... 67
לא שנו אלא... .... 67, 153
לאתויי מאי? 54
מהו דתימא...קמ"ל 55, 188
מימרות 9-10

סברא 14, 19
סלקא דעתך אמינא...קמ"ל 166, 179-180, 188-189
קבע 21
שכלול .... 1, 18 n. 33,
שקלא וטריא 10
ותני והדר ומפרש 55

Index of passages cited (**bold** = passages discussed in text)

Mishnah (M) and Tosefta (T)

M Berakhot
1:1 88
3:1 84

M Shebi'ith
10:3-4 28

M Shabbat
1:4 30

M Erubin
3:3 22

M Yebamoth
10:1 .... **37-42**

T Yebamoth
8:4 .... **99-100, 117-120**

M Ketuboth
5:6 103-104
5:7 .... 98, 209 n. 43
7:6 .... 164 n. 27, 168 n. 42
9:2 182

T Ketuboth
12:3 .... 177 n. 72

M Sotah

3:4 .... 212, 217

M Gittin
1:6 .... 194, 198-199
2:1 16
4:1 11-13
4:3 28
5:1 177-178
5:2 178

M Baba Kama
1:1 .... 40 n. 102

M Makkot
2:1, 2:4 .... 217 N. 52

T Makkot
2:8 .... 194, 203, 216

M Eduyot
1:5 30

M Arachin
1:1 .... **51-53**

Talmud (b=Babylonian; p=Palestinian)

b Berakhot
3a **85-89**
18b **79-85**
62b 143

b Erubin
32b **21-25**

b Succah
7a .... 67 n. 69
38b-39a .... 66 n. 68

b Megillah
7b 65

Index

19a ... 66-67

b Yebamoth
46a ... 193
53b ... 167 n. 40
60a-b ... 172 n. 61
91a ... **37-42**

b Ketuboth
61b-63b ... **97-130**
67b ... **133-134**
72a ... 164 n. 27
84a ... 182-183
87b ... 177 n. 73

b Nedarim
25b ... 161
50a ... 100-102, 117-120

b Nazir
62a ... 54

p Sotah
5:7 ... 142

b Gittin
15a-b ... 16
12a-13a ... 55, **193-223**
19b ... 171 n. 58
32a ... **188-189**
32b-33a ... 11-13
33a-b ... 55 n. 32
34b-35b ... 67 n. 71, **153-192**
36b ... **28**
39a ... 217 n. 53
46a ... 177 n. 74
49b-50a ... **177-187**
57b ... 175 n. 71

b Kiddushin
29b ... 102-103

b Baba Kama
13b ... 55
50b ... 55
106a ... 162-163, 168 n. 44

b Baba Metzia
92b ... 194 n. 4

b Sanhedrin
3a ... 14
100b ... 167 n. 40

b Shavuoth
26a-b ... 161

p Shavuoth
5:6 (37a) ... 174 n. 69
6:5 (37a) ... 163

b Abodah Zara
2a-3b ... 56 n. 34
36a ... 30

b Horayot
2b ... 55

b Zebahim
20b ... 55
68b ... 55

b Bekhorot
28a ... 64-65

b Arachin
2a ... **51-55**

b Temurah
2a-3a ... **58-63**

b Nidah
83a .... 62 n. 49

Midrash

Sifri
Deut. 112 28

Gen. Rabbah
19:9 138-141
95 113-115

Lev. Rabbah
6:3 .... 163, 174 n. 69

Eichah Rabbah
1 (Buber 46) 171

Pesikta Rabati
113b .... 174 n. 69
132b 163

Tanhuma (Buber)
Lev. 16 174-175

www.ingramcontent.com/pod-product-compliance
Lightning Source LLC
Chambersburg PA
CBHW030232170426
43201CB00006B/188